Nazi Labour Camps in Paris

Nazi Labour Camps in Paris

Austerlitz, Lévitan, Bassano, July 1943–August 1944

Jean-Marc Dreyfus and Sarah Gensburger

Translated from the French by Jonathan Hensher

Berghahn Books
NEW YORK • OXFORD

Published by
Berghahn Books
www.berghahnbooks.com

French-language edition
©2003 Librairie Arthème Fayard
Des camps dans Paris
By Jean-Marc Dreyfus and Sarah Gensburger

English-language edition
©2011 Berghahn Books

Library of Congress Cataloging-in-Publication Data

Dreyfus, Jean-Marc.
  [Des camps dans Paris. English]
  Nazi labour camps in Paris : Austerlitz, Lévitan, Bassano, July 1943–August 1944 /
Jean-Marc Dreyfus and Sarah Gensburger.
     p.   cm.
  Includes bibliographical references and index.
  ISBN 978-0-85745-139-2 (hardback : alk. paper)
  1. Jews—France—Paris. 2. Holocaust, Jewish (1939–1945)—France—Paris.
3. France—History—German occupation, 1940–1945. 4. Concentration camps—
France—Paris. 5. Paris (France)—Ethnic relations. I. Gensburger, Sarah. II. Title.
  DS135.F85P245813 2011
  940.53'18544361—dc22

                                                                    2011014735

British Library Cataloguing in Publication Data

A catalogue record for this book is available from the British Library

The translation of this book has been made possible thanks to the financial support of
the Fondation pour la Mémoire de la Shoah, the Fondation du Judaisme français, and
the Centre National du Livre; all three institutions are in Paris

Printed in the United States on acid-free paper

ISBN 978-0-85745-139-2 (hardback)

CONTENTS

FIGURES, ILLUSTRATIONS, AND TABLES

Figures

Illustrations

Tables

FOREWORD TO
THE FRENCH EDITION

WHILE EVERYONE HAS HEARD of the Final Solution and the Holocaust, the Parisian camps have fallen victim to a strange process of forgetting, a 'memory hole'.

Not so long ago, when I mentioned them to an official from the Mission Mattéoli, someone deeply involved in research into the expropriation of France's Jews, a process in which these camps were a vital hub, I received the reply, already heard so many times before, that he had never heard of them, but...

I was seventeen years old and living under false papers. Throughout 1944 I would, from time to time, go and visit my grandfather in a strange place, called Quai de la Gare. There were metal fences, uninterested-looking soldiers with slanted eyes wearing German uniforms and, behind the fences, men and women who I could see were quite well-dressed, even though we already knew about Drancy and where it led. I would come back from these visits weighed down with medicines (this book will explain why). It was a bizarre situation, the troubling strangeness of which I could feel. This camp really did exist.

My grandfather was long dead when in 1996 I discovered a bundle of yellowed letters that I read with amazement and emotion. The time had come for me, as for so many survivors of my generation, to let the doors of memory open.

On 23 January 1997, a front-page article in the newspaper *Le Monde*, following an earlier piece in the German magazine *Die Zeit*, referred, in relation to the construction of the new French National Library, to the existence of Austerlitz camp.

A few months earlier, also in *Le Monde*, a rather strange anonymous advertisement had been printed. Not without some difficulty, I managed to make contact with its authors, the 'Artistes des Frigos', Marie Guastalla, Claude Bensignor and Jean-Michel Frouin, who had discovered that their threatened workspace was located near a concentration camp.

It was through them that I was able to meet some survivors of the Parisian camps, in particular Mira Lessovoï. In 1987 she had attempted to set up an association for former inmates, although this project had come to nothing. For a number of reasons, a great feeling of kinship sprang up between this extraordinary elderly lady and myself. She gave me the job, in a way, of continuing her campaign. The historian Claude Maignen, who had found the diary of Yvonne Klug in a junk shop, was planning her own work on the subject. In 1993 an article by Lucien Steinberg was published in *Le Monde juif*, along with several personal testimonies referred to in the present book.

In this way the Amicale Austerlitz-Lévitan-Bassano was born, an association that received official governmental recognition on 14 January 1998. Roger Mayer, a former internee, accepted the post of president. The object of the association, as declared in its founding statutes, is to 'retrace the history of the Parisian internment, labour and transit camps, and to preserve their memory.' Serge Klarsfeld lent his support, becoming a member and helping us to access documents and lists that were added to the Centre de documentation juive contemporaine, and that constituted our archives. The Fondation du judaïsme français also lent us their support.

The first meetings were, of course, opportunities for reunions, for friendly conversations amidst a warm hubbub. We placed advertisements in the press and sent out letters, and soon former internees or their descendants made their way to us. However, it became clear that what was needed was a truly rigorous study of the subject, a study that we wanted to be of a serious academic standard.

Quite naturally, we first contacted the major French historians of this period, with no success. By contrast, a simple email to Radu Ioanid, the director of the Holocaust Museum in Washington, was all that was needed for his representative in Paris, Peggy Frankston, to put us in touch with two qualified French researchers, Sarah Gensburger and Jean-Marc Dreyfus. This book is the outcome of their collaboration.

Sarah Gensburger is a sociologist, Jean-Marc Dreyfus a historian. This complementary combination has allowed this book to be at once absolutely rigorous, attesting to the vast amount of research it required, while also portraying with humanity and warmth the everyday reality of the lives of the internees of these Parisian camps and the history of these forgotten places. Thank you, Sarah and Jean-Marc.

Of course, not all of their questions could be answered, but the issues they raise are extremely important: the passive collaboration, voluntary or otherwise, of French companies in the looting of furniture; the definition of Jewish identity, so much more complex than it appears today; and, finally, the whole vexed question of individual and collective memory and its mechanisms.

This work would never have come to fruition without the support of the Fondation pour la mémoire de la Shoah, as well as that of the SEMAPA, the organization in charge of the redevelopment of the ZAC-Paris-Rive gauche, the area in which Austerlitz camp stood, who took it upon themselves to offer us their help. We must also thank the Centre de documentation juive contemporaine and all of those who, through their testimony, their generosity and the opening of their private or sometimes public archives, made this possible.

This book is dedicated to the former internees of the Parisian camps, those forgotten slave labourers, unwilling participants in this extraordinary enterprise of twentieth-century pillage, this vital link in the chain of the Final Solution.

Denise Weill
Secretary of the Amicale Austerlitz-Levitan-Bassano.

INTRODUCTION

Over five hundred art historians, antique dealers, restorers, joiners, clockmakers, furriers and couturiers brought in from Drancy and guarded by a contingent of Indo-Chinese soldiers were employed day after day, in fourteen-hour shifts, to put the goods coming into the depot in proper order and sort them by value and kind…
—W.G. Sebald, *Austerlitz*

And so, said Austerlitz, we began a long, whispered, conversation in the *Haut-de-jardin* reading room, which was gradually emptying now, about the dissolution, in line with the inexorable spread of processed data, of our capacity to remember…
—W.G. Sebald, *Austerlitz*

Yes, I know what was in the Lévitan store. Jewish women were put in there before being deported to the camps from the Gare de l'Est. It was truly horrible.
—*Eye-witness account from a woman living near Lévitan camp*

O N 18 July 1943, 120 Jews from the concentration camp at Drancy were transported into the middle of Paris, to a building in the rue du Faubourg-Saint-Martin, virtually opposite the *mairie* (town hall) of the 10th *arrondissement*. It housed a furniture store by the name of Lévitan. They were the first detainees of three new satellite camps of the main camp at Drancy. Between July 1943 and August 1944, nearly 800 prisoners spent anything from a few weeks to a year in one of these buildings, which had previously been used to store furniture. Here, they were subjected to forced labour. They were made to sort, clean, repair and pack furniture and other objects of value that had been methodically looted by the Germans from tens of thousands of Jewish apartments in the occupied zone of northern France. The booty was sent off by the trainload to Germany. The fate of the detainees was supervised by the chief ideologue of the National Socialist régime, Alfred Rosenberg, whose shadow loomed over the stacks of crates piled up by the Jewish inmates standing to attention before the Nazi dignitaries who often came to visit these satellite camps of Drancy.

It should be made clear from the outset that writing this work on the camps of Austerlitz, Lévitan and Bassano has been anything but a routine piece of academic research. The conditions under which it was carried out – namely the silence enveloping these events, which have come to be seen as increasingly important for our understanding of the persecution of France's Jews – were most unusual. The Parisian camps – let us call them this, for want of a better term – were known to historians of this period. They had been referred to at the time of the Liberation, but so briefly that it was impossible to find anything more than a few lines written on them. The Parisian camps escaped – as, to a certain extent, they still do today – simple and straightforward descriptions, or clear perceptions. But the reason for this was not the fog of memory. While many internees of the Parisian camps gave little in the way of testimony, others left very precise accounts of events. The absence of any collective memory, any 'social frame',[1] perhaps explains the lack of attention paid to them by the most authoritative voices on the subject. Sixty years after the events, expressing this memory remains a complex, sometimes painful process, and speaking it a struggle. Perhaps the marginal status of the Parisian detainees – who were, for the most part, the spouses of Aryans, wives of prisoners of war, half-Jews – has something to do with this. Such identities can appear out of step with the canons that structure representations of the Occupation.

The history of the persecution and deportation of France's Jews is well known, having been written, read and debated. The official stamp marked '*Juif*', the index of Jewish families ('*le fichier*'), the yellow star and the looting of works of art have become infamous symbols of the collaboration of the French state and of the murder of a quarter of France's Jews; Drancy, the *Vél' d'Hiv'* and Auschwitz are enshrined as *lieux de mémoire*, places of memory. Yet the three Parisian satellite camps of Drancy have been subjected to the silence of both memory and history.

Austerlitz, Lévitan, Bassano: three names that we have learnt to recite in order, as if to convince ourselves that they really existed. Austerlitz evokes both a Napoleonic battle and a Parisian railway station, the name of which begins and ends like Auschwitz. Lévitan now only evokes, for the older generation, the name of shops selling furniture 'which lasts a long time',[2] and Bassano is just a quiet street in the well-to-do 16th *arrondissement*, barely registering as another of Napoleon's victories near a town in the Veneto.

'Satellite camps of Drancy': this term, if never officially used, seems to have condemned the three sites to a marginal position. The historical vacuum into which they have fallen is thus not entirely surprising. Given that fewer than one thousand inmates passed through them in a period of little more than a year and

---

[1] On the notion of the frames necessary for the expression of a collective memory, see M. Halbwachs. 1994. *Les Cadres sociaux de la mémoire,* Paris: Albin Michel.

[2] The store's slogan, engrained on memories across France, went as follows: 'Un meuble signé Lévitan… est garanti pour longtemps' ('Furniture signed Lévitan is guaranteed for a long time').

that they held, for the most part, people who were neither 'perfectly' Jewish nor 'completely' Aryan, and that they were neither simply prisons, nor deportation camps, these camps fall outside the usual system of classification. It is true that there were places that superficially resembled these camps in Central Europe, where 'privileged' Jews packaged the products of Aryanisation and expropriation. However, none was exactly like the Parisian camps.

These satellite camps were not situated in far-off lands. By referring to them we bring the Holocaust into the very heart of the capital, whereas its epicentre in France was, could only be, or so it was thought, the distant suburb of Drancy. Their addresses – 43, quai de la Gare, near the Gare d'Austerlitz; 'Lévitan', 85-87, rue du Faubourg-Saint-Martin; 2, rue Bassano – show that these camps were geographically central, yet they have become historically marginal. Places of oppression and confinement, they were not as terrible for their inmates as the other French camps, as Drancy, even, and were not true concentration camps. They remained in the realm of the 'almost', where 'almost-Jews' found themselves 'almost' protected in 'quasi-camps'. All of this is difficult to explain.

For a historian, of course, nothing is marginal, as the dimensions of an event tell us nothing about its historical significance. Microhistory has just as much to say as 'grand narrative': it seeks both to complement the latter and, through 'scale-play',[3] to allow us to see it differently. The Parisian camps were not merely subsidiary sites but played a crucial role in the classification of Jews into distinct categories and in the looting of apartments, in what the Germans called 'Operation Furniture'. As places both of racial internment and of the sorting of valuables, they are situated at the intersection of the two great currents that formed the logical basis for the implementation of the Final Solution. Likewise, they were created out of the convergence of the objectives of several distinct administrative agencies. On the one hand, they provided the labour needed by the authorities overseeing the looting of apartments. On the other, they allowed space to be freed up in Drancy in order to facilitate deportations. Since they were at once vessels for economic expropriation and links in the chain of physical extermination, the Parisian camps show us how these two processes, all too often studied in isolation, could fit together and mutually reinforce each other. On the margins of the historical narrative, they are therefore at the heart of historiographical reflection.

Why did we know nothing about them? After all, a few documents, surviving witnesses and physical traces were there for those who wished to see them.[4] Isolated articles dating from the immediate postwar period, tens of thousands of filed requests for compensation for looting from the 1960s... What is striking is the absence of any single narrative and any collective, public memory rather than some desire to hide the truth, or to repress it. Objects of individual or fam-

---

[3] J. Revel (ed.). 1996. *Jeux d'échelles: la micro-analyse à l'expérience,* Paris: Seuil.

[4] C. Ginzburg. 2002. *Wooden Eyes: Nine Reflections on Distance,* London: Verso.

ily memory, these Parisian camps have become *non-lieux de mémoire*. The old Lévitan shop now houses a well-known advertising agency, in an airy, minimalist architectural setting that contrasts with the confined, cluttered spaces of the camp between 1943 and 1944. The town house belonging to the Cahen d'Anvers family, which housed Bassano camp, has been splendidly renovated and split into offices – there too, nobody knew about its past. While the Austerlitz building on the quai de la Gare has been destroyed, two plaques have long indicated its position, although they refer to a discordant, almost imaginary reality: '1943–1944. On these premises taken and occupied by the enemy were interned thousands of victims of Nazi persecution. Many of them were deported and perished in the extermination camps.'[5] Where it exists, then, this memory is unable to find its own frame and often prefers to slip into those highly structured representations that are most resonant today, such as the memory of mass deportation. Establishing a narrative of the events that formed the frame of these three camps thus also involves probing the mystery of how they were almost forgotten.

From the very outset, writing the history of Drancy's satellite camps meant stepping outside established frameworks. This project was, from start to finish, quite different. It took us to varied locations – to airports, to archives in the United States and Germany, but also to the very centre of France, to Le Blanc, a small town in the *département* of l'Indre where the railway station is now closed and that today lies well off the beaten track even though it is only 350 kilometres from Paris.[6] The research, begun by former inmates of the Parisian camps whose association is based in Paris, had to extend beyond France in order for the link between this association and the authors of the present book to be established. We met in the United States, at the Holocaust Memorial Museum in Washington; we were put in touch with the association by Peggy Frankston, the museum's representative in Paris.

The most important archives for our research, those of the Dienststelle Westen (the Western Service) of the Ministry of the Occupied Eastern Territories, have not been located. No file exists, we were repeatedly informed. It was therefore necessary to approach these camps 'indirectly'. The archives of the Union Générale des Israélites de France (the official body representing Jews in France, created by the Nazis in autumn 1941) and those of the Dépôt central de la justice militaire (Central archives of military justice) proved the richest in information. While the former had long been available via the Centre de documentation juive contemporaine, gaining access to the latter required almost a year of negotiations and patience.[7]

---

[5] Plaque fixed to the wall of 43, quai de la Gare in the 1950s, now removed.

[6] Le Blanc houses the central archives of France's military justice system.

[7] We were not granted access to the archives of the SNCF (French national railways) concerning the Parisian camps and the hundreds of trainloads of furniture that were shipped to the Reich.

The list of puzzles and discrepancies unearthed by this research is a long one: these too contribute to the history of these Parisian camps for which we have tried belatedly to provide a frame. It took a long time to locate with certainty the site of Austerlitz camp: three different positions had been suggested. A symbol of the floating nature of these places' position in the memory and history of the persecution of France's Jews, this internment centre drifted around in the space between the Bibliothèque nationale de France (French National Library) and the Paris ring road. The contrast between this shifting emptiness and the huge accumulation of objects in the midst of which the detainees existed for more than a year could hardly be greater.

CHAPTER I

OPERATION FURNITURE

NAZISM WAS IN PART an immense looting project, carried out on a pan-European scale. From 1933 onwards, the dignitaries of the National Socialist party resorted to a vast array of methods to reward both themselves and their loyal followers.[1] As the régime consolidated its power and the territory controlled by the Reich expanded, this looting took on a systematic character. The number of administrative bodies with a hand in this policy grew, and the ministries created special bureaus for the detection, confiscation, sorting, transportation and, finally, distribution of the vast plunder. The entry of German troops into France marked a new escalation of this enterprise. From June 1940 onwards searches were being organised with the aim of seizing works of art and other 'cultural goods'. For example, a *kommando* from the German Ministry of Foreign Affairs, the Sonderkommando Künsberg, undertook the mission of recovering the French diplomatic archives of greatest interest to the Reich;[2] the German embassy worked until autumn 1940 to locate works of art.[3] The Reich's central security bureau, the military high command and numerous more or less separate sub-bureaus – purchasing offices and the like – participated in the plunder. The Devisenschutzkommando (literally, the 'office for currency protection'), which was assigned to Hermann Göring's Four-Year Plan, was given the mission of recovering foreign currency, gold, precious metals and bonds. All these administrative bodies found themselves more or less in competition with one another, and arbitration became necessary, often issued by Hitler himself. However, the bureaus that established themselves most solidly in France were those placed under

[1] See N. J.W. Goda. 2000. 'Black Marks: Hitler's Bribery of his Senior Officers during World War II', *The Journal of Modern History*, 72(2), 413–452; and G.R. Überschär and W. Vogel. 1999. *Dienen und Verdiesen: Hitlers Geschenke an seine Eliten*, Frankfurt am Main: S. Fischer.

[2] The most complete account of the plundering of works of art and cultural goods in occupied France is A. Heuss. 2000. *Kunst- und Kulturgutraub: Eine Vergleichende Studie zur Besatzungspolitik der Nationalsozialisten in Frankreich und der Sowjetunion*, Heidelberg: Universitätsverlag C. Winter. For the Sonderkommando Künsberg, see 285–333.

[3] See B. Lambauer. 2001. *Otto Abetz et les Français ou l'envers de la Collaboration*, Paris: Fayard, 151–158.

the control of Alfred Rosenberg. It is true that the 'theorist' of National Socialism was the man best placed to put an ideological veneer on this project of organised pillage. The Einsatzstab Reichsleiter Rosenberg (ERR) plundered works of art.

The Einsatzstab Reichsleiter Rosenberg

The entire history of the Parisian satellite camps of Drancy is dominated by the troubling figure of Alfred Rosenberg. His 'great work' – his written output having been enormous – was incontestably *The Myth of the Twentieth Century*, published in 1930 and widely disseminated and translated. In it he set out his theory of history, driven as he saw it by the confrontation between Aryans and Semites.[4] Born in 1893 in Tallinn, Estonia, this Baltic German had studied in Riga and Moscow, qualifying as an engineer and architect before emigrating from Moscow to Munich in 1919. He became a naturalised German in 1923 and joined the National Socialist Party on its creation. During Hitler's imprisonment following the Munich Beer Hall Putsch, Rosenberg temporarily took the reins of the movement.[5] This pioneer of Nazism, who had a particular penchant for lengthy theoretical disquisitions of a pseudoscientific character, also developed a theory of art that explained that Jews were incapable of any real artistic creativity and that their possession of Aryan works of art was therefore an act of usurpation.

In April 1933, Rosenberg was put in charge of the foreign policy bureau of the National Socialist Party. On 24 January 1934, he was given the title of 'Führer's representative for the supervision of the intellectual and moral instruction and education of the Nazi Party'. He could not lay claim to the role of spiritual guide of the German people, as this was Hitler's preserve, but in this way he took official control of cultural policy. In June 1934 he created the 'Rosenberg bureau' (Amt Rosenberg), which would oversee numerous new administrative bodies, among them the famous ERR, which was dedicated to the plunder of Jewish cultural goods, first in the Reich, then across all of occupied Europe. He also created, on 10 November 1938, an institution with great ambitions: the Hohe Schule (literally, 'high school') represented nothing less than a new university system, the Nazification of the historic German universities being considered an unrealistic ideal. Rosenberg was thus a great creator of ideological agencies that together produced dozens of reports on the occupied countries, on the United States, on England, on the Jewish question, the racial question and the education of the New Man. The need of these new administrative bodies, the Hohe Schule

---

[4] On Alfred Rosenberg's ideology see A. Molau. 1993. *Alfred Rosenberg: der Ideologe des Nationalsozialismus: eine politische Biografie*, Koblenz: S. Bublies; and J. Billig. 1963. *Alfred Rosenberg dans l'action idéologique et administrative du Reich hitlérien*, Paris: Éditions du Centre.

[5] See the entry for 'Rosenberg' in I. Gutman (ed.). 1990. *Encyclopedia of the Holocaust*, New York: Macmillan, 1304–1306.

in particular, for teaching materials furnished a permanent pretext for operations involving the looting of documents, archives, artworks, books and the like.

As the Reich expanded, Rosenberg set up new *Sonderstab* or *Kommandos,* essentially organisations specialising in theft. At the beginning of the month of July 1940 (on either 5 or 17 July),[6] a branch of the ERR was set up in Paris in order to supply books to the Hohe Schule, in the first instance by appropriating the collections of the major libraries.[7] It was at this point that the question of how to transport the stolen objects to the Reich was raised. The soldiers of the Heeresgruppe A lent their assistance, as did the Organisation Todt.[8] However, from the end of August 1940, opposition from the high command in Paris and the embassy forced the ERR to seize only those possessions belonging to individuals and not to libraries or public collections. The ERR's mission was extended to cover works of art in September, and depots were opened in which these works would be brought together, sorted, inventoried and assigned to new owners. The main depot was in the Jeu de Paume museum, which Göring visited on numerous occasions. The majority of the works placed there had belonged to Jewish collections.

At the beginning of 1941, the ERR moved its offices from the hôtel Commodore, on the boulevard Hausmann, to a town house confiscated from a family of Jewish bankers, the Gunzburgs, at 54 avenue d'Iéna.[9] The head of the ERR in Paris also changed: Ebert, an economics specialist, was replaced by Gerhard Utikal. The organisation's administration was split into a political branch, headed by an individual named Ingram, and a branch placed under the control of Baron Kurt von Behr, who received the rank of *DRK-Feldführer.*

Kurt von Behr was a curious character. Walking about in a bizarre uniform, described as being that of the Red Cross, he was neither a soldier nor a member of the SS. The inmates of the Parisian camps who spent time in close proximity to him on a number of occasions noted his strange manner, which affected martialness without ever quite succeeding. Von Behr apparently spoke good French, which he had learnt in Paris – where he had lived for many years in the rue Raynouard, in the 16th *arrondissement* – and understood the slang of the working-class districts. Born in Hanover in 1890, although brought up in Berlin, he had been an officer in the Imperial army, was taken prisoner in France during

---

[6] Both dates are cited in documents.

[7] Heuss, *Kunst- und Kulturgutraub,* 102–103.

[8] The Organisation Todt was a vast military and civil construction enterprise that provided materiel to the German armies. In France, the organisation bought vast quantities of raw materials and finished goods, kept thousands of businesses running and, most visibly, constructed fortifications all along the French coastline, which became known as the Atlantic wall.

[9] On the Gunzburg family, see J-M. Dreyfus. 2000. *L'Aryanisation économique des banques pendant l'Occupation et leur restitution à la Libération, 1940–1952,* PhD thesis supervised by Pr Antoine Prost, Université de Paris-I, Sorbonne, 258–261.

the First World War and had spent more than three years in captivity. His profession prior to the Occupation is not recorded. One female detainee of Lévitan and Austerlitz, Gilberte Jacob, would describe him after the war as a 'spectacular' man.[10] He seems to have behaved like a caricature of a Prussian *Junker*. He would wear a corset, highly polished riding boots, a well-cut uniform and 'an indispensable monocle'.[11] A terrible snob, he could be cruel with it. He claimed to be the vice-president of the German Red Cross, whose insignia he wore on his uniform. Fiercely ambitious, he had an English wife, who was apparently often at his side, and who declared that she hated England.[12] Frau von Behr was evidently a rapacious character and helped herself to many items from the depots.

Kurt von Behr seems to have arrived in Paris along with the German troops and immediately entered service with the ERR. He had had some difficulties with the NSDAP, of which he had been a member since the 1930s; in 1938 he had been brought before a party tribunal for misdemeanours that remain unclear but that we know occurred outside Germany.[13] His file was subsequently cleaned up, probably following his rise to power within Alfred Rosenberg's administration.[14]

Special bureaus (*Sonderstab*) of the ERR were created in Paris, with powers extending to Belgium and the Netherlands. Each of these departments, run by experts, 'specialised' in certain types of objects. There were seven of them: the 'Churches' bureau visited religious institutions, while the 'Eastern' bureau dealt with the libraries of immigrants from Eastern Europe who had settled in France.[15] There was a 'Prehistory' bureau and a 'Central Library of the High School' (Sonderstab Zentralbibliothek der Hohen Schule) bureau that looted, in particular, the books of the great Jewish institutions, including the Alliance israélite universelle and the rabbinical seminary, but also private collections such as that of the Indianist Sylvain Lévi. The largest bureau, the Sonderstab Musik, was placed under the direction of Dr Herbert Gerigk, a musicologist, who got his hands on a large number of antique instruments as well as musicians' libraries and scores.[16]

---

[10] Dépôt central de la justice militaire, Le Blanc, Indre, 'Dossier Utikal et autres', document 1/D/II, 'procès-verbal d'audition de Gilberte Jacob, née Lévy, 6 juin 1945'.

[11] Private archives of Christian de Montbrison, Memoirs of Colette de Dampierre, née Cahen d'Anvers, 33–37. Christian de Montbrison is the nephew of Mme de Dampierre.

[12] Dépôt central de la justice militaire, Le Blanc, Indre, 'Dossier Utikal et autres', sub-dossier A, 'Ordre d'informer'.

[13] Bundersarchiv Berlin, NSDAP file of Kurt von Behr, Mitglied Nr 3 391 527.

[14] This was also the opinion of the American officer who examined the file in 1945.

[15] Heuss, *Kunst- und Kulturgutraub*, 129.

[16] On the 'Music' bureau, see W. de Vries. 1996. Sonderstab Musik: *Music Confiscations by the Einsatzstab Reichsleiter Rosenberg under the Nazi Occupation of Western Europe*, Amsterdam: Amsterdam University Press.

ILLUSTRATION 1. Alfred Rosenberg arriving in Paris (n.d.).
Dépôt central de la justice militaire, Le Blanc, dossier Utikal et al.

The ERR had local offices in Belgium and the Netherlands, as well as branches in the provinces.[17] It confiscated numerous premises for use as depots in Paris and other large towns. This structure would be duplicated with the setting up of 'Operation Furniture', which organised the looting of Jewish apartments from spring 1942 onwards.

The Context of the Decision (December 1941–March 1942)

The activities of the ERR, which continued up until the Liberation, nonetheless slowed after the summer of 1941 because the major part of the work was complete: the great Jewish collections and libraries had been sent off to Germany, and the ERR was not allowed to touch French public collections. Operation Barbarossa, on 22 June 1941, changed this situation. Alfred Rosenberg was made minister of the Occupied Eastern Territories, taking charge of a new ministry created to administer and exploit the vast tracts of land conquered by the Reich's

---

[17] For a summary of the ERR's depredations, see I. Le Masne de Chermont and D. Schulmann. 2000. *Le Pillage de l'art en France pendant l'Occupation et la situation des 2000 œuvres confiées aux musées nationaux: Mission d'étude sur la spoliation des Juifs en France*, Paris: La Documentation française.

armies.[18] As was the custom under the National Socialist regime, Rosenberg kept his previous position along with his new powers.

The deportation of Jews from the German Reich towards the East began in October 1941. They were sent to ghettos in the General Government of Poland and other Baltic countries. Since they left behind various possessions in need of new owners, the Eleventh Decree to the Reich Citizenship Law was passed on 25 November. This text stated that all the possessions of Jews no longer living in Germany would pass into the ownership of the Reich, regardless of whether their owners had emigrated or been deported. Unoccupied apartments, along with the furniture in them, needed to be assigned to new owners. It was the job of the tax authorities, the Finanzämter (Tax Offices) to recover this property. The Finance Ministry, which oversaw them, reserved the right to bypass this process and take any property that might be of use to it. Declarations were processed centrally in the Berlin offices of Moabit. Once a family had been taken away, the keys to their apartment were given to the building's concierge, who made them available to the Tax Offices.[19] Works of art and cultural goods, meanwhile, were to be handed over to the ERR; jewellery, other valuables and stamp collections to the central pawnbrokerage office in Berlin; currency and bonds went the treasury. The Gestapo quickly obtained priority access to furniture, which they could take directly from apartments. Rosenberg's ministry, in need of furniture for its administrative offices in the conquered territories, was also allowed to help itself to the contents of the Finance Ministry depots.[20]

In the changed context of December 1941, the plunder in Western Europe not only grew in scale but also took on a new ideological dimension. In many respects, this month marked a turning point in the policy of the maintenance of order in occupied France and, consequently, of anti-Semitic repression. The first isolated attacks against German soldiers had taken place that summer, and more occurred in autumn. On 29 November, a French law established a single organisation to represent all France's Jews, the creation of which had been demanded for more than a year by Theodor Danneker, Eichmann's representative in Paris. It was to be called the Union Générale des Israélites de France (UGIF). On 12 December the third round-up of Jews took place: 743 well-to-do people, among them many well-known figures, were arrested in Paris. After being held briefly in the École militaire on the Champ de Mars (next to the Eiffel Tower), they were imprisoned in the camp at Compiègne-Royallieu; some of these detainees would

---

[18] The German name for this ministry was Reichsministerium für die besetzen Ostgebiete.

[19] R. Hilberg. 1985. *The Destruction of the European Jews*, New York, London: Holmes & Meier, 2 volumes, II, 409–412.

[20] In small towns, furniture was sold directly to the public, in the street, in front of the building it had been taken from.

later be sent to the Parisian camps. At Drancy, Dannecker selected 300 Jews, also wealthy, and sent them to Compiègne.

In Berlin, Hitler personally called for harsh reprisals against France. However, General Otto von Stülpnagel, head of the general staff in France, on the avenue Kléber, was torn: his policy was to maintain calm in the country with as few police forces as possible, precisely by avoiding excessively visible reprisals. He nonetheless had to appear willing to the Führer and put forward a plan for the deportation of Jews to the East, probably to camps and ghettos, although it was not yet a question of their extermination.[21] On 14 December, Stülpnagel announced new punitive measures, in particular against the Jews, seen as potential enemies of the Reich. A collective fine of one billion francs was imposed on them, and it was up to the Union Générale des Israélites de France to organise its payment. Deportations to the East were announced, along with the execution of 'one hundred Jews, communists and anarchists, who [had] proven links with those who carried out the attacks'.[22]

One of the great unresolved questions of the historiography of the Holocaust is that of the decision. Was there a single decision to murder all the Jews in Europe, and if so, who took it, and when? No document attesting to the existence of such an order has yet been found. It is in any case far from certain whether this order was ever written down. The latest research nonetheless shows that, if there was such an order, it was issued later than had been thought for many years: between the beginning of December 1941 and the end of January 1942.[23] It is impossible to say whether Rosenberg was aware of any such decision and whether he passed this information on to his faithful lieutenant, von Behr, but on 18 December 1941, the 'thinker' of National Socialism sent Hitler a note requesting permission for his staff in Paris to take furniture from apartments in the western occupied countries no longer inhabited by Jews. He stressed that there was a drastic lack of furniture in the eastern territories placed under his control. This initiative would in fact seem to have come from von Behr, who saw it as a path to promotion. This

---

[21] On the negotiations and tensions between the various authorities in occupied France between August and December 1941, see U. Herbert. 1998. 'Die deutsche Militärverwaltung in Paris und die deportation der französischen Juden', in U. Herbert (ed.), *Nationalsozialistische Vernichtungspoltitik 1939–1945: Neue Forschungen und Kontroversen*, Frankfurt am Main: Fischer, 170–208.

[22] The text of the announcement is reproduced in S. Klarsfeld. 1993. *Le Calendrier de la persécution des Juifs de France 1940–1944*, Paris: Les fils et filles des déportés juifs de France and the Beate Klarsfeld Foundation, 169.

[23] On these questions, see C. Gerlach. 1998. *Die Wannsee-Konferenz, das Schicksal der deutschen Juden und Hitlers politische Grundsatzentscheidung, alle Juden Europas zu ermorden*, Hamburg: Hamburger Edition HIS Verlag; and M. Roseman. 2002. *The Villa, the Lake, the Meeting*, London: Penguin.

was in any case what Gerhard Utikal, whose assistant von Behr was at this point, would later declare. It is uncertain whether those who instigated the operation had in mind the mass extermination of the Jews when they proposed seizing their furniture, but it is quite clear that the Jews could no longer live in France: after they had left, voluntarily or otherwise, they would not be coming back.

Hitler gave his approval and ordered the transfer of furniture from West to East to begin, a decision put down in writing on 31 December 1941 by Hans Lammers, the chief of the Reich Chancellery. The operation was given the name Möbel Aktion (M. Aktion), literally 'Operation Furniture'.

On 14 January 1942, Rosenberg put von Behr officially in charge of implementing the operation, which had in the meantime been extended to Belgium and the Netherlands.[24] On 19 January, the high command in Paris received the order to place itself at the disposal of the Einsatzstab Reichsleiter Rosenberg in order to assist with transporting the fruits of this plunder. The question was raised by the German embassy in Paris as to whether a special decree would be necessary for the operation to be implemented. The French government was at this point preparing a decree (published on 3 February) ordering the seizure of furniture abandoned by Jews who had fled or been arrested.[25] Was Vichy aware of these German projects? This is not clear. Numerous French initiatives involving expropriation and looting were undertaken in order to prevent the Germans from appropriating goods that Vichy considered to be French. For example, the Ministry of Industrial Production was mainly concerned, from December 1940 onwards, with placing provisional French supervisors at the head of Jewish companies. In any case, Otto Abetz intervened to prevent the French authorities from being warned of German plans. These problems delayed the start of the operation, just as von Behr was actively working to organise it.

The high command was still working, in February, on the wording of a decree on the confiscation of furniture. Abetz again intervened to prevent the property of interned Jews from being included in the operation, in order not to complicate any further the issue of settling debts and overdue rent payments. As von Behr was becoming increasingly impatient, the question was passed directly to Hitler, who came down on the side of discretion. The idea of a decree was abandoned. On 8 February 1942, Hitler ordered that only unoccupied Jewish apartments should be looted, and that furniture left with storage companies should not yet be touched, leaving the question of the property of American and English Jews unresolved.

The running of Möbel Aktion – Operation Furniture – was taken out of the hands of the ERR on 25 March 1942 and given to the Ministry of the Occupied

---

[24] Heuss, *Kunst- und Kulturgutraub*, 125.

[25] Lambauer, *Otto Abetz*, 477.

Eastern Territories.[26] A new body was consequently set up in Paris, the Dienststelle Westen (Western Service). On 1 April, the French minister of the interior
passed on the order from the German military high command to the prefects
of the French regions forbidding until further notice the sale by auction of 'the
contents of Jewish apartments or Jewish furniture'.[27]

The Creation of the Dienststelle Westen

The official date of the creation of the new agency was 17 April 1942, and offices
were almost immediately set up in Belgium and the Netherlands.[28] Von Behr's
main problem was organising transport. On 7 April, the German high command
in Paris had given notification of the imminent launch of Operation Furniture
to the various German authorities in the occupied zone, namely the *Komman-
datur* of Greater Paris, the *Feldkommandanturen*, the police services, etc. It was
specified that, following orders received from Berlin, the furniture of unoccupied
Jewish apartments would become the property of the Reich (*Reichseigentum*); no
receipt needed to be issued. The property of German Jews or Jews who had possessed German nationality was to be confiscated according to normal procedure.
Property that had been confiscated by the Wehrmacht should be handed over to
the Dienststelle Westen.

Von Behr did not have to move offices and in fact retained his position with
the ERR, at least until the beginning of 1943. The Einsatzstab moved its offices to 12, rue Dumont-d'Urville. In Paris, von Behr was the target of constant
hostility from the other occupation authorities. He needed to gain support and
informed Göring directly of his changing administrative situation. He knew the
Reichsmarshall well, and the latter paid regular visits to Paris, coming to the
ERR depot opened in the Jeu de Paume museum in order to select works for his
personal collection. On 30 March 1942, Göring mentioned these contacts to
Rosenberg, who replied on 18 June, restating his desire to oversee the plunder
and announcing that the lists of artworks seized up to that date would be revised.
He then asked Göring to support his project of emptying Jewish apartments.

The launch of Operation Furniture also took some time in Belgium, where it
was necessary to coordinate the efforts of the *Feldkommandanturen*, in particular
that of Antwerp, and various branches of the military administration in Brussels.

---

[26] Most of the documents concerning the decision behind and implementation of Möbel Aktion were assembled in a report published by the United Restitution Organisation (URO) in
1958. We have only been able to locate part of this report.

[27] Centre de documentation juive contemporaine, CVII-55.

[28] Centre de documentation juive contemporaine, LXIII-17, Vereinbarung des Reichsministerium für die besetzen Ostgebiete, 17/04/1942.

The departure of the first convoy to Germany was thus cancelled twice.[29] Again, on 5 July 1942, Lammers circulated a note addressed to 'the highest authorities of the Reich' asking them to lend all the necessary logistical support to Alfred Rosenberg's scheme.

At the beginning of March 1942, the first few lorries arrived at a depot in the rue de l'Abondance, at Boulogne-sur-Seine in the western suburbs of Paris. Their contents were to be distributed among victims of the Allied bombing of the Renault factories. From April onwards, trains began to leave for the East. It is not certain whether the convoys got as far as eastern Poland and the conquered Soviet territories, as had been planned. Evidence exists that at least some loads arrived in Ukraine. In any case, the destination of the plunder changed in June 1942 with the raid on Cologne, the first massive bombing against a large German city.[30] The furniture convoys were sent there and distributed among bombed-out families.

In the Netherlands, the direction of the Dienststelle was placed under the orders of Schmidt-Stähler.[31] It collaborated closely with a German body that had no equivalent in Belgium or France: the Central Bureau for Jewish Emigration.[32] This was based on the organisation created in Vienna, following the Anschluss, by Adolf Eichmann. On 20 March 1942, the Central Bureau published a notice in the *Joodsche Weekblad,* the community's official newspaper, ordering Jews to request authorisation in writing from the Jewish Council if they wanted to retain possession of their furniture. The publication of this notice contrasted with the fact that Möbel Aktion was supposed to remain secret in the Netherlands, to the point that employees of the Dienststelle had to sign an agreement saying that they would not speak about the activities they had taken part in, even after the expiry of their contract with their employer. The centralisation of these operations was even more pronounced in the Netherlands than elsewhere. A single office of the Dienststelle was created in Amsterdam, and no regional branches were established. A detachment of the Sicherheitsdienst, or SD (the SS intelligence service), was placed within the Central Bureau in order to coordinate the looting. From summer 1942 onwards, truckloads of objects arrived at the port of Amsterdam, to be loaded onto ships and delivered to German ports.

There was, then, a shift in these first weeks of 1942. Visible in the decision to plunder apartments, it was a shift from a systematic project of economic Aryanisation – of the exclusion from society, the pauperisation of the Jewish population of Western Europe – towards their complete dispossession, the theft of their furniture and most basic everyday objects. Operation Furniture was an integral

---

[29] URO. 1958. *M. Aktion Frankreich, Belgien, Holland and Luxemburg, 1940–1944,* 69.

[30] Cologne was pounded by 1,046 bombers throughout the night of 30–31 May 1942.

[31] G. Aalders. 2000. *Geraubt! Die Enteignung jüdischen Besitzes im Zweiten Weltkrieg,* Cologne: Dittrich Verlag, 359–370.

[32] Zentralstelle für jüdische Auswanderung.

part of the Final Solution. It was rooted at the intersection of expropriation and extermination. It called for the creation of highly centralised administrative bodies, which in turn solicited services from other organisations that thus themselves became involved in the policy of persecution, if this was not already the case. Von Behr had at his disposal an instrument that, while small, was becoming all the more effective as the number of beneficiaries of the anti-Semitic policy grew ever larger. As a direct consequence of Operation Furniture, every German victim of Allied bombing raids became a potential beneficiary of the plunder and murder of the Jews of occupied Western Europe.

CHAPTER 2

THE IMPLEMENTATION OF OPERATION FURNITURE

The Structure of the Dienststelle Westen

The new Dienststelle Westen was attached to the newly created Ministry of the Occupied Eastern Territories. On 20 April 1941, in the context of the preparations for Operation Barbarossa, Alfred Rosenberg had been given the title of 'delegate for the central handling [*Bearbeitung*] of questions regarding the eastern-European space',[1] which was added to his previous responsibilities. The new ministry, created in July 1941, had no real executive powers in the strict sense but was a civil authority that, in parallel with the military occupation of the conquered countries, was meant to deal with the political education of ethnic Germans living there, with Germany's *Ostpolitik*, with the implementation of various ideological measures and with the political surveillance of prisoners of war. Propaganda and the control of the press also fell within its purview. While the Jewish question was not mentioned explicitly, on 20 January 1942 the ministry sent two representatives to the Wannsee conference, where the Final Solution was debated and orchestrated. These were Alfred Meyer, *Gauleiter* of North Westphalia, who bore the title of *Reichsamtleiter* (administrative director) of Rosenberg's new organisation, and Georg Leibbrandt, who ran its political department. The ministry was installed in Berlin. The two main buildings were at 33 and 134 Kurfürstenstrasse, in the western part of the city, a fair way away from the traditional ministries concentrated around the Friedrichstrasse. The ministry had a secondary head office in Ratibor, a town in Poland that had been part of Prussia until 1919.[2]

The new administration saw its own research departments multiply. It never had a very large staff and, within the organisation, the Paris-based Dienststelle Westen was, relative to its size, highly influential. The justification given for this administrative modification, namely the transfer of the responsibility for Operation Furniture from the ERR to the Ministry of the Eastern Territories, was that

---

[1] *Beauftragter für die Zentrale Bearbeitung der Fragen des ost-europäischen Raumes.*
[2] Situated between Oppeln and Katowice.

the goods recovered in France and later Belgium and the Netherlands would serve to furnish both the homes of the German colonists who would settle in the conquered space and also the German authorities, including Rosenberg's organisation, which were also moving there. In fact, Rosenberg found himself confronted from the outset with material difficulties in organising the vast move that was envisaged. He had been counting on greater logistic support from the national authorities, support that the party was either unable or unwilling to offer him.

Kurt von Behr left his post at the ERR and was made head of the Dienststelle Westen, which moved into the same premises at 54, avenue d'Iéna. The ERR moved out. The new service was therefore run by von Behr, from the same premises of the ERR, and was overseen by Alfred Rosenberg. There can be no doubt that from the very beginning there was a degree of confusion regarding the administrative affiliation of the Dienststelle Westen, which has often been mistaken for the ERR. This confusion lasted throughout the war, continuing into the post-Liberation trials and even making its way into the most specialised works of today. Yet – and this was stated on several occasions in internal documents of the Ministry of the Eastern Territories – the Dienststelle Westen was an entirely separate administrative entity from the ERR.[3] It was in fact a branch of the German government, whereas the ERR was attached to the National Socialist Party. The Dienststelle and the ERR nonetheless collaborated quite closely, for a very simple reason: from the beginning, it had been decided that the Dienststelle would deliver to the ERR all the works of art, valuable books and musical instruments that it unearthed in apartments lived in by Jews.

No. 54, avenue d'Iéna was a fine, horseshoe-shaped building that had belonged to the industrialist Émile Deutsch de la Meurthe, who with his brother had been a pioneer of the French oil industry. Built in 1890, the house comprised fifty rooms over five floors, with one apartment per floor except for the attic, which contained twenty-nine servants' rooms.[4] In 1940, its owners were Pierre de Gunzburg and his wife Yvonne, the daughter of Émile Deutsch de la Meurthe, whose dowry the house had been. Before being requisitioned by the Germans, all the apartments had been occupied by members of the family. The couple spent the war in New York.

The Dienststelle Westen was paid for out of the funds of the Ministry of the Eastern Territories, and a detachment of staff from the ministry was sent to it from Berlin. The use of these funds was authorised by the German Finance

---

[3] This confusion was one of the main difficulties encountered in our research. It took long months of work just to clarify the administrative affiliation of the ERR and then look in the archives of the Ministry of the Eastern Territories. We were unable to locate the complete archives of the Dienststelle Westen, which were burned in August 1944 in the depot at Aubervilliers.

[4] The details of the building are taken from: Archives de Paris, 4W 103, dossier 5431, 'Réquisition du 54, avenue d'Iéna'.

Ministry, and the Dienststelle was regularly inspected by officials from the parent organisation. The Reich's auditing authority also monitored its spending. On at least three occasions, inspectors from the Ministry of the Eastern Territories were sent to Paris in order to make checks.[5]

For our description of the internal organisation of the Dienststelle Westen, we possess only one postwar document, the statement of Arthur Garbas, who was sent from Berlin to run the personnel department. Garbas, born in 1909, was a civil servant in the Finance Ministry, from which he was transferred to the Ministry of the Eastern Territories following the creation of the latter. Promoted to bureau chief, he arrived in Paris in January 1943. When interrogated after the war, he drew the organisational schema of the Dienststelle from memory. The Dienststelle answered directly to the central directorate of the ministry, i.e., the director Degenhard, who reported to Alfred Rosenberg. This central directorate may have been something like a ministerial cabinet, whereas other directorates were organised by geographical area. Von Behr therefore found himself two steps below Rosenberg in the hierarchy. He had a personnel and accounts office at his disposal, along with another dealing with general administration (cash and kitchen arrangements) and a department for special tasks (*Sonderaugaben*), headed by two men and one woman, a certain Miss Nehring. This department will be dealt with in greater detail later.

The rest of the Dienststelle's organisation was geographically split. There was a directorate for the Netherlands, another for Belgium and northern France (the two French *départements* of the Nord and the Pas-de-Calais were administratively attached to the high command in Brussels), and yet another for the occupied zone of France. Regional sub-offices were gradually set up in various towns. They often only consisted of one or two people, and not all of them really functioned. By far the most active was that in Nancy, headed by an individual named Brecht. From spring 1944 onwards, with the plans to extend Operation Furniture to the southern zone, a new directorate was created in Marseilles, with two sub-offices in Cannes and Nice. There were offices, or at least representatives, of the Dienststelle in Angers, Auxerre, Besançon, Bordeaux, Dijon, Nancy, Orléans, Reims, Rennes, Rouen and Troyes.

Finally, an '*Abtransport*' department, dealing with removals, was placed under von Behr's direct control. Six subsections corresponded to the depots for furniture and looted objects: Aubervilliers, Ost (meaning Lévitan, next to the Gare de l'Est), Austerlitz, Bassano, Fresnel and the Musée d'art moderne (Museum of Modern Art), on the avenue du Président-Wilson. Three of these depots would be transformed into internment camps. The heads of these subsections thus became camp commandants.

---

[5] See for example the report of the inspection of 15 September 1943: Bundesarchiv, ERR NS 30.

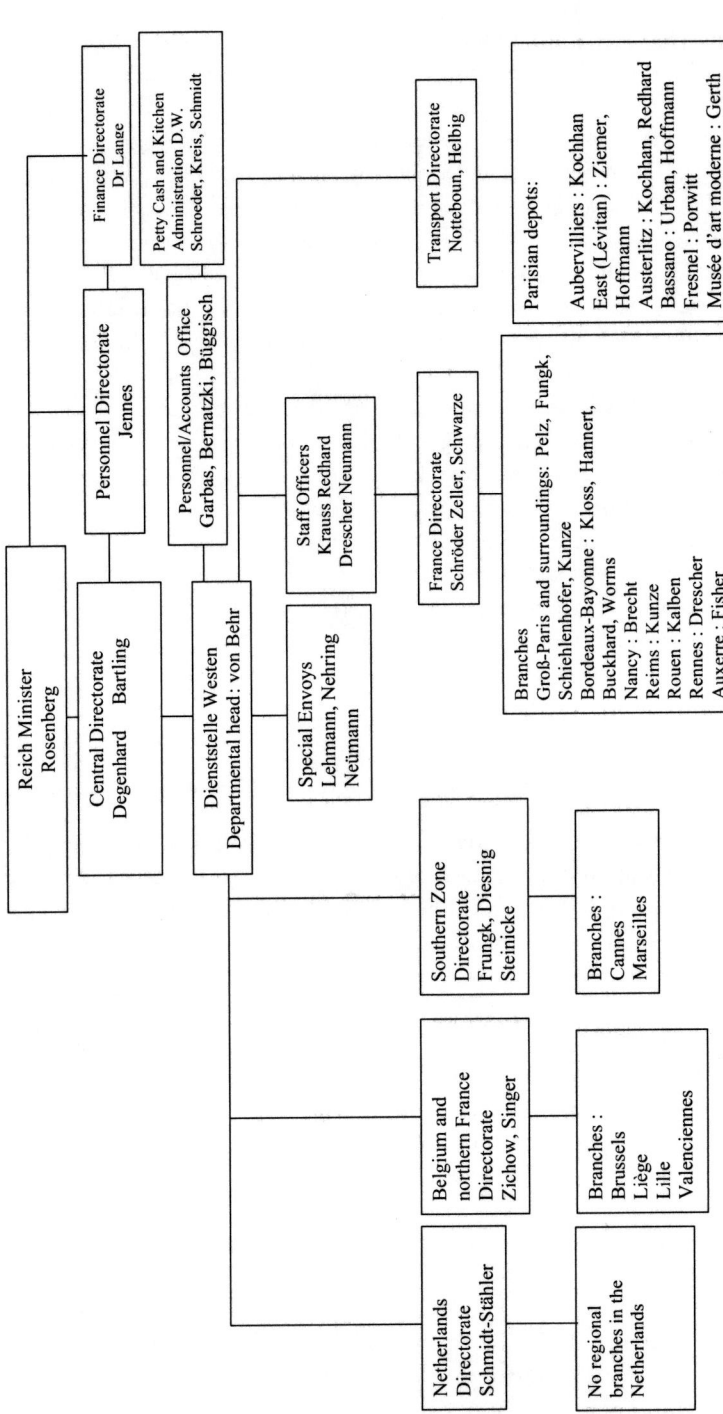

Figure 1. Organisational Schema of the Ministry of the Occupied Eastern Territories, Dienststelle Westen. Drawn by Jean-Marc Dreyfus from the testimony of Arthur Garbas.

There were never many staff working at 54, avenue d'Iéna: 120 on average, including 30 women. The working budget was provided directly by the Ministry of the Eastern Territories; it will be seen later how the latter recovered this expenditure. Von Behr enjoyed a great deal of independence in this organisation he had built to suit his own needs, an independence that he was able to retain until the very end, both because he benefited from the support of Alfred Rosenberg and because he freely distributed the fruits of the plunder around numerous German departments and dignitaries in order to buy their indulgence. By May 1942, the Dienststelle had come to the attention of Martin Luther, the head of the Germany division of the Ministry of Foreign Affairs. Concerned by the potential political consequences of Operation Furniture, Luther recommended to Foreign Minister Ribbentrop that he should intervene directly and contact Lammers, at the Reich Chancellery, in order to get the Dienststelle transferred to the control of the embassy in Paris. He did not succeed. The embassy had to make do with demanding regular updates on the evolving situation.

Once the Dienststelle had been created, Kurt von Behr's first concern was obtaining logistical support. Since he could not rely on the army, owing to the rivalry between the different occupation authorities, he looked for other means to obtain the necessary workforce and equipment. As these resources were needed locally, he quite logically turned to French removal firms, relying greatly on the assistance of their professional body.

The Organisational Committee for Removal and Storage Businesses

For more than two years, the streets of Paris were criss-crossed almost daily by lorries on their way to pick up furniture and other objects from looted Jewish apartments. Both their drivers and the removal teams were French. The vehicles were normal removal vans. Von Behr's department used the tools and expertise of a profession that, while loosely structured, was well equipped. In this time of economic hardship, this activity certainly represented the major part of the work of Parisian removal firms. The intermediary between the Dienststelle Westen and these companies was the profession's Organisational Committee.

The law of 16 August 1940 had attempted to circumscribe economic activity strictly, setting out a programme of centralised control that involved the creation of 'organisational committees', bodies for the self-regulation of different professions. There were 250 of these by the Liberation. Their power and level of activity varied from one profession to another. They often paralleled or replaced existing managerial unions. They were obligatory intermediaries in any dealings with the state and especially with the powerful new Ministry of Industrial Production founded in December 1940. They often played a role in controlling access to the profession, suppressing competition and also in sharing resources, contracts and raw materials.

The Comité d'organisation des entreprises de déménagement et de garde-meubles (Organisational Committee for Removal and Storage Businesses) was created by a law dated 29 May 1941.[6] It set up its offices on the premises of the Chambre syndicale (managerial union), which was well-established, having been founded in 1890. It consisted of a president, Adrien Bedel (soon replaced), whose firm was based on the rue Monsigny, and six members.[7] When the committee received a letter from von Behr dated 25 February 1942, announcing that removal firms would be required for Operation Furniture, this was not its first encounter with anti-Jewish legislation. Jews' access to their possessions left in storage had been limited from June 1941 and then forbidden entirely by the decree of the military high command of 17 December, the same decree that had imposed the billion-franc fine and given Rosenberg the signal to proceed with Operation Furniture. From then on, the Dienststelle would tell the committee each day how many lorries and men were required and indicate an assembly point in Paris. The committee would then send a requisition form to dispatch one or more firms to a new location.

Once the work had been carried out, the Dienststelle paid the requisitioning costs to the committee, which distributed the money among the removal firms. There were days when up to eighty lorries were requisitioned. The committee took a percentage of the reimbursement money to cover administrative costs.[8] This money allowed it to buy equipment, furniture and other supplies, and also to move.

It set up new offices in a fine building on the rue Chauchat, at no. 20, between the rue Lafayette and the boulevard Hausmann, right in the banking district but also not far from the rue de la Victoire, where the managerial union was situated. At least a hundred Parisian removal firms were requisitioned at one point or another over a period of two and a half years. The committee was keen to distribute the Dienststelle's manna to its members in these difficult times. The majority of the 185 Parisan firms belonging to the committee thus worked for Möbel Aktion.

The operation's coordinator was Eugène Grospiron *père*. After the war, there were rumours within the profession that he had agreed to serve as an intermediary between the removal firms and the Dienststelle Westen in the hope of getting his son released from German captivity.[9] The committee also passed on informa-

---

[6] *Journal Officiel de la République française:* 1/06/1941.

[7] From July 1942 these were: M. Léon Galand, president; members, M. Adrien Bedel, Maurice Corvisier, Edmond Dazin, Georges Marcel, Marc Redmontet, Mme Cécile Delafraye (widowed).

[8] Archives de la Chambre syndicale de déménagement, letter from Raymond Cornuau, general secretary of the managerial union, to Henri Lévy, president of the Bureau d'information du Fonds social juif unifié, 10/12/1957.

[9] Archives de la Chambre syndicale du déménagement, letter from the Messageries nationales Waldbaum SA, Reims, to the Chambre syndicale, 24/10/1967.

tion needed for the looting of objects in storage. Possessions stored in depots by Jewish families were one of von Behr's targets; however, these were difficult to locate. Again, the removal and storage firms assisted, on the instructions of the committee. A circular dated 12 March 1942 and signed by Adrien Bedel instructed the firms to send lists of all the furniture they were storing directly to 54, avenue d'Iéna. Circular no. 18 specified that

> [t]he lists must be accompanied by figures indicating:
> 1 total number of items of Jewish furniture (or thought to be Jewish)
> 2 total volume
> 3 total amount of insurance
> 4 total value of boxes stated to clients
> 5 total owed ending March 1942.[10]

When the furniture was taken, the problem was paying the storage costs to these firms. In order to avoid legal problems, these payments were made by the Dienststelle Westen, again using the committee as an intermediary. A special form was printed for this purpose.

Coordination between von Behr's offices and the committee was efficient. Some reticence began to be expressed by the removal firms, but only from 1944 onwards.[11] In the meantime, these procedures had become second nature and the looting of apartments proceeded without a hitch.

The Looting of Apartments

In the first few weeks of Operation Furniture, German soldiers and military lorries joined in with the removals. From spring 1942, the diligence of the requisitioned companies having been demonstrated, only French vans were involved. Operation Furniture quickly took on a routine character. A small team would go to the home to be targeted. It would consist of between one and three employees of the Dienststelle, occasionally with an interpreter, who would get the keys to the apartment from the concierge, or from the police station if the family had been arrested. A summary inventory of the apartment's contents would be drawn up; then the door would be sealed.[12] The summary inventory was passed on in triplicate to the Dienststelle, which then organised transport, sending a number of vans corresponding to the amount of furniture to be taken and drawing

---

[10] Archives de la Chambre syndicale du déménagement, Circular no. 18.

[11] Bundesarchiv Berlin, NS 30, 12, Abschluss-Bericht der Einsatzleitung Nordostfrankreich, 5/10/1944, p. 2.

[12] URO, *M. Aktion Frankreich*, inspection report (*Geschäftsprüfung*) of the Dienststelle Westen, 15/09/1943.

up a preliminary list of what to take. The requisition forms for vans were then sent out.

A team from the Dienststelle would meet the removal men at the appointed time. These teams would generally comprise an officer, an interpreter and two or three employees from the avenue d'Iéna. A transport order was filled out for each apartment, mentioning the place and date of the removal. The *préfecture de police* in Paris (the central administration of the city's police) and the *préfectures* (regional government offices) in the provinces were informed of each removal in order to take charge of the apartments that were left empty. There were up to eighteen teams working at any one time. The vans' contents arrived at the Dienststelle's depots – each more or less specialising in particular types of objects – where they were sorted and packed into crates. These then left by the trainful for the Reich. When an apartment belonging to a Jew was opened, it would be thoroughly looted by the Dienststelle, who would take away virtually everything it contained, from the largest pieces of furniture to the smallest, most everyday objects, from kitchen dressers to school exercise books, from stoves to books and ashtrays.

The avenue d'Iéna's *Abtransport* bureau received daily updates on the activity in its six Parisian depots, allowing it to organise convoys to Germany on a weekly basis. While the depots' inventories were constantly updated, the same was not necessarily true of the inventories relating to apartments. Once they entered the Möbel Aktion system, objects were no longer identifiable by origin. Keeping track of the loot was no longer the objective; only the efficiency of the sorting process and the despatching of items to the Reich mattered now. And this efficiency was remarkable, even if the staff were constantly complaining of being overloaded and teams occasionally found that apartments had already been emptied (this happened in 110 cases in Paris after September 1943), quite possibly by their owners.

The question of how von Behr's offices located these apartments needs to be asked. Only patchy information is available on this subject. Officially, teams from the avenue d'Iéna served as 'beaters', going from one building to the next, interrogating concierges to find any empty Jewish apartments. It is also likely that the Paris *préfecture de police* provided lists of vacant Jewish housing, especially following arrests.[13] The Sipo-SD may have been a source of information, while the Commissariat général aux questions juives (Central Commissariat for Jewish Matters) also provided a certain amount.[14] For instance, in November 1943 the commissariat received a report sent by the *préfecture de police*'s sub-office for Jew-

---

[13] The Préfecture de police de Paris informed us that they have no archived material relating to this question.

[14] Formed in March 1941, the Commissariat général aux questions juives was a French ministerial organisation dealing with all questions linked to the state anti-Semitism of the Vichy régime.

ish affairs regarding an apartment located at 128, avenue d'Italie in Paris, which had been occupied by M. Salomon K., a naturalised Jew of Russian origin. The commissariat sent it on to the Dienststelle Westen on 18 December.[15]

Since Jewish apartments were being progressively placed into provisional French legal administration, and the administrators were appointed by the Commissariat général aux questions juives, it was only logical that the Dienststelle should turn to this source of information. From January 1943, if not earlier, the commissariat passed on lists of unoccupied apartments. On 27 April, a circular was sent to the provisional administrators of these properties requesting them to declare 'without delay' to the commissariat which of them were 'apartments abandoned by Jews but [still] furnished'. Many administrators were called to the avenue d'Iéna. A constant exchange of information took place with the commissariat: the latter dealt with the Aryanisation of business properties, and the Dienststelle busied itself with the seizure of domestic properties. This division of tasks was generally adhered to, even in the case of an apartment on the boulevard de la Reine in Versailles, where the victim had been running a business from his home. On 20 August 1943, the Dienststelle informed the commissariat that the premises had been thoroughly emptied, but that there was a workshop, with its machines, in the garden. The machines were not taken away by the removal men, and the Commissariat général aux questions juives appointed a provisional administrator.[16] The cross-referencing of these sources by the offices of the avenue d'Iéna allowed them to get their hands on the majority of these apartments in Paris and its suburbs. One point should be restated: only *unoccupied* Jewish apartments could be emptied.

The Dienststelle regularly asked the commissariat for clarification regarding the 'racial status' of an individual, meaning how this person would be classified according to German and French anti-Semitic law. An office within the commissariat, the 'directorate of the status of persons', issued rulings based on family trees and documents in its possession. This directorate would become extremely important once the Parisian camps were opened.

The Commissariat général aux questions juives had negotiations with Kurt von Behr on a number of occasions. The seals placed on Jewish apartments before or after they were emptied prevented the provisional French administrator from carrying out the task of selling the property, if the owner was Jewish, or from re-letting it, as the seal made it impossible to organise visits by potential buyers. Another recurring problem was the removal of furniture not belonging to Jews. There was no means of appeal. This is how the papers of the writer Jules Romains

---

[15] Archives Nationales, AJ 38 404, Commissariat général aux questions juives, 'Correspondance avec la Dienststelle Westen concernant les appartements juifs à Paris, 1942–1944'.

[16] Ibid., letter from the Dienststelle Westen to the Commissariat général aux questions juives, direction de l'aryanisation économique, section VII.

ended up being taken by the Dienststelle, despite his not being Jewish.[17] He had left France for the United States, leaving his books and papers (including some manuscripts) with an acquaintance, doctor Jean Poreaux. This doctor had had a Jewish mother-in-law, from whom he had inherited some furniture, which he placed in a house on the rue des Lilas in Paris, along with Jules Romains' papers.[18] At the beginning of September 1943, the Dienststelle took away all the objects and furniture in this house. The papers of the author of *Les Hommes de bonne volonté* and *Knock* ended up in one of the depots of Operation Furniture, where they disappeared without a trace.

The Dienststelle's activities attracted the attention of certain private individuals who saw an opportunity to buy up properties at knock-down prices. Their requests were refused. There were also many landlords whose Jewish tenants – whether deported or in hiding – had left and were no longer paying their rent. With the furniture still in the apartments, it was difficult to re-let them. The commissariat advised landlords to inform the offices of the avenue d'Iéna of this fact, whereupon these properties were very helpfully cleared.

Particularly from the summer of 1943 onwards, the activities of the avenue d'Iéna grew in the provinces. In Bayonne, the head of the branch of the Dienststelle was a German by the name of Worms (from September 1943).[19] The branch had been set up in the villa Lafourcade at the end of 1942. Worms set about plundering country houses belonging to Jews in the surrounding region, and several wagonloads of furniture were despatched to Paris. There was also an office in Angoulême run by Helmut Alisch, then by Dr Edgar Wittfeld. The latter had crates of stolen objects sent directly to his home in Königsberg.[20] Bordeaux was comprehensively plundered: the branch office of the Dienststelle was located on the rue Ravez and rue Croix-de-Seguey. From there, instructions were passed to the German transport firm Kuhne & Nagel, 60 *bis,* quai des Chartrons, which organised removals from Jewish apartments. Sixteen Bordeaux-based companies were requisitioned, transporting at least 8,200 cubic metres of furniture.[21]

The Nancy branch, on the rue Hermite, was opened in January 1943. In the town, the SD had already begun looting apartments.[22] Dr Wittfeld had also

---

[17] His real name was Louis Farigoul.

[18] Archives nationales, AJ 38 798, 'Correspondance', letter from Dr Jean Poreaux, 3, avenue de Clichy, to the Commissariat général aux questions juives, 8/09/1943.

[19] Dépôt central de la Justice militaire, Le Blanc, 'Utikal et autres', documents 29a3E/D/II, 'Enquêtes effectuées dans les régions d'Angers, Bordeaux, Dijon, Marseille, Nice, Nancy, Orléans, Reims, Rouen', statement by Chief Rabbi Cohen.

[20] Ibid., statement by Jean Kneib, fifty-four years old, driver for the Dienststelle.

[21] Ibid., item 17/g, report by the inspector of the Sûreté nationale Pallier to the divisional commander, head of the regional service of the *police judiciaire.*

[22] Ibid., document 32/D/II, report by the enquiry in Nancy.

worked there. With the help of two local removal firms – the Société lorraine des transports and the établissements Prudent – he placed all the furniture in the local *Magasins réunis*. The crates were sent either to Paris or directly to Germany. Some of the items, in particular paintings, were sold on the spot to antiques dealers. In Troyes, the head of the branch was called Willy Fischer, based at 48, rue Thiers between late 1943 and August 1944. The Besançon office covered numerous *départements*, thirteen in total, two of which straddled the demarcation line. It emptied 10 apartments in the Meuse, 60 in the Vosges, 20 in Haute-Saône and 105 in the Doubs (the final total for this region was 514), even going into towns as small as Chaumont.[23]

Despite Hitler's calls for discretion, it was difficult to have vans driving across Paris and its suburbs emptying hundreds of apartments without attracting some attention. Various French authorities quickly became aware of what was going on. For instance, storage firms were writing to the Commissariat général aux questions juives, as in the following example (the name of the firm is not indicated): 'As far as we are aware', its director wrote, 'these removals, announced by a simple telephone call from, we believe, the offices of the avenue d'Iéna, are not the subject of any proper requisition order from the occupying authority, any order from the Organisational Committee of our guild and give no redeemable receipt to depositing clients.'[24] He added that he was notifying the authorities of the existence of the operation, which he did in a letter sent to the *préfet de Police*, in order to cover his civil liability 'with regard to possible claims from owner-depositors.'

The French government was quick to lodge quite vigorous official protests. Their opposition to the looting of works of art had been stated on many occasions, such as on 25 July 1941, when Xavier Vallat, the *commissaire général aux questions juives* (general commissioner for Jewish matters), had written to Werner Best, the head of the administrative department of the military high command. On 5 September 1942, the French delegation to the Franco-German Armistice Commission lodged an official complaint.[25] The removal of furniture was prejudicial to the French state and to Aryan persons (the creditors of dispossessed Jews, for example):

These removals seem to be an initiative of the occupying authorities alone as the French office and even the German office of the Aryanisation of Jewish property

---

[23] Bundesarchiv, NS 30, 12, p. 17, Abschluss-Bericht der Einsatzleitung Nordostfrankreich, 3–4.

[24] Archives de la Chambre syndicale du déménagement, communication sent by pneumatic tube with acknowledgement of receipt to the Commissariat général aux questions juives, 23/6/1942.

[25] Archives nationales, AJ 40 1366, 'Sachgebiet 34, Deutsche Waffenstillstandkommission, Judenfragen und Behandlungen ausgebürgerter Franzosen', item 160.

have no connection to them.[26] They cannot be considered as requisitions in kind because they do not involve objects necessary to the upkeep of occupying troops, no order is presented by the person carrying them out and no requisition voucher is given to the individuals concerned. Additionally, they are carried out without any attempt by the soldiers supervising them to determine whether the furniture seized belongs entirely or partly to Aryan persons and also whether the building in which the sealed-off rooms are situated belongs to an Aryan person.

By September 1942, 4,000 apartments had already been emptied. The French delegation demanded the immediate cessation of the operation, the removal of seals and the valuation of the furniture that had already been seized. The German delegation passed on this demand to the military high command, which replied that it had nothing to do with the removals – which was true. At the beginning of August 1944, Léon Bérard, a representative on the Franco-German Armistice Commission, wrote to General Vogl, his German counterpart, to reiterate this demand, to which no reply had so far been provided.

A final report of the Dienststelle Westen gives the destination of the trains filled with furniture that left the Gare d'Austerlitz for the Reich. It is organised by *Gau* (administrative region) and indicates for each train the city of destination and the number of wagons. The entire Reich was served in this way, from Strasbourg (50 wagons in 1944) to Königsberg in East Prussia (135 wagons in total). Hamburg received 2,699 wagons, a huge figure explained by the scale of the bombing of the city and the arrival of a particularly large number of convoys from the Netherlands. Certain large cities such as Dresden and Leipzig were not served directly, but the trains started to come in as the destruction from bombing increased. In general, cities in the West received more deliveries of furniture: being more industrialised, they were the victims of air raids earlier in the war, especially given that cities in the East came into bombing range only after the Allied landings in Sicily in July 1943. Bomb-damaged cities were therefore the main destination for Jewish furniture from the West.

The news that large quantities of furniture were available spread quickly throughout the various German administrations, and the fact that most of it came from Paris can hardly have lessened the interest that these cargoes provoked. Von Behr was quickly flooded with requests. Karlsruhe, the target of intense bombing, sent two representatives to Paris. Otto Abetz, the German ambassador in Paris, was from the city and personally recommended his two emissaries to the Dienststelle Westen, which received their requests favourably.[27] By March 1942, employees at the embassy were also demanding their share in the booty.[28]

---

26 Meaning the Wi 1 department of the German military high command.

27 Centre de documentation juive contemporaine, LXXI-120, interrogation of Abetz.

28 Lambauer, *Otto Abetz*, 479.

Illustration 2. Möbel Aktion train arriving in Oberhausen (n.d.).
Stradtarchiv, Oberhausen, 712-404.

However, the cities of the Reich were not the only beneficiaries of Rosenberg's largesse. 'National' depots, where the loot was distributed across the entire region, were also recipients. According, again, to the final report, 8,191 wagons arrived in the following depots: Berlin, Kehl, Scholding, Goch, Koenigswusterhausen, Stettin, Hams, Ruenthe, Zentoch, Hoyminden, Saerbeck. Other towns are named in a report by the Belgian office: Holzminden, Oberhausen, Wanne-Eickel, Gladbeck, Bottrop, Soltau, Olsen, Winden/Luhe, Celle. Small towns were thus also served, despite not having suffered any bombing. Municipal authorities simply handed out furniture to large families or the needy.

The final category of beneficiaries consisted of German civil and military organisations. The railways received 1,576 wagonloads for their own use, the Postal Service 196, the Gestapo 231 and the SS 577. Another category of beneficiaries, however, does not appear in the official summary of Operation Furniture as published by Rosenberg's offices. It consisted of high-ranking individuals in the Nazi hierarchy, or simply people with good contacts in one of the *Reichsleiter*'s administrations, as well as various Nazi organisations. For instance, crates were sent to Göring's headquarters in Berchtesgaden, to the stores of the Ministry of the Occupied Eastern Territories in Landsberg, in Warthegau, to the SS headquarters in Berlin and even to a residence for single women working in the Ministry of the

Occupied Eastern Territories in the Berlin suburb of Grünewald.[29] In fact, while it was announced, in a memo from the Dienststelle Westen dated 20 October 1942, that 60 per cent of the furniture sent to Germany had been distributed to refugees and that the figure should in the future rise to 80 per cent, the final result was more like 50 per cent. As was invariably the case under the Third Reich, the organs of the system, and particularly branches of the party, benefited disproportionately.[30]

The destinations of the furniture trains were decided in the following manner: zones that had been bombed sent a request, via the local town hall, to their *Gauleiter* who, acting in the name of the commissioner for the defence of the Reich (*Reichsverteidigungskommissar*), sent it on to the Ministry of the Eastern Territories in Berlin. Once the wagons had arrived at their destination, the *Gauleiter*'s offices had the task of distributing their contents according to the instructions of the president of the finance office (*Oberfinanzpräsident*). A bill was attached from the Ministry of the Eastern Territories, which was thereby paid, though probably not much, for the service it provided and the furniture it had looted. This money went back to the ministry, which in this way recovered part of its personnel and especially its transport expenses.

The contents of the wagons were very varied, since all Jewish apartments, from the wealthiest to the most humble, were similarly emptied. But the most valuable pieces were put to one side, and few arrived among these trainloads. In July 1943, for instance, the town hall of Aachen acknowledged receipt of cargoes sent by the Belgian office of the Dienststelle Westen.[31] As unloading the twenty-eight wagons had taken six hours and distribution had taken place over the following days, it had not been possible to draw up an inventory of their contents to contradict the list sent with them. However, whereas the wagons had arrived safe and sound, a large proportion of their contents was too substandard and damaged to be distributed to the refugees. Many kitchen fittings were unusable, glass panels being broken and so on. 'I wish once more to insist upon the fact', wrote the inspector at the end of his letter, 'that these remarks must not be taken as criticisms, but as responses to your request for information.' He concluded by pointing out that many objects had been suitable for distribution among the district's inhabitants, who had gratefully received them.

---

[29] It was situated on Wangenheimstrasse. Dépôt central de la Justice militaire, Le Blanc, 'Utikal et autres', item 32/g, 'Déposition de Sigrid Nehring, à Hambourg, 5/03/1948'.

[30] On this point, see F. Bajhor. 2001. *Parvenüs und Profiteure: Korruption in der NS-Zeit*, Frankfurt am Main: S. Fischer; in particular chap. 1, 'Organisiertes Selbstmitleid und Patronage', 17–48.

[31] URO, *M. Aktion Frankreich*, 114–115.

Illustration 3. Jewish armchairs, Oberhausen warehouse (n.d.).
Stradtarchiv, Oberhausen, 712-407.

Shipments by river, which are more difficult to retrace, also took place. For instance, nineteen barges left Antwerp for Germany, including five in June 1944.[32] Faced with growing demand from various German towns and authorities, slowing down the looting process risked posing difficulties. In the summer of 1942, the number of apartments that had been emptied had gone up sharply owing to large-scale round-ups of Jews. The temptation for the organisers of Operation Furniture to request new arrests was great. Thus the Belgian office asked the SD in December 1943 to arrest the Jews of Liège, because the need for furniture was becoming increasingly pressing.[33] In Troyes, meanwhile, the branch of the Dienststelle complained in January 1944 about the slow rate of arrests of Jews. Willy Fischer requested that all the Jews still present in the region should be arrested. In support of his request, he explained that he had realised 'from visits to homes made in a random and superficial manner' that 'in occupied accommodation, there is some furniture in relatively good condition.'[34]

Looting sometimes led to deportations. In the case of France, the link between confiscation and murder was not automatic, as only unoccupied apart-

---

[32] J. Pezechkian. 2002. 'La Möbelaktion en Belgique', *Cahiers d'histoire du temps présent* 10, 169.

[33] URO, *M. Aktion Frankreich*, 140.

[34] Dépôt central de la Justice militaire, Le Blanc, 'Utikal et autres', document 30/D/II, report from the Rheims inquest.

ments could be targeted by the removal teams and the Sipo-SD and the Gestapo coordinated their round-ups with the French police. The Dienststelle was never invited to any of the numerous interdepartmental meetings regarding the latter question. Its work came after that of the other organs of persecution. At certain points, however, the link between the expropriation and the murder of France's Jews grew closer. The creation and running of the Parisian camps was one of these points. Baron von Behr, the head of an expropriation department, became the head of various internment camps.

CHAPTER 3

The Creation of
the Parisian Camps

N ATIONAL SOCIALISM'S OBSESSION with race led the regime, shortly after Hitler's seizure of power, to embark upon a vast enterprise of classification of the country's population, forcing it to confront the question of mixed marriages, mixed couples and their children, and even their grandchildren.[1] The problem was all the more widespread given that the rate of interreligious marriages had risen sharply since the beginning of the twentieth century, from 9.3 per cent for Jewish men (and 7.7 per cent for women) in 1904 to 44 per cent of all German Jews in 1933.[2]

Mixed Couples and Half-Jews

Amongst the multitude of 'Aryan' legislation put in place by the Reich following the spring of 1933, of which the most important was the reorganisation of the civil service in April of that year, were restrictions placed upon Aryans with a Jewish spouse (male or female). Civil servants in mixed marriages could lose their jobs (this did not happen systematically until January 1937); Nazi organisations forbade their members from marrying non-Aryans and progressively expelled all those in mixed marriages.

The medical and legal professions were among the first to strike off members who were married to non-Aryans. The simplest solution to this was obviously divorce, which was advised from the beginning of the regime. The statistics show that the often violent pressure applied, which came from the Gestapo itself, hardly bore any fruit: only 7 per cent of the Aryans in mixed marriages divorced

[1] On the question of Jews in mixed marriages and of half-Jews and quarter-Jews see N. Stoltzfus. 1996. *Resistance of the Heart: Intermarriage and the Rosenstrasse Protest in Nazi Germany,* New York: Norton; Hilberg, *The Destruction of the European Jews,* II, 417–430; H.G. Adler. 1974. *Der Verwaltete Mensch: Studien zur Deportation der Juden aus Deutschland,* Tübingen: Mohr, 202–204 and 278–322.

[2] Stoltzfus, *Resistance of the Heart,* xxvi.

between 1933 and 1945. It is true that these couples had often already had to face the threat of ostracism from their own families and from society, and so had acquired a certain degree of resistance to outside injunctions. From 1935 onwards, divorce procedures were simplified for couples where one partner was Jewish, and it became difficult for engaged mixed couples to marry. The Nuremberg laws, issued on 15 September 1935, systematically outlawed marriage (and even sexual relations) between Aryans and Jews. However, faced with firm resistance from the Ministry of Justice, the clause automatically dissolving mixed marriages was never enforced. From September 1936, Aryans in mixed marriages were no longer allowed to display the Nazi flag. In April 1940 they were expelled from the Wehrmacht, in which some had been serving for years, though promotion had long been forbidden to them.

The explosion of violence on 'Kristallnacht' (9 November 1938), which led, with the attacks on synagogues and jobs, to the internment of 30,000 Jews in concentration camps, forced the Nazi leadership, and Göring in particular as the leader of the Four-Year Plan, to take a firmer line regarding mixed couples. Since their objective was the isolation of the Jews from the rest of German society and the completion of the Aryanisation of the economy, Jews who were married to Aryans were therefore obstacles to the radical implementation of these new measures. It was therefore decided to divide these families into two categories. Mixed couples where the woman was Jewish or that had had at least one child baptised received 'privileged' status. Those in which the man was Jewish or none of the children baptised were not eligible.[3] There were three times more privileged couples than ordinary mixed couples. Both partners in a privileged couple were exempt from the new measures, in particular those forcing Jews to move into 'Jewish houses' from April 1939 and wear the yellow star after September 1941. All the Jews in mixed marriages were spared in the first round of deportations. At the Wannsee conference of 20 January 1942, *Staatssekretär* Stuckhart proposed that a decree be issued pronouncing the automatic divorce of mixed couples, which would allow the Jewish partner to be deported without difficulty. The proposal was discussed during the following meeting on the Final Solution, on 6 March.[4] It met opposition from representatives of the Ministry of Propaganda, who feared the reaction of Aryan families, and the Ministry of Justice, who wanted to maintain departmental prerogatives. It was merely decided that divorce would be pronounced automatically if the Aryan partner requested it.

The question of mixed couples was never really considered by Vichy's anti-Semitic policy. Catholicism formed too central a part of a vision of society that

---

[3] This classification demonstrates the Nazi régime's racial interpretation of Jewishness. The Jewish identity of the woman, considered all-important by Jewish law, was seen as less defining in the Nazi system of classification.

[4] Hilberg, *The Destruction of the European Jews,* II, 428.

was not racial in the strict sense (but whose consequences certainly were) for the bonds of marriage to be placed in question. Furthermore, when Pétain's government discreetly sought the Pope's advice – if not from the Holy See in person then from France's ambassador in Rome, Léon Bérard – on the subject of the First Jewish Statute, the reply came that the Pope was not opposed to the statute, but that he would refuse any restriction on marriages, as had been the case in Italy since 1938. Among the many anti-Semitic laws produced by Vichy, one can find no reference to discrimination against spouses of Aryans. Certain dignitaries of the régime were married to Jewish women, the most famous being Fernand de Brinon, Vichy's ambassador in Paris, who was thus in close contact with the Germans and one of the linchpins of French collaboration. His wife Lisette, along with other aristocrats' partners, was spared having to wear the yellow star by the *maréchal* himself.

For Vichy, the status of mixed couples became an issue only as a consequence of the economic Aryanisation policy. It was necessary to establish the status of the property of a married couple where one of the partners was Jewish, in order to apply expropriation measures (nominating provisional administrators, blocking bank accounts, placing share portfolios in the hands of administrators, etc.).[5] The racial status of the man was the determining factor, in accordance with the subordination of the status of the wife to that of her husband. Only the Commissariat général aux questions juives, which always took a very harsh attitude with respect to the application of anti-Semitic decrees and, more importantly, was very keen to follow German wishes, paid real attention to the status of spouses. Provisional administrators appointed to head Jewish businesses were thus relieved of their functions if the commissariat discovered that they had a Jewish wife. Furthermore, numerous diligent enquiries were pursued regarding the religion of officials' spouses. For instance, a letter dated 23 June 1942 and addressed by the commissariat's directorate for the status of persons to Louis Darquier de Pellepoix, the commissioner no less, relating to a new census of Jews, points out: 'It may interest you to know that M. Ricard, the *sous-préfet* of Saint-Julien, is married to a Jewish woman and has many Jewish relations. His *sous-préfecture* borders on the Geneva canton.'[6]

While the Vichy régime did not issue discriminatory legislation with regard to the spouses of Jews, it did not create a 'privileged' status for Jews married to Aryans either. It was up to the German authorities, the Sipo-SD in particular, to concern themselves with this question, as in November 1943 when SS *Obersturmführer* Wannenmacher wrote to the directorate for the status of persons of

---

[5] On the policy of economic Aryanisation and expropriation, see J.-M. Dreyfus. 2003. *Pillages sur ordonnances: Aryanisation et restitution des banques en France, 1940–1953*, Paris: Fayard. See also the numerous reports of the Mission d'étude de la spoliation des Juifs de France, published by la Documentation française in 2000.

[6] Archives nationales, AJ38 146, Statut des personnes, documentation.

the Commissariat général aux questions juives to ask for the number of mixed marriages contracted in France since 1 January 1942, along with a list of names and addresses of all Jewish spouses.[7] The request was passed on to the Ministry of Justice, which replied that it was impossible to provide this information: to do so would have required checking the registers of all the 36,000 municipal districts in the country.

Nor was any special legal status accorded to half-Jews[8] by Vichy's anti-Semitic laws. It is true that some attempts were made by legislators to define a status that remained rather vague, but these never came to fruition.[9] The problem remained one of determining racial status and the classification of the population into Jews and non-Jews, without going any further in the creation of new categories. Half-Jews arrested during raids had to be able to prove that they were not Jews according to French and German legal texts, without it ever being very clear which of these should take priority. On reading through the individual files of the directorate for the status of persons, one is struck by the vagueness surrounding the status of half-Jews in France, a vagueness that was in fact recognised by various officials of the Commissariat général aux questions juives who were dealing with this question. Thousands of people sought to extricate themselves from the legal restrictions imposed by the Jewish statutes, a desk of the commissariat or German decrees by getting themselves recognised as Aryans. To do so they needed to obtain from the directorate for the status of persons, a department of the commissariat, a certificate of 'non-appartenance à la race juive', in fact a certificate of non-Jewishness, as called in the French administrative jargon of the time.[10]

The status of the spouses of Aryans and of half-Jews nonetheless became more important with the policy of the deportation of French Jews to the death camps. These groups were placed in 'holding' positions, considered to be last in line for deportation on the list of categories set by the German authorities, a list that took various factors into account (age, nationality, possible consular protection, protection by the French state, marital situation). It seems that, at least in the first years of Drancy's existence (the camp was set up in August 1941), spouses of Aryans and half-Jews were sometimes freed. Some were sent to provisional internment centres that were run by the Jewish community, then by the Union générale des Israélites de France – the central body representing Jews in France – housed in the Rothschild old peoples' hospice in the 12th *arrondissement* of Paris

---

[7] Archives nationales, AJ38 146, correspondence with German departments, letter from *Befehlshaber der Sicherheitspolizei und des SD im Bereich des Militärbefehlshaber in Frankreich* to the Statut des personnes, 9/11/1943.

[8] Meaning individuals with one Jewish parent of either sex.

[9] On this subject see 'Le statut du métis juif' in D. Gros. 1996. *Le Droit antisémite de Vichy*, Paris: Seuil, 'Le genre humain' 30/31.

[10] About 10,000 of these certificates were issued, and 3,000 more files were awaiting a response at the Liberation.

and in the rue Claude-Bernard (5th *arrondissement*). Some half-Jews were sent to work in premises requisitioned by the Germans. For instance, twelve were put to work on the pig farm situated (rather incongruously) at 47, avenue Foch, where the Gestapo were based, while six worked in the garden of 63, rue de Courcelles. The detainees slept on the premises.[11] Their fate depended on the decisions made in Berlin regarding mixed German couples. Jewish spouses of Aryans were in great danger from February 1943 onwards.

On 11 November 1942, the head of the Berlin police unit with the job of arresting Jews was replaced. The young SS *Hauptsturmführer* Aloïs Brunner (then aged 31) brought in new methods that were effective, imaginative and brutal.[12] Moved in from Vienna, where his organisational and policing skills as Eichmann's former personal secretary between 1938 and 1939 had been noted, he had been called to the capital by Hitler himself, it was rumoured at the Gestapo headquarters. An Austrian born in Röhrbrunn, he had joined the NSDAP in 1931. A trained policeman, he joined the ranks of the SS in 1938. Surrounded by a group of faithful henchmen, he criss-crossed Europe, implementing and accelerating the Final Solution.[13]

In Berlin, Brunner ordered the arrest of several dozen Jewish spouses of Aryans, breaking the subtle balance maintained in the capital by Goebbels. The latter, who had in the past experienced periods of relative disgrace in Hitler's eyes, was once again in favour with the régime. To his functions as minister of propaganda he had added those of *Gauleiter* of Berlin. Highly sensitive to public opinion, he pursued the objective announced by Hitler of winning over the Germans ideologically to the National Socialist cause, and was very worried by currents of dissent within the German population, which at times had to be treated gently to strategic ends, in the midst of the Battle of Stalingrad. In his eyes, repression was not enough; only propaganda could really lead the new ideology to victory, even when it came to its anti-Semitic dimension.

The Rosenstrasse Protests in Berlin

There were 16,760 mixed couples in the Reich on 31 December 1942, 4,803 in Austria and 6,211 in the protectorate of Bohemia-Moravia.[14] Thousands of Jewish spouses of Aryans remained in Berlin, subjected to forced labour in arms

---

[11] Centre de documentation juive contemporaine, documents UGIF, 23-756, 'Befreiungen von Mischehenjuden (Halbjuden)'.

[12] He introduced the use of Jewish agents to bring arrests. He also instituted the practice of making street arrests on the strength of 'facial features'. Brunner employed these methods in Berlin, then Paris and Nice.

[13] On such envoys of the Holocaust, see H. Safrian. 1993. *Die Eichmann-Männer*, Vienna: Europaverlag.

[14] Hilberg, *The Destruction of the European Jews*, II, 427.

factories. These Jews were the most difficult of all to deport: they had links with non-Jews and their work was considered vital when increasing productivity for the war effort was an absolute priority. Brunner concentrated on organising the final round-ups. On 26 February, Moritz Henschel, the president of the Zentralrat, the Central Council of German Jews, was summoned to Gestapo headquarters, where he was ordered to prepare internment areas for the city's last remaining Jews.[15] Among these was a building of historical significance for the community from which various social services had been run for decades. It was situated at 2-4, Rosenstrasse, a narrow old street in the centre of the city, in Scheunenviertel, the district where Jews had first established themselves. The final destination of these Jews is not known for certain. It would seem, according to a recent study, that they were meant to replace the workforce drawn from the 'fully' Jewish population rather than being transported to the East.[16]

The great round-up began on 28 February 1943, a Saturday. It is generally referred to as *Fabrik-Aktion,* 'Operation Factory'. Five thousand people were arrested, many of them in their workplaces. The spouses of Aryans and the half-Jews were nearly all sent to the building on the Rosenstrasse. But their husbands and, more often, wives, had prepared for this eventuality and the news had circulated quickly. The women arrived in front of the building, determined to obtain information about, or even the release of, their husbands. The round-up went on for several more days, but the women stood their ground, in spite of the threats and assaults of the police. Since Goebbels was away from Berlin, no firm decision could be taken over this unheard-of situation: a public demonstration of civil disobedience against Nazi rule. It was the only demonstration of this type to occur under the Third Reich.[17] It is unsure though that those Jews in mixed marriages were doomed to deportation. Their interest in the Rosenstrasse may have been just for screening their statute.

Eventually, Goebbels stepped in and gave the order to release the Rosenstrasse Jews and half-Jews. He had considered the detrimental consequences of a massacre in the centre of Berlin, shortly after the capitulation of the German Sixth Army outside Stalingrad. It was 6 March 1943. The women's demonstration had lasted a whole week. On 9 March, Goebbels went to visit Hitler in his headquarters in the East, the 'Wolf's Lair'. The Führer congratulated him on his decision, which was only supposed to be provisional, as the final fate of Jews in mixed marriages was to be decided at a later date. Although the question was consequently

---

[15] Stoltzfus, *Resistance of the Heart,* 208.

[16] No archival evidence of such a demonstration has been found. To clarify this complex question, see W. Gruner. 2005. *Wiederstand in der Rosenstrasse: Die Fabrik-Aktion und die Verfolgung der "Mischehen" 1943,* Frankfurt am Main: Fischer.

[17] On the circumstances of this demonstration, see also W. Gruner. 1997. *Der geschlossene Arbeitseinsatz deutscher Juden: zur Zwangsarbeit als Element der Verfolgung, 1938–1943,* Berlin: Metropol, 310–323.

debated on several occasions, no real decision was ever taken, and Jews who were married to Aryan citizens of the Reich were saved. This movement had consequences throughout Europe, establishing the principle that it was forbidden to deport Jews in mixed marriages to the death camps, even if exceptions did occur due to local circumstances.

In March 1943 there were 1,500 Jews in Drancy who were not 'deportable',[18] as opposed to 500 who were destined for extermination.[19] This imbalance was about to be corrected, for the German authorities, in particular Röthke, Theodor Dannecker's successor and Eichmann's representative in Paris, were actively preparing the second major phase of deportations of French Jews. A document preserved in the Centre de documentation juive contemporaine shows the concern generated by Jews in mixed couples. On 21 April 1943, Röthke wrote to division IV B 4a of the Reich Security Bureau, headed by Adolf Eichmann and as such responsible for the deportation of Jews across Europe.[20] Citing the situation of forty-one Italian Jews married to Aryans, who were protected by their country's consulate and so could not be deported or returned to Italy, he asked for instructions to follow regarding Jews in mixed marriages. The reply arrived on 1 June, specifying that no decision could be taken before the situation of Jews in mixed marriages living in the Reich had been resolved.[21] Jews in mixed marriages living in France were thus temporarily protected from deportation. They had to be placed at the bottom of the list of 'deportability', a list that had been constantly redrawn since summer 1942 as different criteria were taken into account.

The fate of the spouses of Aryans, and that of half-Jews in France, then, depended on decisions taken in Berlin concerning mixed German couples. Hannah Arendt, reflecting on this question at the Eichmann trial, explained: 'nothing was ever done about the *Mischlinge;* "a forest of difficulties," in Eichmann's words surrounded and protected them – their non-Jewish relatives, for one, and, for another, the disappointing fact that the Nazi physicians, despite all their promises, never discovered a quick means of mass sterilization.'[22] The summer of 1943 marked a turning point in German attitudes towards these half-Jews and the spouses of Aryans. Since these people's fate was left up in the air, the decision

---

[18] Forty-six had been arrested on 20 August 1941. Centre de documentation juive contemporaine, UGIF 90-655, 'État des internés conjoints d'aryens présents au camp de Drancy arrêtés le 20 août 1941', 15/05/1943.

[19] Klarsfeld, *Le Calendrier,* 771, entry for 9 March 1943.

[20] Centre de documentation juive contemporaine, XXV-101, cable from Röthke to the Reichssicherheitshauptamt, 21 April 1943. This communication follows earlier correspondence with division IV B b that has apparently not been preserved.

[21] It would seem that an order forbidding the deportation of Jews in mixed marriages had been issued by Eichmann as early as March 1942 and restated the following summer. See R.H. Weisberg. 1996. *Vichy Law and the Holocaust,* New York: New York University Press, 64–65.

[22] H. Arendt. 1994. *Eichmann in Jerusalem: A Report on the Banality of Evil,* Harmondsworth: Penguin, 159.

was taken to incorporate them into forced labour units. On 13 October 1943, on Hitler's orders, Fritz Sauckel, the head of workforce mobilisation, announced that civilian half-Jews and spouses of Aryans would be used by the Organisation Todt, with the exception of those already working in war-related industries.[23]

In Paris, the Dienststelle Westen complained constantly in its reports and communications that it lacked the resources necessary to fulfil the task assigned to it. On the one hand, as the protection extended to various different categories of Jews by nationality diminished, in particular for French Jews, whom the Germans considered deportable from spring 1943 onwards, the scale of potential plunder increased. On the other, the Paris Dienststelle's activities were becoming increasingly widely known in the Reich, and it found itself faced with growing demand for furniture and other objects from *Gauleiter* and Nazi organisations. It therefore had to work more quickly. The removals were proceeding with few difficulties, thanks to the assistance of the Organisational Committee for Removal and Storage Businesses. Identifying Jewish apartments, though, was proving harder, and various collaborationist agencies were called upon for help. The sorting and packing of objects remained the organisation's weak point. It was decided to use Jewish labour.

In a report to the Führer dated 8 August 1944, von Behr himself revisited what appears to have been the major problem confronting his department: a lack of workers.

> Given the small workforce which was available to the Western Service, it was impossible for us to prevent French workers from committing acts of sabotage which in fact became an increasing problem.[24] In order to put an end to this irritating situation, two large clearing depots were created and the workforce (700 Jews) was provided by the SD. The members of this workforce were interned in various camps. Up until then, the service possessed no workers specialised either in the loading or the repair of damaged furniture. When we created these 'Jewish camps' we also set up workshops housing cabinet-makers, clock-makers, leather-workers, electricians and radio-technicians, upholsterers, etc.[25]

The problem with the workforce was, as we shall see, one of both quantity and quality. Not only did the Dienststelle Westen lack manpower, it lacked workers able to repair furniture.

---

[23] B.M. Rigg. 2002. *Hitler's Jewish Soldiers: The Untold Story of Nazi Racial Laws and Men of Jewish Descent in the German Military*, Lawrence: University Press of Kansas, 222.

[24] The use of Jewish prisoners, who thus lived under the threat of deportation, did not, however, eliminate sabotage, as will be described later. These accusations of sabotage by French workers were not accompanied by proof, and this sentence from the report may have been used as a further pretext to justify the creation of the Paris camps.

[25] Dépôt central de la justice militaire, Le Blanc, Indre, 'Dossier Utikal et autres', report on Möbel Aktion, document FA 16, translation of document L188.

How could camps for Jews have been created in the middle of Paris in summer 1943, as the many round-ups of Jews and the changing military situation were rendering French public opinion increasingly sceptical, and the orders issued from the German authorities were calling for greater discretion, a discretion that was certainly visible in the running of the Parisian camps?

France was the only one of the three Western European countries involved in Operation Furniture to see the creation of special camps in which Jews were used in the packing process. This did not occur in either Belgium or the Netherlands. A possible explanation for this is that, in these latter countries, the looting process remained entirely under German control: it was thus easy for the German occupation authorities to access funds generated by economic Aryanisation and looting to pay for the handling and packing of the furniture and objects plundered from Jewish apartments. In France, the Aryanisation policy was run by the collaborationist authorities, which sought in this way to assert their independence from the occupier and attempt to safeguard interests that were considered to be French. A large proportion of the money realised through the sale of assets remained blocked in banks or with lawyers, or transferred into blocked accounts at the Caisse des dépôts et consignations (where disputed funds in legal cases, refundable deposits and so on are kept in France), out of the immediate reach of the Germans. Alfred Rosenberg's offices thus never gained access to the money generated by the expropriation of Jewish property, so they had to find a workforce for free. This workforce would therefore have to be Jewish. And so the Parisian camps were established.

Finally, if the decision to use Jews only partially resolved this problem, it is important to recognise that this is because it was not a normal workforce but a group of men and women forced to endure physical persecution and extermination. While the organisers of Operation Furniture were able to draw on the population interned in Drancy, they were constrained in how they could operate. The argument that workers were needed in order to expedite the process of economic expropriation only led to the creation of new camps when it converged with the priorities of the German administration responsible for the arrest, detention and extermination of the Jews.

Brunner at Drancy

On 11 February 1943, Eichmann paid a brief visit to Paris. He wanted to prepare the ground for the second phase of the deportation of France's Jews, but he needed first to confer with the police chiefs Knochen and Hagen. In order to prepare for mass arrests and the deportation of 100,000 Jews, he had to proceed with caution. Röthke estimated that he could deport between 8,000 and 10,000 Jews per week by April. This would require the help of the French police, as had been the case the previous summer. In order to get around the prevarications of the French government, the idea was put forward to request the denaturalisation of a certain number of French Jews, who would thus no longer enjoy the protection of the national authorities. A long series of negotiations was begun, discussing proposed changes in the law. Secretary of State for the Police René Bousquet composed a text following his meeting with Himmler, who had made a flying visit to Paris on 3 April. Minister of Justice Maurice Gabolde, General Commissioner on Jewish Matters Louis Darquier de Pellepoix, Pierre Laval and Pétain himself all examined this knotty question. In May, the proposed change to the law, as worded by Bousquet, was handed to the Sipo/SD. The negotiations seemed to be proceeding smoothly. The final text retained 1927 as the cut-off point: any naturalisations made after that date would be revoked. Fifty thousand people would be affected. Laval and Gabolde signed the text at the beginning of June 1943.[26]

The legal and material preparations for the deportations were moving forward quickly. In order to coordinate collaboration with the French police and generally oversee this vast operation, Eichmann sent Aloïs Brunner to Paris. He arrived on 1 June, having spent the previous four months in Greece, organising with incredible efficiency the deportation of all the 43,000 Jews of Salonika. Taking only a few days to assess the situation, he decided to make a thorough inspection of the camp at Drancy, whose internal organisation he changed completely. Meetings between French and German officials continued until the end of June. On June 30, Brunner even met with two officials from the Union Générale des Israélites de France, André Baur and Léo Israelowicz, head of the liaison department with the Gestapo; following this, Brunner created a Jewish authority at Drancy. He tried to introduce the same methods of arrest used in Austria and Berlin to France, and he implemented a new categorisation of the detainees.[27] From the beginning of July 1943, the new categories were as follows:

A) 'Aryans' interned for assisting Jews, spouses of Aryans, half-Jews (nondeportable);
B) the main body of Jews, those who were not protected in any way;
C1) the camp cadres, who headed the various departments and offices. They were theoretically not deportable and almost all French citizens;
C2) foreigners protected by their countries: Swiss, Turks, Spaniards, Greeks, Romanians, Hungarians, Yugoslavs. Their fate varied but the protection they enjoyed was usually fragile;
C3) wives of prisoners of war, who were not immediately deportable;
C4) Jews waiting to be reunited with their families. They in fact functioned as bait for the other members of their family. When the whole family had

---

[26] Klarsfeld, *Le Calendrier*, 817, entry for 8 June 1943.
[27] A. Kaspi. 1991. *Les Juifs pendant l'Occupation*, Paris: Seuil, 274–275.

been brought to Drancy, all its members were placed in category B and deported;

C5) detainees in a position to be released, if they could prove that they were not Jewish.[28]

This system of classification thus divided detainees into two main groups: the deportable and the nondeportable. However, the latter could itself be split into two sections: those detainees whose status was dependent on the decisions of Brunner and the Gestapo, meaning the whole of group C with the exception of sub-category C3, and a core of nondeportable prisoners composed of sub-category C3 and group A, whose status could not be altered by Brunner. The idea of detaching this core from the others formed the basis of the creation of the satellites of Drancy.

The wives of prisoners of war, in theory, benefited from a protected status stemming from the Reich's official concern, in Western Europe at least, with following international law, including the Hague convention on the treatment of prisoners of war and their families. As far as the spouses of Aryans and half-Jews were concerned, the question was linked to internal German politics and the inability of the various German authorities to agree on the fate of these particular Jews.

This classification of the internees into different categories was carried out in Drancy itself, by the personnel service composed of Jewish functionaries in category C1. Inmates' identity papers were often sufficient to place them in a given category, but a simple verbal statement was sometimes enough to obtain a provisional classification that would then have to be justified by sending a letter out of the camp to request that administrative documents be sent in – in particular a certificate of non-appartenance to the Jewish race. The possibility of being placed in a privileged category, and particularly in category A, which was the safest, thus depended on the information possessed by the person who had been arrested, information that could have filtered out of Drancy or even been communicated inside the camp by members of the personnel service, for example. Rumours about the fate of spouses of Aryans had been circulating since May 1943.[29] The Jews working in the administrative offices of the camp had been replaced by the spouses of Aryans;[30] on 30 June, the rumour went round that the spouses of Aryans would be freed.[31]

The Germans took over official control of the camp on 2 July, leaving only the task of guarding the perimeter to the French. The camp regime changed radically.

---

[28] Klarsfeld, *Le Calendrier*, 835.

[29] G. Kohn. 1999. *Journal de Compiègne et de Drancy*, Paris: Éditions des FFDJF. Entries for 10 May 1943, 17 May 1943, 24 May 1943.

[30] Ibid., entry for 9 June 1943.

[31] Ibid., entry for 30 June 1943.

'Internees are beginning to be sorted into categories', wrote Georges Kohn in his diary entry for 3 July.[32] The Jews were subjected to humiliating treatment by their captors, far worse than anything they had experienced under the regime of the French *gendarmes*. Very rapidly, building work commenced and workshops were set up. The prisoners of Drancy, during their pre-deportation internment, began to be subjected to forced labour. The great round-up of denaturalised Jews was scheduled for 15 July. The only delay was in publishing the official French decree. As tens of thousands of people were due to arrive in Drancy and Aloïs Brunner was most concerned with maintaining the camp's neat and orderly appearance, he decided to free up some space and began to assemble the internees even before the round-up began. The Jews in the Rothschild hospice were sent back to Drancy, and the camp at Beaune-la-Rolande was closed. Owing to the Vichy government's delay in announcing the Jewish Denaturalisation Law, the round-up was rescheduled for 24 July.

This was the context in which the three Parisian camps were created.

Austerlitz, Lévitan, Bassano

On 9 July, a convoy of 300 Jewish spouses of Aryans was sent to work for the Organisation Todt in the camps on the Isle of Alderney[33] in the Channel Islands.[34] A second convoy was sent on June 16. An initial group of 120 spouses of Aryans left Drancy for the camp at Lévitan on 18 July, the same day that convoy no. 57 left for Auschwitz. The remaining nondeportable detainees were progressively transferred to the three Parisian camps run by von Behr's organisation, the Dienststelle Westen. On their arrival, they found themselves in buildings used as furniture depots, with no amenities prepared for them. The first of these was the Lager Ost.

The building housing Lévitan camp, at 85–87, rue du Faubourg-Saint-Martin, had previously been a large shop. Its tiled façade still carries the inscription '*Aux classes laborieuses*', reminding passers-by that it was originally built to sell cheap clothing to the inhabitants of this working-class district. In 1936, the premises had been purchased by Wolff Lévitan, who turned them into a large, modern furniture store. This entrepreneur proceeded to build up a small Parisian furniture-

---

[32] Ibid., entry for 3 July 1943.

[33] C. Cruikshank. 1975. *The German Occupation of the Channel Islands*, London, New York: The Trustees of the Imperial War Museum, Oxford University Press, 203–204. On the Channel Islands concentration camps, see also A. Briggs. 1995. *The Channel Island:. Occupation and Liberation 40–45*, London: BT Batsford Ltd, Imperial War Museum, 68; M. Bunting. 1995. *The Model Occupation: The Channel Islands under German Rule, 1940–1945*, London: HarperCollins, 148–158. There were four camps on Alderney.

[34] Kohn, *Journal de Compiègne et de Drancy*, entry for 9 July 1943.

selling empire using the new retailing methods of standardisation and advertising.[35] Wolff Lévitan, born in Russia, had fled to Cannes at the beginning of the Occupation. A provisional administrator, Robert Mioque, was appointed for the six properties belonging to him and his brother Adolphe. Mioque ran a decorating business on the boulevard de Magenta; several furniture businesses were put under his management.[36] It was not until 29 September 1942 that Mioque sent his first report on the Faubourg-Saint-Martin premises to the Commissariat général aux questions juives; he judged that it was 'of antiquated construction but solidly built, well maintained and in excellent condition'. The plot, covering about 1,390 square metres, had the uncovered passage du Désir running along its right-hand side, which linked up with the rue du Faubourg-Saint-Denis. 'This building comprises three arches looking onto the rue du Faubourg-Saint-Martin, with four floors above ground and two below', continued Mioque.

> The interior comprises several floors of shops and arcades for commercial use. There is a roof terrace at the top. The interior is fitted out for furniture retailing and a great deal of modifications have been made. There is, in particular, a ramp down which large lorries can drive, an electrically-driven turntable, three powerful goods lifts serving all the floors. Inside the shop, fitted out with furniture display stands, there are two lifts for clients' use. In the basement are heating boilers and the very large electric motors which run the goods lifts and passenger lifts, along with a very extensive electrical system for lighting and power.[37]

It appears that the shop continued to function normally up until at least 1942. The building on the Faubourg-Saint-Martin was then subjected to the usual procedure of economic Aryanisation, as was the Lévitan furniture company and the other properties belonging to the family.[38] The provisional administrator undertook to sell the building, whose price was set by the Comissariat général aux questions juives at 3 million francs, even though an architect's survey carried out in October 1942 estimated its value at 4.3 million. After several false starts, the building was sold by notarised deed on 21 July 1943 to a French company, Liebig, for 3 million francs. The Liebig soup company thought they had got a bar-

---

[35] Marcel Bleustein-Blanchet has evoked the atmosphere of the large Lévitan store, where he worked as an apprentice. He was the nephew of Wolff Lévitan, whose wife was called Berthe Bleustein. See M. Bleustein-Blanchet. 1960. *La Rage de convaincre,* Paris: Robert Laffont; reissued by Livre de Poche, 1974.

[36] On the Aryanisation of this specific furniture store , see the files of the Commissariat général aux questions juives; Archives nationales, AJ38 2626, dossier 24 195.

[37] Idem, Report of the provisional administrator.

[38] On the Aryanisation of the Lévitan company, see P. Verheyde. 1999. *Les Mauvais comptes de Vichy: L'aryanisation des entreprises juives,* Paris: Perrin, 191–194.

ILLUSTRATION 4. Lévitan building façade (1939).
Sales catalogue Lévitan.

gain, but the sale was not homologated by the German Military High Command in Parisor by the commissariat.[39] On 15 July 1943, the building in its entirety was requisitioned by the Dienststelle Westen. Robert Mioque immediately informed the commissariat of this.

When the detainees arrived, they found themselves in a furniture shop that could have opened to customers. The window displays on the ground floor were

---

[39] From July 1941, it beame usual for a homologation clause to be inserted into the final contract for Jewish properties and companies sold according to the economic Aryanisation laws. The written agreement of the Commissariat général aux questions juives, which often consulted with the German authorities before issuing it, was required to make the contract binding and thus transfer the funds, blocked up until that time, along with the property.

left as they were in order not to attract the attention of passers-by and neighbours in a very busy street in which, virtually opposite the shop, stood the town hall of the 10th *arrondissement.* The proximity of the Gare de l'Est, only 200 m away, also increased the number of people in the street. It was perhaps this proximity to the station, as well as the modernity of the building's fittings, that led von Behr's offices to choose Lévitan as an internment camp. The administrative designation of the camp was Lager Ost, 'East Camp', perhaps in reference to the station. The camp at no. 2, rue de Bassano was also housed in a fine building, but one with a very different layout.

The rue de Bassano is very well-heeled; it runs down to the avenue d'Iéna, where it comes out opposite the very elegant place des États-Unis. The buildings of this part of the 16th *arrondissement* are not very old but enjoy a wonderful position at the centre of a triangle formed by the place de l'Étoile, the Trocadéro and the place de l'Alma. Wealthy Jewish families such as the Gunzburgs and the Deutsch de la Meurthes had moved into the area at the turn of the century. No. 2, rue de Bassano is at the corner of the rue Georges-Bizet,[40] which leads down to the avenue Marceau. The building, which dates from 1883, resembles a classic Parisian town house, even if the difficult configuration of the plot meant the main entrance had to be placed on the side. Hippolyte Destailleur, its architect, had demonstrated some skill in building on such an irregularly shaped, if large, plot.[41] The main entrance, on the rue de Bassano, opens onto a large hall with a courtyard behind it. Cars could drive out onto the rue Georges-Bizet.

The impressive size and spacious feel of the ground-floor rooms give an idea of the wealth of the building's original owners, as well as their taste for entertaining. The decoration attests to the eclectic style in which the Parisian bourgeoisie liked to live and receive visitors. The Cahen d'Anvers family, to whom the house belonged, had become very rich in the nineteenth century. They were among the wealthiest of the Parisian bankers. Born in Germany, Joseph-Meyer Cahen brought his business over to Paris in 1848, as did many German Jewish bankers at this time. Cahen had added the aristocratic 'd'Anvers' to his name fairly illegitimately, but he was far from alone in doing so. He made many successful deals and built up a considerable fortune, which he left, on his death in 1881, to his four sons. Raphaël and Louis Cahen d'Anvers took over the family business.[42] It was Louis who had the house at 2, rue de Bassano built, and he moved into it with his wife and five children.

---

[40] Renamed thus in 1906.

[41] Interview with M. Roquelaure, the architect who carried out renovation work on the building in 2000, 05/06/2003.

[42] On these banking families see: L. Bergeron. 1991. *Les Rothschild et les autres: la gloire des banquiers,* Paris: Perrin.

ILLUSTRATION 5. Bassano building façade (2003).
©Gilles Roquelaure.

The decoration of the reception rooms was impressive.[43] Some of the ceilings and panelling had been taken from Parisian mansions from the seventeenth and eighteenth centuries. Some of the woodwork had been purchased from the hôtel de Mayenne, built at the beginning of the seventeenth century by Charles de Lorraine and then extended before 1709 by the prince de Vaudémont. Other decorative elements were commissioned from contemporary artists, including the painters Bonnat and Carolus-Duran. In the entrance hall, a white marble bust of Minerva on a plinth of veined red marble greeted visitors. Light fittings in the shape of little cherubs framed the staircase. Renoir was commissioned to paint the children's portraits.[44] The two paintings that were finished, one showing Élisabeth and Alice and the other the oldest daughter, Irène, did not please the family and were, it is said, hung in the servants' quarters for a while. Irène went on to marry Moïse de Camondo in 1891.

The Cahen d'Anvers family held parties and balls in their residence, which was built with entertaining in mind. The newspaper *Le Gaulois,* for example, reported in its famous society column on the ball held on 20 March 1895:

---

[43] See illustrations for photographs of the building.

[44] P. Assouline. 1997. *Le Dernier des Camondo,* Paris: Gallimard, 155–156.

The ball held the night before last at the home of the comtesse Louis Cahen d'Anvers in her ravishing house on the rue de Bassano was among the finest ever given. The King of Serbia graced it with his presence. The young sovereign, in the company of his father, King Milan, and the Serbian Minister in Paris, made his entrance at half-past eleven and immediately mingled with the many guests. One and all admired the verve and grace of this accomplished dancer. The *cotillon,* which the King danced with the young comtesse de Camondo was among the liveliest ever seen; ribbons, scarves, fans and, especially, flowers were generously distributed.[45]

There then followed a description of the dinner, held in the first-floor dining room, then the list of guests.

The fortunes of the Cahen d'Anvers declined after the death of Louis. The house on the rue de Bassano passed to Charles, Louis's youngest son, then was put up for sale a few years before the Second World War, without success. By 1938, it had already been emptied of its furniture. It was known to be a 'Jewish building' since, on 19 May 1941, a certain M. Audiffret-Pasquier, living at 10, rue de Bassano, wrote to the department for economic Aryanisation at the Commissariat général aux questions juives to ask for the name of the provisional administrator in order to enquire about purchasing the property.[46] This letter led to the appointment of a provisional administrator in the person of Gabriel Blancke, architect, of 10, avenue Ingres (Paris, 16th *arrondissement*). Blancke was given this job on 25 June 1941 and undertook a brief enquiry into the real owners of the building. It belonged to two people: Lydie Cahen d'Anvers, the wife of Anthony Gustav de Rothschild, banker, living in London, and Marie Cahen d'Anvers, the wife of Hubert Conquère de Montbrison, living in Paris at 14, avenue d'Eylau. Very conscientiously, the provisional administrator indicated to the commissariat that two-thirds of the building was owned by a person who, it had to be assumed, was English, given her marriage. This information was sent to the Majestic, to the department of enemy property, in a letter dated 10 November 1941.

A new provisional administrator, a M. Simon, appointed on 29 January 1942, tried to inspect the building, as his job required. He was unable to gain access, but when he went to 54, avenue d'Iéna, von Behr informed him that the building was in a poor state of repair and was being used to store furniture. He also learnt, by enquiring at the solicitor's, that the building comprised around thirty rooms, with six on the ground floor and six on the first floor. There was also a concierge's lodge, storage rooms and servants' quarters, as well as two large garages, each of which could hold five or six cars. Negotiations for sale had been opened in 1938, with an offer of 5.5 million francs, but this had been judged too low by the owners.

---

[45] Quoted in Assouline, *Le Dernier des Camondo,* 185.

[46] Archives nationales, AJ38 2423, dossier 8839 'Cahen d'Anvers. Immeuble 2 rue de Bassano, 16e'.

ILLUSTRATION 6. One of the rooms in Bassano building (2003).
©Gilles Roquelaure.

In March 1944, Bassano camp held sixty Jews. The choice of this building as a place of detention had been logical, as it was already being used as a furniture store for Operation Furniture. It also possessed a useful quirk of construction: the great height of its roof concealed its eaves. There was a fourth floor invisible from street level, a large area of around 300 square metres directly beneath the roof, with no windows: an ideal place to hold Jews in secret. Furthermore, as the building was very near 54, avenue d'Iéna, it was convenient to put the largest pieces of stolen furniture there.[47] On the other side of the avenue d'Iéna, the house at no. 4, place des États Unis, which belonged to the Deutsch de la Meurthe family, had also been requisitioned as a furniture depot. Colette de Dampierre, née Cahen d'Anvers, would be interned, as the spouse of an Aryan, at Lévitan camp; Antoinette Vernes, née Goldet, the grandaughter of Émile Deutsch de la Meurthe and the wife of an heir of the Protestant bank of the same name, would be sent to Lévitan.

In November 1943, the third camp, called Austerlitz or 'Quai de la Gare' was opened in the 13th *arrondissement*. The setting was very different. The build-

---

[47] No. 56, avenue d'Iéna is at the corner of rue Georges-Bizet.

ings used as a furniture depot and internment centre were in an industrial area surrounded by factories, a site bordered by the quai de la Gare and the sidings behind the Gare d'Austerlitz. At the confluence of the Seine and the river Bièvre, a large industrial zone had sprung up at the beginning of the nineteenth century. The area had officially become part of Paris in 1790.[48] The name of the *quai* (quay, or platform) – 'la Gare' – did not in fact come from Austerlitz, but from a *gare d'eau*, a riverside quay, the construction of which had begun in 1764 but was never completed.[49]

The advent of the railway, along with the city's continuing growth, led to the construction of immense warehouses where the tons of food and other merchandise consumed by Paris could be stocked. In 1860, Jacob Émile Pereire obtained from Napoléon III a monopoly over the provision of storage in the capital. He set up his warehouses on land he had inherited, along with some buildings dating from 1833.[50] Baron Hausmann presided over the board of the Compagnie des entrepôts et magasins généraux de Paris (General Warehouses of Paris) from 1873 to 1890. In 1879, the Entrepôts Trotrot built some imposing structures in the quai de la Gare. Demolished between the wars, these were replaced by two buildings constructed by the Grands Moulins de Paris and by a more modern warehouse belonging to the Magasins généraux. This was no. 43, quai de la Gare.

The entire zone was taken over in 1940 by the Germans, who needed this infrastructure to stockpile, pack, and finally send off to the Reich all the material they had looted or bought from France. The Dienststelle Westen chose several buildings, in particular nos. 5 and 6, which had been used as bonded warehouses, as the main storage depots for the stolen furniture. These provided the space required and also, most importantly, a railway siding next to the buildings allowing wagons to be brought right up to the warehouses. This was where the Jews arrived in November 1943. The zone was busy during the day, full of thousands of workers from the surrounding businesses, all of which were more or less under the economic control of the occupier. At night, however, it was empty. There was virtually no housing nearby, except for a few apartment buildings on the quai de la Gare, towards the Gare d'Austerlitz. The buildings of the Magasins Généraux and the Grands Moulins were surrounded by the steel warehouses of the steel company Compagnie des forges Châtillon-Commentry (at 89, quai de la Gare), a warehouse belonging to the Vichy-État mineral water company and located near the Bergès stationery warehouse (at no. 55).

---

[48] On this district, see G.-A. Langlois. 2000. *De la Salpêtrière à la Bibliothèque national de France: Histoire d'un quartier de Paris*, Paris: Somogny.

[49] J. Hillairet. 1997. *Dictionnaire historique des rues de Paris*, 2 vols, 10th ed., Paris: Éditions de Minuit, I, 568, entry for 'Gare (quai de la)'.

[50] On the history of the Magasins Généraux, see E. Philipp. 2000. *Histoire d'une entreprise de son temps: Compagnie des Entrepôts et Magasins généraux de Paris*, Paris: EMGP-Textuel.

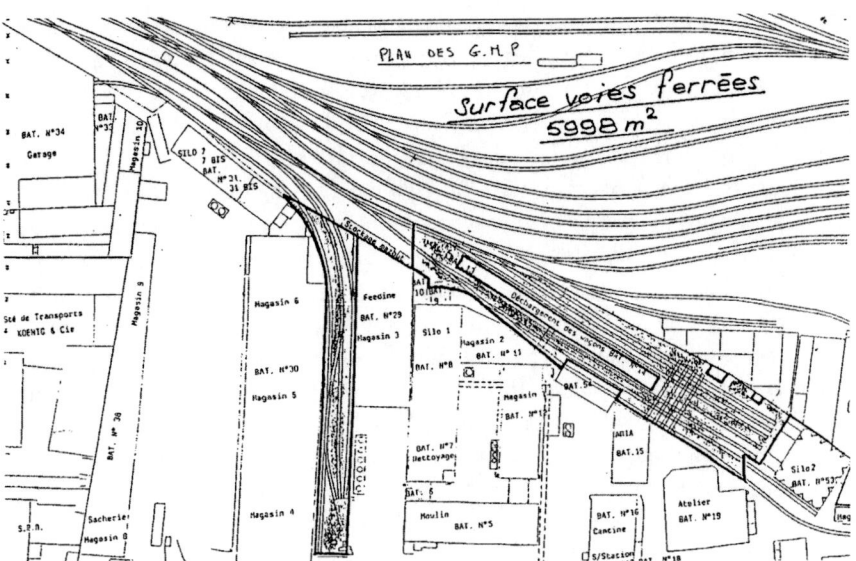

ILLUSTRATION 7. Map of Austerlitz camp district.
Private document given to Jean-Marc Dreyfus.

The passing of the Denaturalisation Law of foreign Jews took longer than expected. In the end it was never adopted, thanks to a volte-face by Pierre Laval. On 25 September, in one of his letters, Knochen concluded that 'it is now certain that the projected measures for the denaturalisation of foreign Jews will not produce significant results.' By 31 July 1943, 7,053 Jews had been denaturalised on an individual basis from summer 1940 on. The invasion of the Italian occupied zone in the meantime had also maintained a sufficient flow of inmates into Drancy. In October, any hope of seeing the French government sign the denaturalisation decree had faded completely. Röthke had the idea of arresting nondenaturalised French Jews and banked on a large haul. Thus the creation, on 1 November 1943, of the satellite camp of Austerlitz was once again linked to the rationale of freeing up space in Drancy for new, immediately deportable internees.

With Brunner's arrival, the Union générale des Israélites en France (UGIF) was invited to assist with the running of Drancy, which raises the question of the UGIF's possible role in setting up the Parisian camps.[51] If, in the summary of the 15 June meeting of the UGIF council, the possibility of 'work for Jews' came up, this seems to have stemmed from a German proposal. Under the heading 'Organisation of work for Jews', the idea of taking detainees out of Drancy to put

---

[51] Centre de documentation juive contemporaine, UGIF 3-114, transcript of the meeting of 30 June 1943 between Brunner and Bruckler on one side and André Baur and Léo Israelowicz on the other.

them to work is mentioned. The UGIF, in an abortive attempt to spare detainees deportation, did negotiate directly with Dannecker to send Jews to agricultural colonisation projects in the Ardennes.[52] However, the transcripts of the meetings held in June and July 1943 between Brunner and the officials of the UGIF Nord do not mention the creation of the Parisian camps.[53]

While the UGIF may not have played an active role in the creation of these satellite camps, it is certain that it kept the number of internees they held as high as possible, thus preventing or delaying their deportation. It took particular care to follow those detainees whose special status meant that something could be done for them. In March 1943, when the spouses of Aryans had been moved to Beaune-la-Rolande, the UGIF had assigned women to look after their needs and maintain contact with them. The internal memo from the general secretariat to UGIF *service* (department) 14, dated 6 March 1943, read thus: 'Following the departure of all the spouses of Aryans from Drancy camp to the camp at Beaune-la-Rolande, it is absolutely essential that we establish a link with the camp authorities similar to that which already exists for Drancy camp.'[54] Furthermore, in the spring and summer of 1943, the UGIF made a huge effort to draw up lists of spouses of Aryans, hoping that their situation would change. In May and June 1943, it sent out questionnaires to their families in order to establish complete files. It regularly notified the Sipo-SD of cases of spouses of Aryans interned in Beane-la-Rolande and Drancy. Simply put, the UGIF played the card of keeping detainees in France by means of work, paying for the detainees' food and upkeep.

Service 14 of the UGIF, headed by Kurt Schendel, dealt with relations with the various German authorities. It was engaged in work such as collating, and sending on to the authorities at Drancy, documents such as certificates of non-appartenance to the Jewish race issued to internees' spouses. It also followed the fate of Jewish wives of prisoners of war, whom it was possible to assist.[55] The participation of the UGIF carried on after the setting up of the satellite camps. For instance, on 15 March 1944 its offices sent the chief internee at Austerlitz an envelope containing 'photos of the certificates of non-appartenance to the Jewish race nos. 9074 and 9075 relative to M. Roger Louis and Mlle Anne Marie Golub which we would be most obliged if you could pass on to M. Abraham Golub, presently working in your camp'.[56]

---

[52] On this painful episode, where nonprotected Jews were put to work with the help of the UGIF, see M. Rajsfus. 1989. *Des Juifs dans la collaboration. 2. Une Terre promise?* Paris: L'Harmattan.

[53] Centre de documentation juive contemporaine, UGIF 3-99 and UGIF 3-125.

[54] Centre de documentation juive contemporaine, UGIF 17-815.

[55] See for example Centre de documentation juive contemporaine, UGIF 17-590 and UGIF 28-1054.

[56] Centre de documentation juive contemporaine, CDXXV-2.

The specific document ordering the creation of the Parisian internment camps has not been found. It may well not exist. In the Nazi decision-making process, it was not always necessary to issue written orders. In any case, here, as elsewhere, Brunner demonstrated his efficiency and his inventiveness. Faced on his arrival with a complicated situation, through a single initiative he solved the problem of overcrowding in Drancy, the fate of nondeportable Jews married to Aryans and von Behr's constant requests for more manpower. The Parisian internment camps would exist for one year, in a most unusual situation that written memoirs, oral testimony and also numerous historical documents allow us to describe.

CHAPTER 4

Forced Labour in Paris

'THE DEUTSCHE DIENSTSTELLE, on the quai de la Gare was the craziest, most unthinkable place there has ever been. It was the biggest operation of organised removal, hoarding and theft imaginable: all the possessions and furniture stolen from the Jews came there to be sorted and sent off to Germany.'[1] This was Yvonne Klug's first impression on her arrival at Austerlitz labour camp. She conjures up a powerful image before our eyes, identical to that described by all the former inmates, even if behind this dominant overall memory of the work they had to perform lay a strict division of tasks. The position each internee occupied within this organisation depended on various factors. Their recollections therefore often differ according to individual circumstances. As a 'camp worker' (*ouvrier de camp*), Michel Behr moved around the whole of the building at 43, quai de la Gare.[2] Interviewed, he admits, however, that he is 'pretty hopeless' when it comes to describing its exterior, that is to say the rest of the site, which he barely had any opportunity to see. Likewise, although she was interned in Lévitan from its creation until its evacuation, Odette Dassonville is unable to describe the work carried out on the second floor, since she 'never saw' it.[3]

The Arrival of the Workforce

At Drancy, detainees were placed in various categories. This system of administrative classification was also implemented geographically by allocating different groups to different sections of the blocks. After the war, André Cohen, a former internee in Austerlitz, would describe his arrival at Drancy on 6 April 1944:

---

[1] Yvonne Klug, *The 8616 came back or Doors that open only from the outside* (typed manuscript). Carton de l'Amicale Austerlitz-Lévitan-Bassano, Centre de documentation juive contemporaine.

[2] Interview with Michel Behr, Angers, 05/02/2003.

[3] Interview with Odette Dassonville, Orly, 04/11/2002.

We were led into an office that we called the 'Kanzlei'. The Nuremberg Laws were applied to each prisoner in turn, with reference to their file. Each would receive, depending on their status, a little red slip for A's (spouses of Aryans [of which Cohen was one]), purple for B's (deportable) or green (C's, assigned to work for the Organisation Todt). According to these categories, we were placed in designated buildings. ... Category A from [blocks] 13 to 19.[4]

In a letter sent from Drancy, Simon Sarfati, whose wife was not Jewish, told how, out of the 103 people with whom he arrived in Drancy, only two went with him into his block.

Yvonne Klug, who was later deported to Auschwitz, provided a short but minutely detailed account of her arrest and deportation, written in March 1945. In it she describes her arrival at Drancy at the beginning of November 1943:

After being searched, we went into another office called the Kanzlei where you had to fill in a form giving every detail of your pedigree and, according to the replies we gave, we were placed into numerous categories. A was for workers, this was the best one, B was for deportees and it was, unfortunately, the largest group, C was for those whose situation required clarification or those awaiting their papers. We were put in C and sent to dormitories assigned to this category.[5]

Yvonne Klug's transfer to Austerlitz camp only occurred after her category changed

on 2 December, a day when a big revision was carried out not by Weisel but by a certain Roetke [sic] ... We had to stand in front of him as if we were in court and after interrogating us and also having my husband examined by a doctor who was present for that purpose, he decided to accept that my husband was an Aryan and let him go ... while I had to make do with being placed in category A, the best one. For me this meant working in a place designated by the Germans and better treatment ... I carried on sewing my bags until 13 December, the date on which a group of one hundred women and men was chosen to go and work in Austerlitz. My name was on the list and I left Drancy.[6]

Brunner selected the internees he sent to Lévitan, then Austerliz and Bassano, from the category of nondeportable prisoners. The records of transfers from

---

[4] Centre de documentation juive contemporaine, statement dated 01/03/1945 by André Cohen to the Nice division of the Fédération des sociétés juives de France, CCXVI-55.

[5] Klug, *The 8616 came back*, 4.

[6] Ibid., 9.

Drancy clearly show, even down to the typography they use, the link between the status of the internees and their transfer to the Parisian camps. For instance, on 21 and 7 May 1944, the transfers file records, respectively: '*Transfer of C1: Departure to Dienststelle West*, HEIM Roger, Matr. No. 909', and 'Transfer of C1: *Transferred to Dienststelle WEST* 782 Goldfarb Elias.'[7]

Not all of the internees in these categories were transferred to the satellite camps. Lists were drawn up to allow Brunner's men to select the workforce. Although transfer to Lévitan, and later to Austerlitz or Bassano, was hardly ever mentioned in detainees' personal records at Drancy, one occasionally finds 'German list' marked on the records of detainees moved to Paris. Odette Dassonville recalls her departure for Lévitan, when the camp first opened, very clearly: 'The Germans designated those who were going. They had lists and called out our names.'[8]

The successive lists that seem to have preceded the definitive list of 1 November 1943, the date on which Austerlitz camp opened, are quite instructive with regard to the Germans' methods.[9] On that day, 136 internees were taken to Austerlitz, joined by a group transferred from Lévitan. The group from Drancy was chosen from a list of internees in category A. On this list, each detainee's profession was marked next to his or her name, date of birth and camp number. Students and artists, whose names were absent from the definitive list, were transferred only in subsequent detachments. The need for a specialised workforce therefore guided the selection process. Indeed, some internees were transferred to Lévitan despite not belonging to either of categories A or C3.

Detainees' professional skills were thus one of the criteria that decided their departure to the satellite camps. In some cases they were the only reason for their transfer. Erna Herzberg, despite being an Austrian Jew, and married to a Jew who was himself interned at Drancy, was transferred to Lévitan as soon as it opened.[10] She describes how 'one day, a call went round, they were looking for workers, craftsmen: seamstresses, potters, clockmakers'. She came forward and went through an interview in which she was able to explain her *haute couture* dressmaking qualifications. Before the war, she had been the head dressmaker at

---

[7] Centre de documentation juive contemporaine. 'Transfer of C1' should read 'transfer of C1 to A'.

[8] Interview with Mme Odette Dassonville, detainee no. 233 at Lévitan camp. The list of the first group transferred from Drancy has not been found.

[9] Centre de documentation juive contemporaine, CCCLXXVI-4. The lists that have been found include numerous mistakes that reveal the relatively disorganised nature of the selection process. For example, Michel Behr's name is not on any of them. Yet he was transferred to Austerlitz on 1 November with his father and brother, as testified not only by other internees' accounts but also by correspondence dating from this time.

[10] Interview with Mme Erna Herzberg, interned at Lévitan and Bassano, then deported to Auschwitz.

Paquin, a noted Parisian fashion house.[11] She was therefore selected to 'go and work in Paris', along with her husband. Her account tallies exactly with that of Félix Lichtenauer, sent to Lévitan as a cabinetmaker despite being officially designated as an unmarried German Jew.[12] They both recall that the ability to speak German may have been required, but are not entirely certain on this point. Being moved to the quai de la Gare could also depend on a detainee's qualifications, as was the case for Jacques Altman, who was neither a member of the 'spouses of Aryans' category nor a 'half-Jew' but was a mechanic, a profession useful to the running of the camp. He left Drancy for Austerlitz, where he stayed from November 1943 to February 1944 before being deported.[13]

The precise organisation of these transfers and the means of transport used to make them are not fully known. If, in detainees' accounts, reference is made to the presence of French *gendarmes,* the descriptions of the vehicles used vary. Odette Dassonville, who was part of the first transfer to Lévitan, refers to a group of buses surrounded by French police, as is confirmed by the war memoirs of the countess de Dampierre.[14] Sent to Austerlitz with the second group, on 1 November 1943, Bernard Behr also talks of a journey made in 'Paris buses', 'guarded by French policemen'.[15]

Yvonne Klug mentions a 'removal van, inside which, like the objects they would be sorting, the internees were piled up', whereas Maurice Wolf, sent to Austerlitz on 27 November 1943, describes a Black Maria in which his group of eight prisoners was guarded by French policemen[16].

The first detachment of workers arrived at 85-87, rue du Faubourg-Saint-Martin on 18 July 1943. Baron von Behr welcomed them in person with a short address, in which he explained the tasks they were to perform and threatened them with collective punishment and deportation if any prisoners escaped.

The building had not been modified to receive its new inhabitants. Everything was as it had been left, even down to the cash registers. The first three floors were occupied by the Dienststelle's stock, while the fourth was cleared out to serve as a 'dormitory' for the internees, although it was hardly worthy of the name. A curtain was all that separated the women's area from that of the men. No proper washing facilities were provided, and only two washbasins were installed. For a

---

[11] At Bassano she would eventually become the deputy-chief seamstress in the Main Salon. See Centre de documentation juive contemporaine, UGIF roll 18.

[12] Interview with M. Félix Lichtenauer, interned in Lévitan.

[13] M. Rajsfus. 1996. *Drancy, un camp de concentration très ordinaire 1941–1944,* Paris: Le Cherche-Midi, 338.

[14] Private archives of M. Christophe de Montbrison (the nephew of Mme de Dampierre), *Memoirs of Mme de Dampierre* (written in English).

[15] Recollections written down by Bernard Behr in December 1989.

[16] *La Mémoire blessée,* memoirs of Maurice Wolf, unpublished.

Illustration 8. Lévitan front entrance. The building is already occupied by the Germans (1943–1944).
Bundesarchiv Koblenz, B 323-311-79.

long time these served the needs of 180 internees. Finally, there were no beds or mattresses. For the first two weeks, the internees slept directly on the concrete floor. Gradually, beds began to arrive, and the camp's carpenters put together rudimentary shelving.

Three and a half months later, Georges Wellers was part of the first contingent to arrive at Austerlitz: 'On 30 October, 1943, after nineteen months, I left Drancy with 250 of my fellow prisoners to go and work in another camp, situated in Paris, at 42, quai de la Gare.'[17] It was not von Behr, but Bruno Kochan, the camp's commandant, who welcomed his 'guests' with a speech detailing the system of punishments inside the camp. Gilberte Jacob has described the same lack of material readiness already seen at Lévitan: 'In Austerlitz, three floors were used for work and we were billeted on the fourth. When we arrived, we had to do a thorough clean-up.'[18] While, as Bernard and Michel Behr have described, very 'rudimentary' beds and cupboards were crammed together to from long rows, here, too, no washing facilities had been provided.[19]

---

[17] G. Wellers. 1991. *Un Juif sous Vichy,* Paris: Éditions Tirésias, 126. The actual address was 43, quai de la Gare. Once again, one can see the perpetual shifting of Austerlitz camp within memory (see Introduction).

[18] Centre de documentation juive contemporaine, XVa-169, statement by Mme Gilberte Jacob to the Department for Research into Enemy War Crimes, 6/06/1945.

[19] Interviews with Michel Behr and Bernard Behr.

The Germans gave a numbered armband to each detainee. This was their camp number. Herself transferred to the quai de la Gare a month and a half later, Yvonne Klug relates her arrival in more detail: 'The back of the lorry was opened: we had arrived in front of a large, grey, stone building into which we were quickly herded. We just caught a glimpse of the rails, and the Seine embankment in the distance. Then we familiarised ourselves with our new residence, its routine and its inhabitants ... We were led up to the fourth floor where the living accommodation was situated, and our names were taken. Then everyone was given an armband with a number: I was number 43 and would stay there for a little over six months.'[20]

On 15 March 1944, the third satellite camp, called 'Bassano', opened its doors to its first Jewish workers.[21] Yet Bassano had in fact been the first of the three buildings used as satellite camps to have been commandeered by the Dienststelle Westen, for use as a storage site. While Bassano was a satellite camp, its workforce was assigned to it in a different manner. It was, so to speak, a satellite of the satellites.

'The camp was split up, some left for Bassano, located on rue Bassano', wrote Bernard Behr in March 1944 from the quai de la Gare. Documents relating to food provisions indicate that there were eighteen people on site, eight of whom appear to have been transferred there from Austerlitz. A text that was never published but was found among the draft material for the camp newspaper *Camp-Camp*, dated to the end of March 1944, makes explicit reference to the transfer of eight internees to Bassano, the Napoleonic echoes of the names Austerlitz and Bassano having evidently struck the text's cultivated author.

> 'Austerlitz...Bassano...
> Names evoking
> glory, the glories
> of the past. Names which are
> today synonymous
> with suffering
> You are leaving. You eight who, having shared for a brief time, this communal life devoid of all joy, are flying off to a smaller and, it would seem, less uncomfortable 'camp'.
> You eight who will take our memory with you to another place.
> Comrades. For some of us, you were, perhaps, more than comrades... You will carry on talking of us a little, we will talk a little of you, and that will be that.

---

[20] Centre de documentation juive contemporaine, Yvonne Klug, *The 8616 came back*, 9–10.

[21] The exact date of the camp's opening has been established through a thorough examination of roll no. 48 of the UGIF archives, kept in the Centre de documentation juive contemporaine. These documents record the amounts of food needed to supply the satellite camps. The entry for 'Bassano' first appears on 14 March 1944. The camp must therefore have opened on 15 March.

The dream that we nurtured together, that beautiful, unique dream, will be the only link still uniting us.

But beyond that dream, stronger still, the other dream must live on.

A land, a flag, a love greater than all the loves that can infuse or rend our human hearts.

A vast, immense love, which soars above us beyond us.

Marengo… Austerlitz… As if somehow predestined, the separation is not total. The sustained link, the historic link holds out to us, above the tumultuous torrent of our suffering, of our passions, the rainbow of this wondrous certainty on a level above the mere human: 'FRANCE WILL LIVE ON!'

Farewell, perhaps forever, comrades.

Faced with an unknown future, our lives go their separate ways today. Think of us a little longer.

Do not forget that the paths of our lives crossed, and why they crossed…

Why does my heart hurt so?[22]

This group of internees seems to have consisted mainly of seamstresses. The final version of *Camp-Camp* (the title plays on the French pronunciation of the Parisian music-hall dance, the cancan, but also on the slang 'cancan', for gossip) featured a drawing that at first sight appears rather enigmatic, but in fact refers to this transfer of prisoners to a place where they would be employed in needlework.

In terms of its administrative organisation, Bassano remained a branch of the main camps. Thus, when a list of internees with the recognised status of 'half-Jews' in Bassano camp was produced in June 1944, it comprised two sections: 'internees detached from Austerlitz camp' on the one hand, and 'internees detached from Lager Ost' (meaning Lévitan) on the other.[23] Likewise, it was the quai de la Gare that, on 24 April 1944, sent a request to the commandant at Drancy that packets of cigarettes be sent 'to the men in Bassano (12 instead of the 10 dispatched)'.[24] From an administrative point of view, Bassano was, right from its creation, a sub-branch, a subdivision of the two main camps. In a correspondence dated July 1944 between Kurt Schendel, the UGIF official assigned to deal with the Germans, and the head of the Bassano internees, the camp, described as a 'shelter group', would ask the quai de la Gare that 'priority [in the coming delivery] be reserved for the "shelter" group in the delivery of [boiler] suits'.[25] At this time, throughout the Third Reich, the system of concentration camps was being divided up in the same way, as the SS opened up Kommandos and sub-Kommandos in the very heart of German cities.

---

[22] Centre de documentation juive contemporaine, UGIF 93-22.

[23] Ibid., UGIF 92-1697.

[24] Ibid., UGIF 93-44.

[25] Ibid., UGIF 23-710.

ILLUSTRATION 9. Lévitan main lobby (1943–1944).
Bundesarchiv Koblenz, B 323-311-80.

Between July 1943 and March 1944, then, three satellite camps were established in Paris, and the workforce progressively moved into them. These were true work camps. That the creation of these sites was a response to the need for cheap workers is clear from the fact that the tasks that gradually began to be carried out by the Jewish internees had previously been done by 'normal' workers. Correspondence from August 1943 relating to Lager Musik – the musical instruments depot – shows this: 'In Lager Bassano 23 crates have been packed. The workers did it very well.'[26] A few months later 'workwomen' and 'packers', all Jewish internees, were carrying out the same work. The creation of the satellite camps allowed the Dienststelle both to enlarge its workforce and reduce expenditure on salaries. While the internees remained dependent on the SD, they were also regarded as workers. In a report, the Ministry of the Eastern Territories described Lévitan, at that point the only functioning camp, as a real part of its workforce: 'In this Lager are employed around 200 male and female Jewish workers, for a modest daily salary of five francs per person.'[27] The Dienststelle thus paid the Sipo-SD for the work done by the internees of the Parisian camps. As in the concentration camp system within the Reich, internee labour was rented out by the SS to private or public companies, who paid a small daily salary for each worker. Naturally, this money did not go to the Jewish labourers. Their work, however, was intensive, hard, and closely supervised.

[26] Ibid., CXLI-168.

[27] Ibid., CCXXXII-30. A worker's average daily pay at this time was 40 francs.

The Sorting Process

The internees spent the greater part of each day working. While the end result of this work might seem simple, namely the sorting and repair of furniture prior to its being sent to Germany, in reality it comprised several stages. In his testimony after the war, André Cohen gave an impression of its nature: 'At the Gare d'Austerlitz, my work consisted of loading wagons to be sent to Germany. We worked between 10 and 12 hours a day. It was hard, unpleasant work which demanded constant physical effort. On the three other days of the week, it was the vans bringing in the furniture ... We had to unload the vans and stack the furniture. [The women] had the job of sorting and packing the crockery.'[28]

This series of tasks thus began with the arrival of the lorries. At Austerlitz, the furniture was delivered inside the site's perimeter, just in front of the building housing the internees. The unloaded crates were brought in on the ground floor of the building. At Lévitan, the vehicles drove straight down into the old loading bays. The concern with secrecy was clear in both cases, the lorries' contents being impossible to see from street level and revealed only within the camps' respective confines. When two women living just opposite Lévitan, at 85–87 rue du Faubourg-Saint-Martin, came forward to testify, they were unable to recall ever having seen any furniture or crates entering the building between July 1943 and August 1944.[29]

These crates arrived constantly and in huge numbers, so they had to be dealt with to avoid an overflow situation. In his deposition, Georges Kohn, the camp chief at Austerlitz and then Lévitan, reckoned their number at '2,400 per working day', coming from Paris and the provinces alike.[30] Georges Geissmann gave details of what was coming in: 'Several thousand crates bring in every day what, very often, once constituted the pride and joy of innumerable households whose members are today deported, imprisoned or in hiding. Linen, clothes, crockery, glassware, silver, toys, books are piled up higgledy-piggledy with lamps, kitchen utensils, rugs, dustbins ... Personal effects, family mementoes, photographs and personal papers.'[31] The crates were emptied by the Jewish internees themselves.

Sorting furniture was a speciality of Austerlitz. This happened just outside the main building. None of the former detainees that we have spoken to was involved in this stage of the process. It seems at first to have been carried out by Aryans,

---

[28] Centre de documentation juive contemporaine, CCXVI-55, statement to the Centre de documentation sur la persécution nazie, Nice, 3/04/1945.

[29] Interviews with two women living in the area, on boulevard de Strasbourg and rue du Faubourg-Saint-Martin respectively, conducted on 15/05/2003 and 16/05/2003.

[30] Dépôt central de la justice militaire, Le Blanc, Indre, 'Dossier Utikal et autres', statement of 6 September 1944.

[31] Dépôt central de la justice militaire, Le Blanc, Indre, 'Dossier Utikal et autres', article in *L'Homme libre,* 15 September 1944.

ILLUSTRATION 10. Arrival of a moving truck, Lévitan (1943–1944).
Bundesarchiv Koblenz, B 323-311-34.

either French employees or German soldiers, in part because of the visibility of this work in a very busy area and also because of the risk of escape, given that it took place outside the camp buildings. In March 1944, the situation changed with the arrival of new German supervisors. In his correspondence with his wife, Simon Sarfati described how 'now we're unloading the furniture vans ourselves, a job done before by Aryans; that way, we're always out in the air.'[32]

The sorting process would begin once the crates were brought inside the buildings. The ground-floor areas were organised around this main activity. Parallel lines of ten people were drawn up. Each internee would go and pick up a crate to sort, then return with it to the line, which stood between two rows: on one side were the crates of mixed objects, on the other a set of specialised crates. The work consisted of distributing the contents of the former among the latter. The result of the operation was a new set of crates, each containing a single category of object. At the end of the line, women internees counted the number of crates that had been sorted.

The furniture arriving at Austerlitz was stacked in another building, and only a few internees remember going into it in order to reassemble sets of bedroom

---

[32] Private archives of Jacqueline Ribot, placed in the Centre de documentation juive contemporaine.

furniture or large wardrobes.[33] Furniture was arranged in rows according to type or in matching sets.[34] Specific sorting exercises sometimes took place, as at Austerlitz at the beginning of August 1944, when work concentrated on 'a big push to pick out textiles'.[35] Instructions for sorting particular objects were also given by the offices of the ERR, with which the Dienststelle continued to work.

The offices of the ERR paid particular attention to recovering works of art and cultural goods. An agreement had been signed in December 1942, putting a depot on the rue de Richelieu at the disposition of the music division for the storage of pianos. The vast number of pianos that had built up was causing space problems. A building on the Austerlitz site was therefore lent by von Behr for this purpose. Instruments, paintings and fragile objects thus passed through the Dienststelle Westen. On 8 November 1943, Dr Gerigk, the head of the music division, reminded the organisers of Operation Furniture that, in the sorting process carried out in the depots, Jewish internees had to put record players, musical instruments and scores to one side for his division. Anything that was incomplete or in poor condition would then be sent back to the Dienststelle Westen.[36]

These cultural goods were sometimes mishandled during removal and sorting. Furthermore, Scholz, the head of the fine arts division of the ERR, was concerned by the quality of the pictures sent directly to the Reich as part of Möbel Aktion, to be used to decorate new apartments for bombed-out families. In March 1943, he had already complained that some paintings were examples of degenerate art, and also that the works of a Jewish painter, Mandel, had been made available for distribution. He considered this scandalous, given that the whole operation was being carried out in the name of Alfred Rosenberg, supposedly the guarantor of ideological purity in occupied Europe. He also complained about the bad taste of the poorer Jews whose apartments had been plundered, and the 'kitsch' character of the artworks being sent to Germany. He had laid his finger on a flagrant contradiction within Operation Furniture: the enterprise was predicated on the idea that Jews had no right to keep their furniture, which would be used to restore the injustices inflicted on the Reich, but there was a risk that the Jewish vices and perversions of their former owners might be rub off on these objects.[37]

Musical instruments and works of art, of course, formed only a tiny fraction of the vast jumble of objects that needed to be sorted. The crates brought in by the lorries attest to the brutally interrupted lives of these apartments' occupants: half-finished plates of soup, scraps of food, unfinished letters. They contained not

---

[33] Interview with Roger Mayer, 08/04/2002.

[34] Photographs of furniture depots created in Germany for Möbel Aktion give an idea of the contents of this store (see illustrations).

[35] Centre de documentation juive contemporaine, CXLI-195.

[36] Centre de documentation juive contemporaine, CDXXXVI-13.

[37] Centre de documentation juive contemporaine, CXLIV-396.

only luxury goods, but also traces of people's lives: crystal glasses and fine fabrics alongside school exercise books and family photos. It occasionally happened that 'sorters' came across objects that belonged to them or their families. Gilberte Jacob emphasises this 'rather curious and painful detail': 'Among all these objects, some internees recognised their own possessions, which they were forced to wrap up for these men.' Robert Fabius realised that his father-in-law had been arrested when he saw the contents of his apartment going through the system; these included framed photos of his own daughter.[38] Odette Dassonvile recognised a drawing done by a member of her family. She hid it and still has it today.

At the end of the war, Marcel Lob, a former internee in Austerlitz, recounted the following events with great emotion in a letter to the descendants of Georges Ascoli, a professor of nineteenth-century French literature at the Sorbonne who was arrested and deported to Auschwitz on 7 March 1944:

> A former student of the École Normale, and a former teacher sacked for being Jewish by Vichy, I was, in March 1944, arrested by the Gestapo and sent to Drancy. As my wife is not Jewish, I was not deported but instead transferred to the Dienststelle … Given my specialist knowledge, I was placed in the book department. One day in July 1944, the personal library and papers of professor Ascoli arrived, a man of whose reputation I was aware. I have been a teacher myself, and I know just how much our books mean to us … As events [the Normandy landings] gave cause to hope that liberation was not far off, I did what I could to save his papers: lecture notes and reading notes, presentations, etc. I camouflaged them inside two or three old bags hidden under tables to prevent them from being pulped. I was unable to do the same for the books.[39]

Whether their owners were famous or unknown, the objects being sorted constituted the worlds of thousands of men and women to whose existence these internees were the last witnesses.

Whether taken from the figures of the Dienststelle Westen, the UGIF, or the postwar lists drawn up by the Allies, all the documents relating to Operation Furniture are striking both for the sheer number and the enormous variety of objects and furniture listed: entire kitchen, dining room, or bedroom suites, rugs, safes, pianos, radios, watches, lamps, gas stoves, desks, sofas, armchairs, books, photos, china…

Once the crates had been sorted, they would be taken upstairs. At Austerlitz, they were at first carried up by hand as, unlike at Lévitan, there were no lifts.

---

[38] Interview with Mme Haymans, daughter of Robert Fabius, 14/12/2002.

[39] Handwritten letter addressed by Marcel Lob to Pierre Ascoli, Rousillon, Vaucluse, 19 September 1946, 2 pages. Quoted in C. Singer. 2000. *Un universitaire face au destin. Georges Ascoli (1882–1944)*, Paris: Association des anciens élèves de l'ENS.

Jacques Altman recalls having been taken from Drancy to Austerlitz as a mechanic in order to help install a lift in November 1943.[40] Six months later, in a letter to a friend, Bernard Behr explained: 'My work is pretty tiring; personally, I'm in charge of the lift and when my team isn't able to work (when there's a power cut), we have to carry thirty or so crates weighing between 35 and 60 kg on our backs (up 3 floors).'[41]

In Austerlitz as in Lévitan and Bassano, once the objects had been taken upstairs, they were arranged on shelves. 'Porcelain', 'glassware', 'kitchenware', 'children's clothes', 'rugs', 'curtains': teams of camp workers had installed counters of a sort on which were piled all the more valuable goods, which had been picked out. At Austerlitz, these counters were arranged so as to look 'a bit like a department store. On each floor there were stands and at these stands were women. I remember that Mlle Politi was at one of them.'[42] At Lévitan, Odette Dassonville recalls having spent some time in 'the cutlery department'. Bassano camp had the finest selection of goods: 'silverware, crystal, porcelain, fine linen, fabrics'.[43] In all three camps, each floor had 'its' counters, which explains the recurrent metaphor of the 'Galeries Lafayette', a reference to the Parisian department store, in the accounts of former inmates, regardless of which camp they were held in.[44] Thus Muriel Schatzmann placed the title *Galeries Austerlitz* above her ironic account of her experiences published just after the war.

Like shop assistants, the inmates in charge of these 'counters', for the most part women, had to clean up the objects they displayed and make them sparkle. Yvonne Klug, held at Austerlitz, and Odette Dassonville, at Lévitan, both recount how polishing the contents of cutlery services took up a large part of their days. In a report on the Dienststelle Westen, an inspector from the Ministry of the Occupied Eastern Territories expressed his satisfaction with this atmosphere of cleanliness: 'It is amazing, given that these crates often seem to be full only of worthless old junk, to see how objects and effects of all sorts, after being cleaned up in the Lager [Lévitan], can be put to good use.'[45]

However, the contents of the crates as they came did not always end up on these counters. The piece of furniture or object might, on the one hand, be in such a hopeless state of repair that it was simply thrown on the bonfire that

---

[40] Rajsfus, *Drancy, un camp de concentration très ordinaire*, 338–339.

[41] Private archives of Bernard Behr, letter dated 28/05/1944.

[42] Interview with Michel Behr. Mlle Politi was Vivette Politi, later Mme Bahaklia.

[43] Dépôt central de la justice militaire, Le Blanc, Indre, 'Dossier Utikal et autres', statement by Georges Geissmann. His account is corroborated by the organisational schema of Bassano found in the archives of the UGIF.

[44] M. Bonnet, J. Jacob-Delmas, M. Lessovoï. 1993. Testimony published in *Le Monde juif*, 146 (January–March), 37.

[45] Centre de documentation juive contemporaine, CCXXXII-30. Report dated 15/09/1943.

burned every day at the back of the building at the quai de la Gare or, on the other, be in sufficiently good condition, or sufficiently valuable, to warrant its being repaired. The placing of objects on these shelves constituted the final stage before sending them to Germany, which was, in theory, the objective of Operation Furniture. But above all, it gave an opportunity for German dignitaries and their friends to take their pick of the items on display.

Jean Reich's job at Austerlitz was to act as an interpreter for the German NCO in charge of handling 'special orders'. In his statement, he gave precise details of the names and addresses of whom these were sent to.[46] The recipients were German civilians and soldiers of various ranks and in various places, from detachments of the SS to bakers and teachers, from film stars – like Maria Paudler – to anonymous friends of camp commanders, whose own personal addresses feature at the top of the list. This aspect of the handling of the plunder thus involved networks (of acquaintance or friendship) of officials of the Dienststelle, apparently regardless of their status within the hierarchy. Generals Grün, Blocher, von Salmuth, Aschenbrenner, Guderian and Fromm, for example, received deliveries at their home addresses. Hitler had given estates in East Germany to many of these men, such as Guderian, who in 1942 received a property in the Warthegau, part of Poland annexed by the Reich. Furniture was needed to fill these newly acquired houses.

Several statements, including those from camp guards, also mentioned parcels being regularly sent to addresses in Germany, and written and oral testimony provides a detailed account of these special assignments.[47] Georges Geissmann recounts what shocked him most: the 'best pieces are reserved for influential figures [among whom were] numerous French collaborators, with choice items of furniture going to the rue Fresnel. Every day, crates were going off to Germany marked with the names of the best-known officials of the régime. Did Minister Rosenberg himself not deign to order an impressive quantity of sheets, towels and other accessories?'[48]

Gilberte Jacob describes this unofficial use of the sorting process with precision. The role played by Miss Nehring, assistant to Kochan, the camp commander, is revealed. This woman was effectively in charge of the 'special tasks department' and the Fresnel depot: 'Fabrics of every type, wool, silk, the contents of entire shops, pharmacies, magnificent libraries, paintings were all stolen by these bosses. *Mademoiselle* Nehring filled her apartment with stolen objects.' Arthur Garbas describes Sigrid Nehring as being of 'the southern type' [*sic*]. Born in Berlin in 1918, she had studied interior design in Vienna. Mobilised by the

---

[46] Statement of 8 April 1947, Dépôt central de la justice militaire, Le Blanc, Indre, 'Dossier Utikal et autres'.

[47] Dépôt central de la justice militaire, Le Blanc, Indre, 'Dossier Utikal et autres'.

[48] Georges Geissmann. 1944. Article in *L'Homme libre*, 15 September.

labour office in Berlin at the end of 1940, she was sent to Cracow in Poland, in March 1941 to work as a secretary in the construction department of the General Government; then, at her request, she returned to Germany a year later. She spent several months without working in Vienna, Munich and Berlin, taking classes in theatre, theatre criticism and French. In April 1943, she became an employee of the Ministry of the Occupied Territories, and was sent to Paris at the end of May to find furniture for the house of Gauleiter Meyer in Dahlem. Ever the conscientious interior designer, she fitted out the whole of the *Gauleiter's* residence. At the end of June, she was sent back to Paris to work in the Dienststelle Westen and was given the sort of special missions that she had proved so adept at carrying out. Her sister Helga, who was blonde, was also occasionally seen in Paris. On the avenue d'Iéna, Sigrid Nehring was known to all as Alfred Rosenberg's niece, which was not true. After the war, Miss Nehring explained that von Behr had told her, when she arrived in Paris, to pretend to be related to the *Reichsleiter*. She denied all knowledge of where these objects came from, and claimed not to have profited personally from them, but did acknowledge that she had 'chosen furniture and other objects from several warehouses'. She admitted receiving orders, from July 1943 onwards, to 'arrange furnishings or entire interiors for high-ranking officers from all branches of the Wehrmacht and for German civilians based in Paris'.

On several occasions, during what he called his 'inspections', Kurt von Behr also allowed both German dignitaries and French collaborators to help themselves directly to the goods on offer. These visits were, for them, an opportunity to pick out the object of their desires, which internees, under the orders of Miss Nehring, then had to wrap up and send off to addresses in France or Germany. The officers of the Dienststelle spread the word about the fruits of Operation Furniture among their contacts and friends. This was a way of winning support and reinforcing relationships, which could, given the competition between the different Nazi agencies, be vital. Kurt von Behr had seen for himself that such links could count for a great deal. However, most looted objects and furniture were neither thrown out nor siphoned off in this way. In theory, the sorted crates and furniture were loaded into freight wagons and sent to Germany.

At Lévitan, the loading was done off-site by Aryan workers at the Aubervilliers depot, which was linked to the national SNCF rail network.[49] At Austerlitz, it was done by the internees, since the site had a direct rail link. In a letter to his wife, Simon Sarfati describes how being assigned to loading, which took place three times a week, represented an opportunity to go outside: 'We were happy, then, because we could go outside and breath some fresh air instead of being cooped up inside with only electric light.'[50] Michel Behr recalls that a group of workers

---

[49] Centre de documentation juive contemporaine, CCXXXII-30.

[50] Private archives of Jacqueline Ribot.

from the camp was stationed outside in order to load crates and furniture into the wagons.[51] Roger Mayer also describes this task, giving details of the role played by cushions and straw. This description is echoed in the ironic glossary included in *Camp-Camp,* the internees' newspaper: '*Stroh* is a material of vegetable origin with a lovely bright yellow colour. It is found in bales or artistically arranged in warehouses, on the doorways of wagons, on the rails, between skin and shirt and, very occasionally, inside wagons… It can also be found in between the furniture loaded at Austerlitz.' For the internees loading the wagons, positioning this straw could be a means of sabotage. According to witness testimony and various official figures, the number of wagons leaving the satellite camps each week can be estimated at between 200 and 300. The message 'Gift from the French for German refugees' seems to have been written on them.[52]

Von Behr had got into some difficulties in the middle of 1943 owing to his wife's nationality. On 10 May 1943, Hitler had made public his thoughts on the necessity of sidelining those German officials 'of the State, of the Party, and of the Wehrmacht whose wives were liable to adopt oppositional stances because of their political opinions or their nationality, along with men from certain backgrounds who, through links with family or with social and economic influences, could reveal themselves to be foreign in spirit.' This meandering pronouncement meant that, given the situation of total war in which Germany found itself, the wives of German officials had to be ideologically irreproachable, immune to any accusations of 'siding with the enemy'. This statement was sent to all the large agencies and organs of the Party. As a result, lists were drawn up of officials whose wives were not German.

Von Behr was on one of them.[53] He was sufficiently highly placed in the hierarchy to be considered a top-ranking official. His wife was described as being English by birth. But von Behr had been able to make himself indispensable and gather wide support. The Ministry of the Occupied Eastern Territories wrote that he was in no way suspect, even if the authorities could continue to 'keep an eye on him'.[54] He thus avoided being simply removed from his post, as certain Nazis in situations similar to his were, along with various members of the nobility, such as Prince Albrecht von Hohenzollern, a lieutenant in the German army, who had nevertheless been a member of the National Socialist Party since 1932.

Even before the establishment of the satellite camps, Operation Furniture had won von Behr many friends. He had been promoted to *Oberstführer* and received a cash payment. This had been awarded to him directly by the finance office of

---

[51] Interview quoted above. See also the statement: by André Cohen, also quoted above.

[52] See in particular the testimony of Odette Dassonville, Michel Behr and Roger Mayer. The written account given by Jacqueline Jacob-Delmas in *Le Monde juif* also mentions this.

[53] Bundesarchiv Berlin, 0.915, 136/326.

[54] Bundesarchiv Berlin, O.915, 136/341.

Illustration 11. Glasses and tableware being sorted, Lévitan (1943–1944). Bundesarchiv Koblenz, B 323-311-32.

the Munich division of the NSDAP.[55] It was meant to mark the third anniversary, on 17 July 1943, of the creation of the ERR; supposedly, Kurt von Behr, during these years of intense work, had received no salary and had given his services on an entirely voluntary basis. Yet he had been leading a life of luxury in occupied Paris, entertaining frequently and lavishly. The recommendation praised his self-denial in accomplishing this difficult task. Kurt von Behr received a total of 6,000 reichsmarks, the equivalent of 120,000 francs at the time. The sum was paid to him in August 1943, a few weeks after the creation of the first Parisian camp.

The Organisation of Tasks

The internees' days were organised according to the work they were doing: ten hours per day on average. In the morning, the prisoners had to be at their posts by 8 a.m. 'Work begins at eight o'clock sharp, we start coming down from the billets to work at 7.50. This is why the time for coffee has been set at seven o'clock', wrote the chief internee at Austerlitz to the UGIF in January 1944.[56] The time at which work ended was less rigid, however. In a letter dated 6 February 1944, Simon Sarfati recounted his daily routine to his wife: 'The work is very tiring. We are carrying crates around non-stop. I'll briefly describe the daily timetable:

[55] Bundesarchiv Berlin, NSDAP file for Kurt von Behr, Mitglied 3 391 527.

[56] Centre de documentation juive contemporaine, UGIF 18.

wake up at six, work from eight until 1.30pm; lunch then back to work at 3pm until 7.30pm.' He himself described the detainees' existence 'as something like life in a barracks'.

Occasionally, either because of the arrival of large numbers of crates, or due to collective punishments, the hours worked could become much longer. Eighteen days later, the same Simon Sarfati wrote: 'Just imagine, since we woke up at six until half past eight this evening we haven't stopped working with only a break between 2pm and 3pm this afternoon.' Sometimes, as a punishment, internees were woken up in the middle of the night and made to work nonstop for twenty-four hours. However, it was usually the arrival of loads that dictated the rhythm of their work, as it was necessary to work quickly so as to keep neither the lorries nor the sorting-lines waiting. Jacques Altman recalls: 'In certain periods, the work was very hard, as the lorries were arriving so frequently that we had to keep working until 10pm. There was no fixed timetable; when a lorry arrived, it had to be unloaded immediately.'[57] At Austerlitz, the hours worked seem to have depended on the German supervisors. When Kochan, the commandant of the quai de la Gare camp, was replaced by Redhardt in March 1944, the latter proved more flexible in terms of output and hours worked, and seemed principally interested in the camp's cleanliness and hygiene.[58]

Internees, then, were required to be at their posts at 8 A.M. But how were they dressed? Were they wearing work clothes? Such clothes do seem to have existed. In their testimonies published by *Le Monde juif*, Jacqueline Jacob-Delmas and Michèle Bonnet, two women interned in Austerlitz and Lévitan respectively, speak in turn of their 'uniform' and 'one-piece suit with yellow star'.[59] Odette Dassonville and Erna Herzberg recall that at Lévitan the men wore smocks, while the Germans had allowed the seamstresses to make uniforms for the women from black fabric found on one of the looted premises. Correspondence between service 14 of the UGIF and the head internees responsible for the three satellite camps confirms that work clothes were requested. On 8 November 1943, for example, the quai de la Gare ordered 108 men's overalls and 86 women's aprons. On 8 May 1944, the German camp commandant wrote to Röthke to remind him that 'to carry out their work, the Jews interned in Austerlitz camp are in urgent need of *200 sets of overalls*', while his counterpart at Bassano would place an identical request two months later.

However, whether in written memoirs or oral testimony, many former detainees do not remember having worn a uniform. This apparent contradiction can in part be explained by the staged 'tableaux' that were an important aspect of these very unusual camps. The frequent visits by von Behr gave rise to a veri-

---

[57] Quoted in Rajsfus, *Drancy, un camp de concentration très ordinaire*, 338.

[58] The spelling of his name is uncertain and changes from one document to another.

[59] Bonnet, Jacob-Delmas, Lessovoï in *Le Monde juif* 146, 37–44.

table ritual in which the internees had to play the role of the perfect worker in a uniform that was almost a theatrical costume. Thus Gilberte Jacob states that 'when the colonel's visits were announced, we had to quickly go and put on our work uniform.' This may also explain why, in the photos we possess showing the unloading of lorries, apparently meant for propaganda use, the internees all wear smocks, despite testimony that this was not the case.[60] This phenomenon of staged 'performances' could sometimes influence the organisation of the work routine. Both Maurice Wolf and Yvonne Klug speak of the frenetic pace of internees' activities, like a speeded-up film, when von Behr paid his visits.[61]

Usually, however, their work was organised fairly simply. When the camps first opened, work teams composed of ten members were created. Thus the Behr brothers, along with their father, belonged to group 11, which contained internees 111 to 120 (the Behrs were 115, 120 and 112). When an internee left the camp, his or her camp number, which in fact denoted a workpost rather than an individual, was re-attributed. These groups of ten initially corresponded to the rows of ten crates that formed the first sorting lines on the ground floor. The place occupied by an internee in the organisation of this work thus constituted his or her identity within the camp. When, on 3 April 1944, Thérèse Bottazzi was transferred from Lévitan to the quai de la Gare, she changed both her camp number and her group. 'She previously had the number 204-group 11, here she has no. 59-group 8.'[62] Drawn up in summer 1944, the list of requirements signed by inmates of Lévitan gave the names as well the group numbers of the eligible internees. It referred to fifteen different groups, meaning fifteen work teams.[63]

Once general instructions had been received from the Germans, the precise distribution of tasks was up to the internees themselves. Michel Behr, for example, remembers that because he was the youngest, his fellow detainees had given him the lightest job, that of general camp worker, in which position he could rely on two older, more experienced and physically robust colleagues. The camp numbers, and by extension the corresponding work teams, were the only real organisational restraint in this respect. As former internees mention repeatedly, and Jacqueline Jacob-Delmas describes: 'Each crate had to be marked with the number of the person who had packed it.' Speaking of the risks involved in sabotage, Gilberte Jacob refers to this numbering system: 'Stringent checks were made. Our numbers were marked on the outside and inside of the packages, crates and wagons.'

---

[60] See plates.

[61] Centre de documentation juive contemporaine, *La Mémoire blessée* (typed manuscript, memoirs of Maurice Wolf); and *The 8616 came back*.

[62] Centre de documentation juive contemporaine, CDXXV-2, letter from the chief internee of the quai de la Gare to Kurt Schendel.

[63] Centre de documentation juive contemporaine, UGIF 92-1675.

Illustration 12. Jewish internees cleaning, Lévitan (1943–1944). Bundesarchiv Koblenz, B 323-311-33.

Despite the threat of sanctions, the way work was organised in the satellite camps of Drancy nonetheless appears to have allowed certain acts of sabotage to take place. Gilberte Jacob continues her account: 'In all the work we did, we performed systematic sabotage, using the limited means at our disposal, especially when we were not being observed. We generally used hammers to damage the stolen furniture and render it, as far as possible, unusable. We demolished anything that looked nice. Unfortunately, it was sometimes impossible to do so.' The hammer appears to have been the instrument of choice for sabotage, which it came to symbolise in internees' memories. Jacqueline Jacob-Delmas describes what she would do: 'Armed with a little hammer concealed in the sleeve of my uniform, I would deliver a sharp blow to the sounding board [of a piano] which would split into an X-shape.' Having been very young, and having gone only once to see his father at the quai de la Gare, Michel Kaplan's son has no other memories of the camp but remembers, as a keen pianist, having been horrified by his father's description of the hammer-blows delivered to instruments in order to make them unusable.[64] Sabotage could take other forms, and scissors could take the place of the hammer, turning fine fabrics into rags.

Initiatives taken by internees to slow down the looting enterprise sometimes took a more subtle form, such as repeated delays in sorting crates containing per-

---

[64] Interview with Georges Delorme, 03/06/2002.

sonal documents or family photos. Hiding certain documents could be a form of resistance, as when Marcel Lob concealed the papers of Georges Ascoli. Finally, sabotage could be performed while wagons were being loaded or furniture was being prepared for shipment. On several occasions, the German authorities complained of the deplorable state of the objects and furniture crossing the Rhine.

Ever-present in witness accounts – whether dating from just after the war or from recent years – the existence of a certain number of acts of sabotage was mentioned by von Behr himself, who nonetheless had an interest in playing down what would be seen as evidence of insufficient monitoring on the part of his own services. On 20 September 1944, in an interview with the *Reichsleiter*, he admitted that 'owing to the number of foreign personnel, it was not always possible to prevent some sabotage actions from occurring.'[65]

Finally, the distribution of tasks could also take certain internees outside the camps. In addition to the main activity, which occurred within the camp walls, most often within a single building, detachments were also occasionally sent out of the camps, as the internees constituted a reserve pool of labour. Jacqueline Jacob-Delmas describes one such excursion: 'One day I was chosen along with another girl and six men to go and work on a special job. That morning, under close guard, we were taken to the place where we worked and brought back in the evening. I was shifting grand pianos on my own there.' She was then 'lent' for three weeks, as a 'housemaid for a German called Gert', to 'cook his meals and, in the morning, serve him his breakfast'.[66]

Between April and June 1944, internees from the quai de la Gare were on several occasions taken to the palais de Tokyo to move pianos.[67] Some were used to run errands for the German command, such as making a delivery to Drancy[68] or working as day labourers. During these movements, surveillance seems to have been very lax. At the palais de Tokyo, some received visits from their wives, with whom they were even able to have sexual intercourse. The threat of deportation of their fellow inmates back at the camp was considered by the Germans to be the best guarantee against escape attempts. During an errand run for Kochan, Jean Levi was thus able to pay a visit to his parents-in-law for fifteen minutes while his German escort and fellow internees waited downstairs.[69] He had the opportunity to escape, but the detainees left in the vehicle would have paid the price.

---

[65] Centre de documentation juive contemporaine, CCXXXII-23.

[66] Bonnet, Jacob-Delmas, Lessovoï in *Le Monde juif* 146, 39.

[67] See interviews with Roger Mayer and Jean Levi, also correspondence from M. Sarfati to his wife (private archives of Jacqueline Ribot).

[68] See the description given by Maurice Rajsfus of the delivery of pigs made by Maurice Wajdenfeld to Drancy: Rajsfus, *Drancy, un camp de concentration très ordinaire*, 337. Similar errands and the lending of workers are mentioned throughout the testimony we have assembled.

[69] Interview with Jean Levi.

ILLUSTRATION 13. Jewish pianos waiting to be given to German families, Oberhausen warehouse (n.d.).
Stradtarchiv, Oberhausen, 712-404-01.

Before the third camp opened, some internees, among them Lichtenauer, a member of the cabinetmaking team at Lévitan, were on several occasions transferred for the day to 2, rue de Bassano, in order to get the building ready. Once the camp had been set up, personnel could still be borrowed from the two main camps in order to provide reinforcements for storage and repair jobs. These internees would be brought back to their original site in the evening.

Craftsmanship, Repairs and Fabrication

The satellite camps also exploited the specialised skills possessed by their internees. This is what had allowed internees of Drancy who did not officially belong to special categories, such as Jacques Altman or Lichtenauer, to be sent there. Attached, respectively, to Austerlitz and Lévitan, they belonged to the camps' technical teams. The main task of these 'camp workers' was the construction of display shelving and partitioning between different areas. Maurice Wolf and Félix Lichtenauer, who had both claimed to be cabinetmakers, recall participating in these activities. Michel Behr worked for a long time on the first floor as part of a team led by the two brothers Bernard and Samuel Jaroussky. Equipped with professional woodworking tools, they fitted out both the camp and the German guards' accommodation. Lastly, Jacqueline Jacob-Delmas has described how she was put to work making the crates used in the sorting process.[70] The task of manufacturing the main tool of the camp's work, the crates, thus also fell to the detainees. This further reduced the costs to the Dienststelle Westen.

Aside from the sorting process, the main tasks were repair and fabrication, which involved a degree of craftsmanship. Georges Kohn has described how '[c]ertain raw materials stolen during these raids such as leather, clothing, furs, linen, were transformed into items for the wives of staff officers, generals and high-ranking German figures in a workshop situated at first in the faubourg Saint-Martin and at the quai de la Gare, then transferred from April 1944 onwards to rue Bassano in the Cahen d'Anvers' mansion.'[71]

The condition of the furniture and other objects sometimes meant that more than a quick dusting-off was necessary. This had led the German administration to set up restoration workshops. The Lévitan workshop included watchmakers and jewellery repairers. A letter dated 19 December 1943, from the chief internee to Kurt Schendel, refers to a shoe repair workshop that seems to have been working at full stretch, since its operation demanded '2 kg of 8mm cobblers' nails, 2 kg of 10mm, 100 men's steel toe pieces, 100 women's steel toe pieces, 100 men's steel heel pieces, 100 women's steel heel pieces. All with fixing-pins. A bottle of special glue for glueing on the pieces. *Bouchou* glue if possible.'[72]

The Germans insisted that only items in good, or at least functioning condition were to be sent out. A striking anecdote illustrates this: Odette Dassonville, who had been at Lévitan since the opening of the camp, recalls that among the plundered objects were the gas masks that each French family had received at the outbreak of the war. The organisers of Operation Furniture wanted to make sure that these functioned correctly. Odette Dassonville has described how certain internees, including her, were regularly taken down to the building's basement and put in a small sealed room. The Germans pumped in gas to test the condition of the masks worn by the internees within. 'They were of high quality because nothing ever happened. We did not become ill', she concludes.[73]

By contrast, the workforce was sometimes given very skilled tasks, such as repairing gramophones or musical instruments. A letter from Dr Gerigk to the *Stabsführung* of the ERR, dated 13 October 1943, refers to a piano repair workshop situated in Austerlitz that, while it mainly operated using specialist Aryan workers, also called on the services of the internees.[74] On 15 April 1944, the management of the music division wrote to the director of the Dienststelle

[70] Bonnet, Jacob-Delmas, Lessovoï in *Le Monde juif*, 146, 39.

[71] Central archives of military justice, Le Blanc, Indre, 'Dossier Utikal et autres', statement by Georges Kohn.

[72] Centre de documentation juive contemporaine, UGIF 18-842.

[73] Interview with Odette Dassonville, Orly, 04/11/2002.

[74] Centre de documentation juive contemporaine, CXLI-178.

ILLUSTRATION 14. A sewing workshop, Lévitan (1943–1944).
Bundesarchiv Koblenz, B 323-311-41.

Westen, on avenue d'Iéna: 'We have urgent need, in order to carry out work in our piano repair workshop in Lager Austerlitz, of two suitable Jewish men or women, able to clean pianos professionally under the direction of messrs. Schumann and Verner.'[75]

In his report dated 21 July 1944, von Behr announced that the workshops set up in the camps had up to that date restored 30 kitchen dressers, 23 dining tables, 56 dining chairs, 43 wardrobes, 65 beds, 10 dressing tables, 30 bedside tables, 12 bookcases, 24 writing desks, 25 armchairs, 25 kitchen cabinets, 15 kitchen tables, 35 kitchen chairs and 1 sofa, while 4 armchairs had been refitted with springs and reupholstered.[76] This was a rather modest total considering the massive quantity of furniture and other objects that passed through the camp.

While these repairs are the only skilled task referred to in official reports, they were far from being the only job done by Jewish craftsmen in these camps, who were also made to produce items from scratch. This was not an isolated phenomenon, as there were similar workshops at Drancy, where Yvonne Klug, later interned at Austerlitz, was 'in charge of a workshop which produced the bags in which the poor deportees kept their provisions'. On his arrival, Brunner had set

---

[75] Centre de documentation juive contemporaine, CXLI-184.

[76] Centre de documentation juive contemporaine, XIII-47.

up a number of workshops to manufacture clothing and other items necessary for the deportation of the Jews to the East.

However, when she arrived at the quai de la Gare, Yvonne Klug was placed in a new sewing workshop that this time was not producing items for internees; here, clothes were being made for German officials and their friends. In Lévitan, Erna Herzberg, who had been immediately selected for her skills as a former head seamstress, was told to organise and manage a workshop. She was given four or five sewing machines for the purpose of making 'little skirts for little German girls', while a similar, male-oriented workshop had to stitch 'little pairs of trousers'. Mira Lessovoï recalls having worked in this workshop under the supervision of a woman 'who spoke German.'[77] Two photographs, apparently taken for propaganda purposes, correspond exactly to the account given by these former internees.[78]

Mira Lessovoï describes how, every day, German officers would come to place orders. This team of nine people only ever manufactured a handful of skirts. These were carefully put to one side, and every time von Behr came visiting accompanied by dignitaries they would be brought out to illustrate the general's boasts of sending off 'a big crate of little skirts and trousers every fortnight'.[79] In fact, these workshops were used to make dresses and suits for the wives of German soldiers and officials. Von Behr's wife, who comes across from descriptions by former inmates as a capricious prima donna, was one of their most frequent clients. This work meant that on several occasions Erna Herzberg left the camp, where her husband remained, in order to go to the avenue d'Iéna and try the clothes on her clients. The fabric was taken from the immense stock of rolls stolen from apartments and shops run by Jews, who were particularly heavily represented in this profession. A room in the basement of 85–87, rue du Faubourg-Saint-Martin was barely large enough to contain them. This stock reached such overwhelming proportions that even the camp guard, an invalided German soldier, had dresses made for his girlfriend and allowed the heads of the workshops to make clothes for themselves.[80] As Gilberte Jacob sums up: 'These big bosses clothed their entire families as well as their wives. Sewing workshops were set up for this purpose using stolen fabric. There was a third camp on rue Bassano, where you had to work quickly to finish the orders.'

In March 1944, Erna Herzberg was transferred to Bassano, where she worked exclusively on made-to-measure clothing for German women in near professional conditions. Also transferred to Bassano, Georges Geissmann described the level of activity in the camp:

---

[77] Bonnet, Jacob-Delmas, Lessovoï in Le Monde juif 146, 42.

[78] See illustrations.

[79] Interview with Erna Herzberg.

[80] See the interviews with Erna Herzberg, Odette Dassonville and Félix Lichtenauer quoted above.

The workshops were unable to satisfy the demand of their clientèle: Baron von Behr ordered dozens of pairs of boots, while the tailors never ceased to make up uniforms for him. Not to be outdone, his wife had an insatiable appetite for the shoes and handbags produced by the expert hands of the internee craftsmen. As for the sewing workshop, supervised by an ex-head seamstress with Paquin, it was quite literally unable to keep up with all these ladies, from the Baroness to the lowliest secretary, who simply went crazy for the flawless taste, the fine workmanship which have brought French haute couture worldwide renown!

The organisational schema of Bassano camp dated 8 May 1944 – a little more than a month after it opened – mentions fifty-one people. The list indicates their functions and how the work was organised.[81] The main activity was indeed tailoring, and it was not only organised in a manner similar to that of the big fashion houses, but also housed in suitably sumptuous surroundings. This department was made up of 19 internees, 12 'seamstresses', 3 'tailors' and 3 'ladies' tailors', to whom must be added the staff overseeing the work of each 'salon', namely a 'head seamstress (main salon)', a 'head seamstress (Austerlitz salon)' and finally a 'head tailor'. Bassano also had a 'fur' department made up of 3 furriers, a 'seamstress for the fur workshop' and a 'head furrier'. As in any fashion house, they also produced and repaired accessories. Along with the seamstresses and furriers there was a 'leather worker (head)' and a 'head cobbler'.

Besides fashion, there was also a cabinetmaking department, apparently set up to restore and perhaps make furniture. This workshop comprised a 'foreman' and two 'cabinetmakers'. Repairs were also done on clocks, watches and electrical items. Thus there was a 'head watchmaker' and a 'watchmaker' under his supervision. The 'electrical and radio workshop' was more crowded, with a 'foreman', a '[female] assistant' and a pair of 'electrician and radio technicians'.

Whereas Austerlitz and Lévitan were primarily depots with some workshops attached, the opposite was true of Bassano. The 'porcelain and crockery depot' was manned by two female detainees, the 'linen depot' by just one. Both the type of workshops and the nature of the depots in the camp confirm that it was given over to activities involving greater added value. Objects seen as valuable or worth repairing were transferred there in order to help the Germans pick them out. It was thus for the purpose of transporting and preparing these more valuable objects that 5 'female porters' and two 'packers and porters' appear on the list.

The von Behrs were the Bassano workshops' best 'clients'. The baron had dozens of uniforms and pairs of boots made. Georges Geissmann adds: 'Baroness von Behr, for all her being, or claiming to be, a fine lady, had no qualms about picking things up second-hand. She was frequently present when crates designated as being particularly valuable were being sorted; not only that, she was not

---

[81] Centre de documentation juive contemporaine, UGIF 18.

afraid to get her hands dirty. The internees would often look on in amazement at the spectacle of the wife of their supreme commander up to her elbows in crates from which she would triumphantly pull out a crocodile-skin handbag or some silk scarves which would straight away have to be carefully put to one side for *Madame la baronne*.'

In the Parisian camps, then, internees were used to sort through stolen objects and furniture, clean them, load them, repair them and occasionally make new ones. The organisation of their work clearly shows how profitable the 'renting out' of the Jewish detainees to the Sipo-SD was for the Dienststelle Westen. It also explains why detainees' memories of each of the tasks carried out shift according to their position in the work organisation at a given time. Despite having been interned at Austerlitz from its opening, Michel Behr, for instance, had never heard of any workshops or of furniture repairs being done in the camp.

All this intense activity was organised, led and supervised by a small contingent of Germans. Their productivity in relation to their numbers was remarkable. Jewish detainees, officials from the UGIF, French removal men and Russian legionnaires together constituted a considerable workforce at their disposal.

CHAPTER 5

A Place of Fragile Safety

THE DIVERSITY OF POINTS of view becomes even more striking as far as everyday life inside the camps is concerned. As Michael Pollak has demonstrated with regard to the (far from typical) case of Auschwitz-Birkenau that '[m]an attempts to create a world in his image by following his own affinities'. These 'micro-worlds' mean that 'there is no shared vision among deportees of this universe but instead perceptions which are highly differentiated both during and after the concentrationary experience.'[1] In the Parisian camps, the past that is evoked always emanates from two points of view: that from which the experience was lived and that from which this experience is reconstituted.

For this reason, 'neither researcher nor survivors possess an "underground map"'.[2] While this phenomenon is visible in the accounts of the tasks performed by internees, its impact is felt with much greater force when it comes to the rest of the internees' everyday universe. 'The social space in which these trajectories run their course and which gives meaning to them has gradually emerged from the accounts of the people who moved within it.'[3]

Two testimonies written down at the end of the war are thus striking for their total contradiction of one another. Yvonne Klug states that, at Austerlitz, 'we were allowed to take as many blankets and eiderdowns from the shelves as we wanted; so we picked out some very fine bedclothes.' Her fellow internee, Gilberte Jacob, declares the opposite, recalling that punishments were meted out to anyone who was even suspected of taking the above-mentioned bedclothes from the counters.

Understanding the apparent contradictions between individual memories amounts to retracing the map of the interior of the camps and of how they functioned. According to Félix Lichtenauer, a German Jew without any family interned at Lévitan, neither visits nor correspondence was permitted. The opposite was true according to Odette Dassonville, a French Jew married to a non-Jew

---

[1] M. Pollak. 1990. *L'Expérience concentrationnaire*, Paris: A.-M. Métailié, 17–18.

[2] Ibid., 21.

[3] Ibid., 21.

Illustration 15. A Jewish internee sorting toys at Lévitan (1943–1944). Bundesarchiv Koblenz, B 323-311-51.

and supported by her in-laws, who stated that inmates could receive visits and exchange letters, if only on an irregular basis.[4]

In spite of this considerable degree of divergence between points of view and personal positions, an overall impression begins to emerge. It relates to the special character of these camps, at once marginal and central. The resulting narrative is sometimes almost surreal, although the facts it recounts are well attested. As Yvonne Klug eloquently put it in her memoirs, 'Everything was unbelievable in that camp, and when we described something of the life we lived there to our visitors, they would look at us as people look at the inhabitants of Charenton.'[5] The diversity and the fragility of these different situations were reflected in a disciplinary régime that was at once protective and threatening. The internees' situation was in a state of continual flux, between security and arbitrary punishment, between varying degrees of liberty and its total absence.

Supervision and Hierarchy

The internees of the satellite camps were guarded by a police contingent that was low in both numbers and quality. As von Behr would write in his report of 22 March 1944, 'a whole section of the Dienststelle Westen's manpower' was

---

[4] Interview with Odette Dassonville, quoted above.

[5] She alludes here to the French psychiatric hospital in Charenton, an eastern suburb of Paris.

composed of 'war invalids'.[6] The German supervisory staff numbered only a few individuals and was made up mostly of soldiers wounded on the Russian front.

Between November 1943 and March 1944, the commandant of Austerlitz camp was Bruno Kochan, a veteran of the Eastern front from where, having fallen ill, he had been sent to France in 1942. Born in Berlin, he had been a tailor before the war. Former internees describe him as a violent man, capable of beating people to death. Georges Geissmann characterises him as 'a nasty, spiteful little man, [who] at the smallest opportunity would inflict severe punishments on prisoners, forcing them to do the most degrading work … He nonetheless pretended that he took the greatest possible care of the workers' well-being and their food but [was] incapable of any real act of pity.' Living in a small billet to the right of the entrance to 43, quai de la Gare, he would personally attend the internees' roll call every morning. He went around between floors and among the detainees in order to keep an eye on their activities. The newspaper *Camp-Camp* alludes satirically to the nature of the internees' supervision:

NEWS IN BRIEF

Omar's circus, whose big top has been standing for several weeks at the Porte d'Ivry, has been forced to interrupt its performances: the magnificent gorilla which was its star attraction has escaped. It is feared that it has sought refuge in nearby buildings. The animal is dangerous, roars ferociously and smashes anything that comes within range of its paws. The management are offering a large reward to anyone helping the local fire brigade capture the beast.

UPDATE

More on 'The Gorilla'-

Following a long and difficult search, the police have discovered the Gorilla's hideout: a large warehouse in the gare d'Austerlitz, where it has already caused considerable damage to the merchandise stored inside.

Some young people who had joined forces with the police sent to the scene, have been captured by the monster, which has barricaded itself inside the building with them. A daring reporter from 'Camp-Camp' was able to catch a glimpse of them by climbing a nearby wall.

The gorilla is forcing them to carry around massive, heavily-loaded crates for hours on end. Rescue operations continue.

Kochan was assisted by a female deputy, Miss Nehring, up until January 1944, at which date she began dealing exclusively with 'special orders'. Two secretaries carried out administrative tasks. Yet it was the two 'caretakers' of the camp, both Wehrmacht soldiers, who left a particularly strong impression on former inmates. One was tall and thin, while the other, shorter and stockier, was nicknamed 'the

---

[6] Centre de documentation juive contemporaine, CCLII-8.

gorilla'. 'The *Oberwachtmeister*', reports Yvonne Klug, 'was simply the NCO who acted as the caretaker and he had a way of speaking that always put me in mind of a dog's bark. Apart from that he was a fairly decent man.' This impression is entirely representative of other descriptions of this man, who remains etched on the memories of former detainees. Kochan was sent to Nice in March 1944 and replaced by a certain Redhardt, who had been left crippled by a wound on the Eastern front. A far more accommodating character, he made it clear that all he demanded was that things run smoothly. The internees remained at the mercy of sanctions and punishments, but the attitude of this new team was more relaxed.

The number of Nazis present on site at 43, quai de la Gare, could increase at certain times. Germans worked in the storage area surrounding the buildings of the camp proper. Like those who were directly involved with the surveillance of the internees working for Operation Furniture, they sometimes used detainees to help in their own logistical operations. On his arrival at the quai de la Gare in June 1944, for example, Maurice Wajdenfeld occupied a rather unusual position. He later described it to Maurice Rajsfus: 'When I arrived at Austerlitz camp, the authorities were looking for an internee to occupy the post of "pig-keeper." So I put my name forward. The piggery was intended to feed the SS at the camp and the German railway workers who had their kitchens in the depot.'[7]

The actual supervisory staff was never very large. Besides the camp commandants and their subordinates, members of the Vlasov army were assigned to guard duties around and within the complex of camp buildings.[8] People living in the vicinity remember these 'Asian soldiers', who probably came from the Caucasus, or even Mongolia. It is, however, difficult to calculate their number. While 200 'Russian legionnaires' were placed at the disposal of the Dienststelle, they were not all employed to guard the camps; some intervened when a fire broke out at the quai de la Gare in May 1944.[9] The presence of the Vlasov troops is also attested at Lévitan, at 85–87 rue du Faubourg-Saint-Martin. Here, too, residents were left with the picturesque image of 'Asians' in the heart of Paris in the 1940s.[10]

Inside the Lévitan building, the German presence was not much heavier than at the quai de la Gare. Fritz Ziemer was the camp commandant. His behaviour and mentality were very much in the same vein as Bruno Kochan's. He was assisted by a certain Rockenfeller, a Wehrmacht captain of about forty who had had one leg amputated. The deputy chief, also a member of the Wehrmacht, was called Fritz Bertl. Like Kochan, these overseers would attend the daily roll call

---

[7] Rajsfus, *Drancy*, 336.

[8] The Vlasov army was composed of Soviet soldiers, usually drawn from national minorities, who had been taken prisoner by the Germans and then used against the Red Army. A certain number of them were posted in France.

[9] Centre de documentation juive contemporaine, CDXXXVI-10.

[10] Interview with two local residents, 15/05/2003 and 16/05/2003.

and watch over the prisoners, particularly while they worked. The internees were supposed in principle to be searched before going up to the fourth floor where the dormitory was located, and where the Germans rarely ventured.

Lastly, Bassano was commanded by a certain Max Hoffmann. Unlike Kochan and Ziemer, he is described by witnesses as a 'rather humane and understanding' man who only applied sanctions or punishments as a last resort. We have been unable to find any details of the other members of the camp's German staff.

Apart from the day-to-day business of command, all three sites were regularly inspected by von Behr. These visits were an opportunity for the head of the Dienststelle to pick out items and demonstrate in situ the work performed by his services in stage-managed displays of his power and authority. Such inspections were relatively frequent in all three camps, and during them the internees were forced to behave according to strict rules. In her memoirs, Yvonne Klug tells of how von Behr could announce his impending visits by telephone at any hour of the day or night. 'So that everything would be ready for him to put on his show for the personalities that he brought along to see the camp, we had to stop work and clean, polish, scrub and sweep. Everything had to be gleaming then we had to stand to attention when he appeared and swivel around so that we would always be looking towards him.' This obligation to keep their eyes constantly fixed on the director of the Dienststelle Westen left a lasting mark on the detainees. Jacqueline Jacob-Delmas evokes these regular 'shows': 'We had to face [him] at all times. This necessitated a circular movement on the spot as he walked around us.'

Judging by former detainees' descriptions, these visits seem to have been drawn straight out of a film like Jean Renoir's classic prisoner-of-war tale *La Grande Illusion*. In an interview, Jean Levi, a former assistant film director and internee, makes explicit reference to Renoir's film: a German officer speaking French, impeccably dressed, staring out from behind his monocle...[11]

At Lévitan, von Behr was proud to show off to General Dietrich all the members of the aristocracy who were included among his 'staff'. These were, it was true, relatively numerous, consisting for the most part of women from Jewish high society who had married into noble families. Years later, in her English memoirs, Colette de Dampierre would in turn ironically bestow upon Baron Kurt von Behr the title of 'His Royal Highness'.[12]

An extract from a poem by Paul Drori, entitled *Visits*, apparently written for the camp newspaper *Camp-Camp* and eventually published after the war, gives an impression of the power and authority that Kurt von Behr wanted to impose upon the internees during his visits. He draws a direct parallel between the imprisoned men and women and the objects that surrounded them. Like puppets, the detainees of the satellite camps were, for von Behr, no more than toys that

---

[11] Interview quoted above.

[12] Memoirs of Comtesse Colette de Dampierre, private archives of Christian de Montbrison.

could be shifted around as work tasks or deportations demanded, that could be whipped or made to stand motionless – in other words, to be smashed or lined up like mere objects.

Visits

So they dance
So they dance/
To the tune
To the tune/
Reich's on the march
Glass eye and all
Baron Colonel von Starch
Sounds the roll-call./
For the greater good
There we all stood
In tears, pain, the noise
Of the whip cracked
And shelves stacked
With toys./

So they dance
So they dance/
To the tune
To the tune/
Side by side
Queen and slave
Jackboot strides
In their veins
There we stood
In the mud
Must always face
The lord of the race./

So they dance
So they dance/
To the tune
To the tune/
We are displayed
We explode
In silence.
The marionettes
Keep their lips firmly set
On the toy racks
As the whip cracks.

Illustration 16. Alfred Rosenberg and Kurt von Behr visiting Lévitan (between 1943 and 1944).

Dépôt central de la justice militaire, Le Blanc, dossier Utikal et al.

Through the metaphor of the marionette, Paul Drori wanted to keep this menacing experience at arm's length, although the visits of von Behr were not the only intrusions that the internees had to fear. When a return to Drancy, usually prior to deportation, had been decided, the transfer was carried out by SS staff from outside. Gilberte Jacob refers to a certain Waisel, who was assigned to Drancy and came to Lévitan to punish certain internees physically or bring them back to the main camp.

These recurrent crises apart, the Germans were too few in number to prevent the internees from enjoying a certain degree of freedom. The humour of the writers of the *Camp-Camp* 'glossary', published with the full knowledge of their jailers, symbolises both the total authority of the Germans over the internees and the relative autonomy given to the latter. In it, *Schnell* is defined as 'literally "quickly". In current usage in the French language of today. Never applies.' Meanwhile for *Los* we are told to 'see *Schnell*. Pronounced with a sweet and pleasant tone, often transformed into a hoarse scream.'[13]

Similar room for manoeuvre was visible in the ability of a specific category of internees to take independent action: these were the Jewish officials, at whose head stood the camp chief. As at Drancy, the 'concrete' running of the camp was left in the hands of officials chosen from among the internees. At Bassano, this function was performed by Edmond Bloch, while at Austerlitz and Lévitan the camp chief changed according to transfers and deportations. Originally given to Raymond Dreyfus, responsibility for the quai de la Gare fell, on 23 November 1943, to Georges Kohn, who had previously led the team of Jewish officials at Drancy; when he in turn was transferred to Lévitan, Roger Lévy and then Muriel Schatzmann replaced him. When the first chief internee of Lévitan, Roger Hartmann, was deported to Auschwitz in convoy 62 on 20 November 1943, the full meaning of the word 'responsibility' in the camps was made clear. The chief could be answerable for the behaviour of 'his' internees – two escapes, in this case. After him, the post was occupied by someone whom it has not been possible to identify, then by Georges Kohn, who ran the camp before escaping during an excursion on 6 June 1944. He was replaced by Colette de Dampierre.

The camp chief's status meant that he or she could leave the camp in order to see to matters such as the provision of food and liaison with the offices of the UGIF. These two tasks, closely linked, constituted the greater part of the chief's activity. On 6 August 1943, the chief of Lévitan camp wrote to the UGIF to request better rations.[14] It was the UGIF's job to supply the satellite camps, and the point of contact for the camp chief was Kurt Schendel's service 14, which dealt

---

[13] Centre de documentation juive contemporaine, UGIF 93-5.

[14] Centre de documentation juive contemporaine, UGIF 92-1662.

with deliveries.[15] Apart from delivering food, Kurt Schendel had 'been formally ordered by Röthke and Brunner' not to 'give any assistance', as he described in his report after the war. On 7 December, Schendel referred to orders received from the Germans in his correspondence with food suppliers. 'I enclose with this letter the original, photocopy and translation of a letter from the Dienststelle Westen concerning the supplementary rations for workers on heavy duties allocated to these internees.'[16]

It was therefore up to the chief internee to carry out liaison both with service 14 of the UGIF and with the German authorities. When the chief of the quai de la Gare worded a request to service 14, he or she would almost always take care to state that this request was made 'with the agreement of *monsieur le Lagersleiter*[17] Kochan.'[18] The orders for overalls placed at the beginning of May 1944 were first sent to Röthke and then to the UGIF.[19] However, on 5 July of the same year, Schendel had to give a negative response to an order for overalls for the 'shelter' group in Bassano camp. He felt obliged to explain himself: 'As we have repeated on many occasions, both verbally and in writing, we must again draw your attention to the fact that we can only accept and pass on orders such as these if they are issued by the Dienststelle Westen and accompanied by a signature and official stamp.'[20]

Nevertheless, as Kurt Schendel stated and, more importantly, many items found in the archives show, the UGIF was omnipresent in the lives of the internees. The chief internee had a privileged relationship with the officials of service 14. As in the case of George Kohn on 23 November 1943, he or she would inform the department if the holder of this office was about to change.[21] The chief internee could leave the camp to talk to them directly. On 10 September 1943, for instance, Roger Hartmann apologised to Kurt Schendel for not having paid him a visit and promised to do so the following Wednesday.[22] On the joint orders of von Behr and Röthke, Schendel himself was given a pass that allowed him to enter and leave all of the camps. He would visit from time to time to share meals with the detainees and test their quality, as the internees and even the Dienststelle

---

[15] Centre de documentation juive contemporaine, CCXXI-26, 'Rapport du 02/09/1944 de Kurt Schendel, chef du service de liaison no 14 de l'UGIF retraçant son parcours et son activité au sein du service de liaison.'

[16] Centre de documentation juive contemporaine, UGIF 92-1677.

[17] Camp governor.

[18] Centre de documentation juive contemporaine, UGIF 23-709.

[19] Centre de documentation juive contemporaine, UGIF 49-1042, 49-1043, 49-1044.

[20] Centre de documentation juive contemporaine, UGIF 23-710.

[21] Centre de documentation juive contemporaine, UGIF 92-1662.

[22] Centre de documentation juive contemporaine, UGIF 18 and 92-1662.

Westen's employees frequently complained about the food.[23] From January 1944 onwards, the chief internees received from the UGIF an amount of money proportional to the number of internees in 'their' camp, which they could use to top up food supplies when they went outside.[24]

The chief internees were assisted in their administrative duties by secretaries and deputies. While we have been unable to establish whether these camps had an administrative department of the type found in Drancy, we do know, thanks to the organisational schema of Bassano camp (dated 8 May 1944), that besides the chief internee the Jewish administrative structure included a female secretary and a '[female] deputy to the chief internee.' Given that Bassano only held sixty internees, it is reasonable to assume that Austerlitz and Lévitan, with their larger populations, must have had a greater number of Jewish officials. The large volume of correspondence sent by the '*chefs internés responsables*' (literally, 'chief internees in charge') of both Austerlitz and Lévitan, found in the archives of the UGIF, confirms the existence of other Jewish staff besides the chiefs themselves.[25] At Lévitan, for example, Andrée Carbonié was in charge of a 'Department of mutual assistance.'

The chief internees also had responsibility for a régime of inspections and general regimentation that in some ways recalls, in admittedly less dramatic form, the Jewish police at Drancy. The memoirs of Colette de Dampierre, who was interned at Lévitan, provide precise descriptions of her everyday duties as camp chief.[26] She slept separately in what was called her 'office', and she would get up each morning before 6.00 A.M. to wake up the other internees. She also dealt with the running of the camp, in terms of both the quantity and quality of work performed, the provision of food and the distribution of parcels and letters. Lastly, she had to make sure there were not too many 'thefts' from the counters and maintain discipline in the dormitories. She states, however, that it was never possible to achieve these last two objectives completely. A large number of testimonies confirm both that 'pinching' occurred constantly and that amorous liaisons between men and women were similarly frequent.

A Degre e of Openness to the Outside World

As the list of tasks performed by the chief internee suggests, excursions from the camp were possible, and letters and parcels could be received. These satellite camps were places of internment but nevertheless enjoyed a degree of openness;

---

[23] Centre de documentation juive contemporaine, UGIF 18.

[24] Centre de documentation juive contemporaine, UGIF 18.

[25] These letters were addressed to the UGIF, to Drancy and to various German departments including the Dienststelle Westen.

[26] Private archives of Christian de Montbrison.

the internees were not completely cut off from the outside world. Several types of movement between the camps' interior and the world outside them existed. This allowed internees to benefit from a situation that was sometimes relatively favourable, if precarious.

Firstly, there was access to outside information. On 22 November 1943, only three weeks after the camp opened, the chief of the quai de la Gare informed the UGIF that '[w]ith the agreement of *monsieur le Lagersleiter* Kochan, we request that you send us each day by the morning or at the latest the midday van, ten newspapers, preferably all different.'[27] Two months later, in a letter dated 29 January addressed to Schendel, he gave a list of the German publications received daily: *Das Reich, Völkischer Beobachter* and *Pariser Zeitung*. Admittedly, the *Völkischer Beobachter* was the official organ of the Nazi Party, and obviously violently anti-Semitic, while the *Pariser Zeitung* was the German newspaper published in Paris. But he also asked for newspapers in French 'for the francophone internees'. In March 1944, the number and quality of these publications increased significantly. To the twenty titles received up until then would be added 4 copies of *L'Œuvre*, 5 of the *Petit Parisien*, 3 of *Aujourd'hui*, 3 of *France socialiste*, 6 of the *Pariser Tageszeitung* and 4 of the *Cri du Peuple*.[28] The internees thus had access to a certain number of daily newspapers. Even if the collaborationist press was overrepresented, it was at least possible to read between the lines. However, this does not mean that all the prisoners got their hands on this material. Several former detainees have stated that 'there were no newspapers in the camp.' Once again, reconstructing the history of their internment involves an examination of the various micro-worlds and different positions that constituted it.

Radio news may also have played a role. In relation to Austerlitz, only two former internees have mentioned the existence of a radio set. In Lévitan, however, the presence of a working radio is well attested. One of the internees, an electrician, had rigged up a set that allowed them to listen to Radio London at night. In her memoirs, Colette de Dampierre recalls with great emotion the joy but also the fear felt by those who, along with her, heard the announcement of the Normandy landings.

A third source of information available to the internees was the news passed on by railway employees and removal men. Many former internees of both Austerlitz and Lévitan have mentioned the exchanges of information made by teams working outside the camps or unloading crates. In the section of *Camp-Camp* under the heading 'What we've seen... What we've heard...', a short dialogue clearly links the job of unloading the wagons to the gleaning of information.

- Any news, mate?
- Everything's fine.

---

[27] Centre de documentation juive contemporaine, UGIF 18.
[28] Centre de documentation juive contemporaine, UGIF 23-708 and 709.

- Yes, but what else? Give me some precise detail[s].
- It's just that, you see, I mostly get fresh news in the evening.
- Alright. Tell me yesterday evening's news…
- Yesterday evening…? Well, yesterday evening there was… nothing new.

Internees have spoken of how Aryans from outside the camps could play the role of couriers. While Odette Dassonville has recounted how she passed silverware to them to finance the Resistance, most internees talk of sending objects and letters to their families and friends using this method.

Finally, writing and receiving letters was an important part of the internees' lives. While sending letters was not allowed at the beginning, receiving them was an established right from the outset. Under normal circumstances, detainees could receive an unlimited number of parcels and letters. In a letter to his wife dated 30 March 1944, Wolf Epstein describes his elation at having received seven pieces of post the day before. Usually, however, only one letter per week could be sent out of the camps. Marc Garguir, internee number 184 at the quai de la Gare, spoke repeatedly of the 'Sunday post' that he would send every week to his wife. As he himself wrote on 9 January 1944, this was a 'little weekly letter to bring you some good news from me.'[29] The lists of articles ordered by the camp chiefs show that the UGIF provided stamps and notepaper. If these stocks of paper ran out, as was the case for other materials, the satellite camps were after all located in shops and warehouses. Thus, when Marc Garguir wrote to his wife on 7 August 1944, he used headed paper.

The frequency of the postal service varied. Some items of correspondence show that sometimes it could be more than once per week, although punishments made the service unpredictable. In November 1943, for instance, Schendel was threatened with sanctions for having taken unauthorised letters out of Lévitan and Austerlitz and had to promise never to do so again.[30] At the end of June 1944, following the Normandy landings and the return to Drancy of all the internees, access to post was disrupted in both directions. Finally, 'new regulations' limited letters to ten lines and remained in force, officially, until the camps were evacuated in August.

Even more so than letters, parcels were a precious lifeline for those internees fortunate enough to receive them, in particular when they contained extra food. Unlike at Drancy, internees in the satellite camps gained, after a certain time, the right to receive food parcels. At Austerlitz, authorisation for this was given a month after the camp opened.[31] The contents of these parcels were described at length in detainees' correspondence. Foodstuffs, in particular meat and butter,

---

[29] Private archives, access provided by Denise Bernard; also placed in the Centre de documentation juive contemporaine.

[30] Centre de documentation juive contemporaine, UGIF 18.

[31] Centre de documentation juive contemporaine, UGIF 18.

and toiletries were the items most frequently sent. Packages were sent through the post or handed in at one of the offices of the UGIF, and occasionally even brought to the gates of the camps.

Exchanges were also effected through the laundry, which had to be done outside the camps by the families or friends of internees. The dirty linen was rolled up by prisoners into packages bearing their names, which were taken away by the UGIF. When the clothes had been washed, the families brought them back to the same place. This allowed not only letters to be smuggled out of the camps, but also objects taken from their stocks of valuables. Yvonne Klug alludes to this: 'Some were able to send home objects of value.' Marc Garguir's daughter remembers for her part a pair of very good quality shoes that her father managed to send her during the harsh winter of 1943.[32]

Links with the outside world could also be established through excursions, which were rare, and visits, which were more regular. As Wolf Epstein wrote to his family on 22 February 1944, 'these are the times fixed for visits: every Saturday between 2pm and 5pm and Sundays from 9am to midday and from 2pm to 5pm.'[33] It appears that they took place on the ground floor of the buildings in a shared area; a German guard would be present. Several Austerlitz internees recall receiving visits from their spouses or mothers, and surviving correspondence allows us to situate some of these meetings with precision. Marc Garguir received several visits from his wife, who lived in the Paris region (24 December, 18 February and 22 April). Simon Sarfati's wife came up on three occasions from Marseilles.[34] In Lévitan, Odette Dassonville was able to see her mother-in-law and her son.[35]

Visits by children also occurred. During the Easter holidays, Simon Sarfati saw his wife and daughter and even spent the night with the latter with Redhardt's agreement. Jacqueline, seven and a half years old, slept in a bed in the men's dormitory, where for a few hours she was the guest of honour. She left the camp the following morning clutching a dolly, amazed by the mountains of crates and objects she had seen.[36] The son of Thérèse Pintel[37] and the daughter of Adèle Warchawski,[38] who were both Jewish wives of Jewish POWs and interned in Lévitan, met their parents in the hall of 85-87 rue du Faubourg-Saint-Martin, where they were discreetly given a set of dominoes and a doll respectively, toys that had been taken by the Germans from other Jewish children. The coming and

---

[32] Interview with Denise Bernard, 29/03/2002.

[33] Private archives of Denise Weill.

[34] Private archives of Jacqueline Ribot.

[35] Interview quoted above.

[36] Interview with Jacqueline Ribot, 24/02/2003.

[37] Interview with Samuel Pintel, 14/03/2003.

[38] Interview with Hélène Grunwald, 15/06/2002.

going of 'hidden' children, who risked arrest for being Jewish, gives an indication of the relatively informal character of these visits. It is hard to imagine that these mothers would have taken such a step if their children's identities had been checked, as is confirmed by the repeated visits of the daughter of Marc Garguir, a young Jewish woman who was living in hiding.[39]

Yet there does seem to have been a degree of formal organisation to these arrangements. On 12 February 1944, the chief internee of the quai de la Gare urgently requested 1,000 visit tickets from the UGIF 'since we are using up a dozen of these tickets a day, and we have no way of printing them ourselves'.[40] It was sometimes necessary to book a month in advance and obtain written authorisation.[41]

In a letter dated 30 April, Simon Sarfati refers to a friend who had seen his sister-in-law for more than half an hour on two occasions: 'Some visits last 4 hours. Today, for the first time, several women are having lunch with their husbands.'[42] The right to visits seems to have been upheld until the beginning of June 1944. Gilberte Jacob's correspondence with Roger Mayer refers to it without interruption from 22 February to 2 June 1944.[43] However, the impression that emerges from testimonies and archives alike is one of a rather arbitrary situation that could improve but also deteriorate at any given moment. Wolf Epstein, Simon Sarfati and Marc Garguir speak in their letters of sudden changes of policy. As Wolf Epstein remarked on 22 February 1944, visits always took place 'on the condition that nobody did anything stupid'. Any escape attempts or other violations meant visits would be suspended.

With the arrival of the new camp commandant, the visiting policy at Austerlitz became more flexible from March 1944 on, although its organisation remained rather informal. Garguir thus wrote to his wife on 23 March 1944: 'Maybe soon you'll be able to visit me for 2 hours and a bit later on for another two hours, although I don't know the date of this reward, for the moment I can't tell you when, just remember this good news.' From June onwards the policy hardened. From 2 July to 18 August 1944, the internees kept announcing that things would be improving, only to say in subsequent letters that they would get worse. When a visit did take place, it was 'allowed as a special favour', as Wolf Epstein wrote in a letter of 25 July.

While they were neither regular nor particularly formally organised, these visits had an important psychological and emotional value for many internees. Simon Sarfati's wife, who lived in Marseilles, was only able to see her husband

---

[39] Interview with Denise Bernard, quoted above.

[40] Centre de documentation juive contemporaine, CDXXV-3.

[41] Private archives of Denise Bernard and Jacqueline Ribot.

[42] Private archives of Jacqueline Ribot.

[43] Private archives of Roger Mayer.

three times. He therefore wrote to her no fewer than forty times from 25 January to 18 August 1944.[44] A letter from Marc Garguir to his wife echoes these sentiments: 'But the best thing of all will be your visit since visit day is the best day of the month, so until Saturday, then I'll have the wonderful pleasure of seeing you.'[45] A sketch written by female internees of Austerlitz and performed on 9 April 1944 was entitled simply 'The Visit'.[46] The very existence of this text demonstrates the importance of these visits in the lives of the internees. The sketch was also an opportunity to refer, through the prism of the music-hall genre and the black humour found in all the camp writings, to the difficulties caused by the forced separation of a couple and the new loves that could spring up during internment. The owner of the surviving programme to the show had judged this sketch to be 'very good'.

The Visit[47]

[*The internee, 'over the moon', has spruced himself up for a visit from his wife, whom he describes to his jealous comrades as 'kind, charming, so sweet'.*]

At this point the curtain rises on the visiting room: some chairs lined up along the wall, a table, a telephone, an ashtray. In a corner, a small table next to which sits the guard. Sitting in an armchair, the internee's wife. She seems far from charming, and rather nervous. He enters.

HER: So 'ere you are at last. You 'aven't changed, always late, always the last one.

HIM: I am so moved by the thought of seeing you again that…

He approaches, gives her a peck on the cheek.

HER: Don't pinch!

HIM: (*Innocently*) Oh, but everyone's at it! But how did you know I'm on sorting duty?

HER: What are you on about? Stop looking like an idiot, I mean don't pinch *me* like that. You've lost your marbles. Go on, look this way. No, you haven't changed, or maybe, yes, I reckon you've put on some weight. Internment's done you some good by the looks of it.

HIM: Oh come now, a bit of unhealthy flab.

HER: Unhealthy flab? You could have fooled me! And what about this wonderful complexion, this relaxed glow?

HIM: I have simply come to understand that one mustn't get worked up about things; it does one no good. We must suffer our fate with patience and resignation. I have a great deal of both, and then if I get a bit down I like to smoke a nice,

---

[44] This correspondence forms the majority of Jacqueline Ribot's archives.

[45] Letter dated 16 April 1944, private archives of Denise Bernard.

[46] See Centre de documentation juive contemporaine, CMXVII-13 for the programme of the 'Austerlitz's folies' show.

[47] Centre de documentation juive contemporaine, UGIF 93-28 to 93-34.

relaxing pipe… And try to forget. On the subject of pipes, have you brought my tobacco?

[*Argument over his tobacco ration*]

HER: You know how fond I am of you, my love, do you often think of me?

HIM: Oh yes, oh yes!

(*She turns his face towards her*)

HER: Tell it to my face, there, like that. Are you behaving yourself in here?

HIM: How could you even think…?

HER: Well, who's that lanky trollop over there for a start… There, sat next to that gigolo? Just look at her! She gave me such a filthy look going past, the haughty cow! Just you wait! I'm gonna give her something on the way out.

HIM: Calm down, dear, calm down, don't make a scene… She's the daughter of an important banker – a great contact for after the war; please stop making that face at her. Smile at her, she could be very useful to me. (*He puts on a fake-looking smile*)

THE GUARD: Only 5 more minutes.

HER: (*Getting increasingly worked up*) Oh, your contacts, I know all about them, a bunch of good-for-nothings you go out with at night to talk business with… You just wait till you get back. I've had enough of being a mug… you'd better change your habits from now on… So he thinks he can pull the wool over my eyes, does he? Well, I've wasted me whole morning, up at six, 25 minutes' walk from the underground station. I have to stand around waiting behind the barrier, expecting to see some poor starved wretch with his head shaved, I was all set to comfort him, pity him, maybe even cry a bit, and then, what do I find? You stroll out, dressed up to the nines and you don't give a fig about me! Ungrateful pig! Monster! Unfaithful swine! Blithering cuckold!

The guard stands up solemnly. The session is over.

(*The curtain falls. At the front of the stage, we see him walk slowly across and meet the group of internees seen previously*) So, your visit's finished already? Feeling happy?

HIM: (*relaxed and smiling*) Oh, yes, ever so happy…

(*With his hands in his waistcoat pockets, looking around wistfully*): 'But it is nice to be back home.'

Some internees were able to visit their families or go and consult their own doctors.[48] Authorisation to leave the camp required a list of ten guarantors who would immediately be deported if the internee escaped. Bernard Behr has described the system of medical passes as follows: 'The Germans allowed internees out if there were guarantors. For a few months, this was possible and each evening the walker ['*promeneur*'] would come back to the camp.' But these excur-

---

[48] Interview with Bernard Behr, 31/03/2002.

sions were soon forbidden. On 28 May 1944, the same internee wrote to a friend: 'Dad went out, but after somebody escaped, these trips have been stopped. I don't think they will be reinstated and in a way it's for the best, because the reprisals and the responsibility always fall on us.'[49]

As Paul Drori evokes in one of his poems from Austerlitz, even when outside the camp, the internee remained a prisoner of his 'cage'.

An excursion

You are suffering, Paris, you are beautiful in your chains,
I love you, my brother, and our suffering is the same
This evening, from my cage, like you I will listen to the Seine,
Like you, from my suffering, I will make a poem.[50]

It does seem, however, that the excursions were later reauthorised; an exit pass in the name of Muriel Schatzmann allowing her to go outside the camp and even excusing her from wearing the yellow star is still preserved today.[51] But was this authorisation only given to her in her capacity as chief internee?

It was also possible to leave Lévitan. In her memoirs, Colette de Dampierre recalls having been let out for a whole day to see her doctor and visit friends. She returned in the evening.[52] Testimony confirms that other internees obtained similar passes. Some chose not to return. The list of deportees from the satellite camps via Drancy provides evidence of this.

Not all detainees remember these camps as being so (comparatively speaking) open. Jacqueline Jacob-Delmas has written, for example, 'Of course, we were never allowed visits.'[53] Once again, the primacy of individual point of view in the formation of memory is clear. Jacqueline Jacob-Delmas may simply never have been offered the opportunity to receive any.

The comparative permeability of the satellite camps paradoxically went hand in hand with the German insistence that they remain virtually invisible; situated right in the heart of Paris, it was imperative that these places and their inmates were not seen from outside. At Austerlitz, the building's windows were blacked out, the interior being illuminated solely by artificial light. An internee deliberately making him or herself visible to those outside would immediately be physically punished. Two detainees 'guilty' of breaking this rule were sent to Drancy and then deported to Auschwitz, where they perished. This same concern with

---

[49] Private archives of Bernard Behr.

[50] P. Drori. 1948. *Matricule 5586,* Paris: Polyglottes.

[51] Centre de documentation juive contemporaine, CMXVII-13.

[52] Private archives: access granted by Christian de Montbrison.

[53] Bonnet, Jacob-Delmas, Lessovoï in *Le Monde juif* 146.

ILLUSTRATION 17. Visitors at Austerlitz (probably winter 1944).
Memorial de la Shoah/CDJC, C III 23.

secrecy may explain why a (for a long time, very brief) walk in the open air was finally incorporated into the camp routine. Gilberte Jacob refers to this: 'Each Sunday at Austerlitz we were allowed to walk around for a quarter of an hour under Kochan's supervision. Given the short period of time allotted, we would do just one lap of the camp. The régime became less strict later on.'[54] The relatively strict control of these exercise periods contrasts with the general disciplinary régime. However, the layout of the quai de la Gare building, which was isolated and surrounded by a fence, minimised the risk of people seeing what was happening inside.

Since the district in which it was located was densely populated and busy, Lévitan camp was harder to hide; yet the Germans seem to have managed to do so. Detainees were not allowed to go near the windows, which had in any case been covered. People living nearby did see some internees when, after some time, the latter were let onto the roof terrace for a quick fifteen-minute walk around (although they would be punished for going near the edge). The shop's ground floor was left as before, from the cash registers to the furniture on display, in order to fool passers-by.

---

[54] The two photographs showing the front of the Austerlitz camp building were most likely taken during one of these walks. See illustrations.

Punishments and Deportations

Although hidden, the satellite camps enjoyed various links to the outside world. Some prisoners exploited these in order to escape. The reprisals were terrible. The detainees would be abruptly and savagely reminded of the precariousness of their situation. Yvonne Klug describes the impression internees had of their condition: 'We were a whole category of internees that they wanted neither to deport nor set free and so we were used in this way. We were still under the Gestapo and we were only being lent to the work department. Hovering above our heads was the threat of being returned to Drancy and deported, either as a punishment, or simply on the whim of these gentlemen.'

The detainees in the satellite camps remained internees of Drancy. On 21 August 1943, Brunner had ordered that henceforth the names of the Dienststelle Westen's internees be checked each evening against the central register at Drancy; they were still attached to the central camp.[55] As such, they wore the yellow star. Numerous letters addressed to the UGIF refer to the importance of this obligation in camp life. The following extract from a letter sent from the quai de la Gare to the UGIF on 13 December 1943 is telling: 'I would be grateful if you could urgently send me about 75 "Jew" stars. On a different note, would it be possible to send fifty kilos of onions?' Requests for yellow stars regularly featured on orders for supplies. Again, on 17 February 1944, Kurt Schendel announced that he would send 200 stars and 100 blankets 'on the orders of *M. le Lagersleiter* Kochan'.

If, particularly when it came to living conditions, the attachment of the Parisian camps to Drancy may have appeared a pure formality, internees would be brutally reminded of their true status when escapes occurred. As Bernard Behr remarks: 'In truth, you'll say to me, it was just a case of internment and the prisoners enjoyed quite a few benefits. But it was also a collective death sentence, with no date set for the execution and applying to every one of us; each day, each night, the terror of deportation was present.'[56]

Only one month after Lévitan camp opened, on 29 August 1943, Georges Kohn wrote in his Drancy diary: 'Jean Mayer and Antoinette Vernes return to the camp from Lévitan. There were three escapes from the camp this morning, and, following a botched intervention by Antoinette Vernes, assisted by Jean Mayer, these two internees were sent back to Drancy, along with an order specifying that Jean Mayer be imprisoned and classed as deportable.' Jean Mayer was deported to Auschwitz in convoy 59, on 2 September 1943, and did not return. Georges Kohn does not specify whether other prisoners accompanied him and Antoinette Vernes back from Lévitan. Antoinette Vernes was eventually freed, thanks perhaps to the social position of her husband.[57]

---

[55] Centre de documentation juive contemporaine, CCCLXXVII-1.

[56] Interview quoted above.

[57] He was a member of the family of Protestant bankers of the same name.

For the two main Parisian camps, evidence exists of escapes bringing awful consequences. Several former internees of Lévitan have spoken of the rooftop escape of two internees in November 1943; the Drancy files mention the escape of Prosper and Georges Ben-Soussan on this date. Robert Hartmann and at least eleven others were brought back from the rue Faubourg-Saint-Martin to Drancy: Charles Jais, Benjamin Herszfeld, Joseph Frandji, Albert Caraco, David Herschensohn, Alfred Levy, Hélène Pige, Jacob Rosenbund, Rudolph Korner, Julien Unger and Jacob Elbaz were deported to Auschwitz in convoy 62 (20 November 1943). Only Julien Unger returned.

Similarly, the escape made from the quai de la Gare on 20 January 1944 by a certain Pariente appears in all witness accounts. Georges Kohn referred to it in his statement of September 1946, and Jean Levi recalled it in even more detail, for understandable reasons.[58] 'One day in January 1944, I went to the infirmary. Another man, Marc Pescarolo, took my place in my work team. It was the day that Pariente chose to break out. My whole team, ten people, was deported. I should have been there. Pescarolo's mother, who was also an internee, wanted to go with her son, she didn't want to leave him.'[59] The team was immediately rounded up and sent back to Drancy. Many witnesses remember the courage of one of its members, Esther Carre, who screamed that Pariente had been right to do it because everybody would end up where they were going. Rosa Pescarolo did in fact ask to join her son in Drancy, a request granted the following day. The latter's status as a half-Jew and his mother's own status as the wife of an Aryan no longer protected them or their comrades. On 3 February 1944, Henri Hilf, Raoul Lyon, George Pinto, Raymond Poguileski, Esther Carre, Guy Lohak, Rachel Chapochnik, Eugène Dumbte, Elissaf Gattegno and Rosa and Marc Pescarolo were deported to Auschwitz in convoy 67. Esther Carre and Rachel Chapochnik were the only survivors.

While other escapes occurred, the archives do not give sufficient details to identify their dates, circumstances and aftermath precisely. Letters sent to family members, owing to their nature, give a euphemistic account of the frequency and scale of deportations from the satellite camps. Some former inmates, such as Félix Lichtenauer and Odette Dassonville, have reported that on several occasions SS men from Drancy came to take away one or two detainees from Lévitan to fill deportation convoys. The reconstituted list of internees and their movements shows that several individuals, who were initially internees of the Parisian camps, were indeed included in deportation convoys without (as far as it appears) belonging to a particular group sent out from the satellite camps. Henriette Maquis, deported in convoy 61, Roland Levy and Alfred Rosenfeld, deported in convoy 71 and Pierre Franck, convoy 73, are some examples.

---

[58] Dépôt central de la justice militaire, Le Blanc, Indre, 'Dossier Utikal et autres', statement by Georges Kohn.

[59] Interview with Jean Levi, quoted above.

Escapes also triggered other punishments. The breakout on 20 January 1944 led to reduced sleeping hours and all prisoners being put on particularly unpleasant duties, including sorting through filthy waste paper.[60] 'We would therefore live in a state of artificial gaiety in order to hide the gnawing anxiety that was deep in our hearts; in order to forget the difficult days we had been through or that were to come, like the days following the escape of 20 January, when we were woken up at 5am and made to scrape at the stairs with sandpaper until 8am as a prelude to the twelve-hour day', Yvonne Klug would write. She was later deported to Auschwitz. The camp's disciplinary régime would also change. The post was affected first, correspondence being forbidden or limited for a certain period.

Internees were also deported for minor transgressions. 'In Austerlitz, there were deportations for stupid reasons. One day, two of our comrades, on seeing their wives, waved at them out of the window, and were then beaten up by the German commandant [Kochan] and we did not see them again; they were immediately deported. Following this, we were punished, being allowed no letters or parcels', wrote Gilberte Jacob. The pair in question were Marcel Lattes and Ladislas Vadasz. Like many others, Geissmann recalled the violence with which Kochan treated them, 'clubbing them with his pistol and fists'. Marcel Lattes and Ladislas Vadasz were deported to Auschwitz on 7 December 1943, in convoy 64. They did not return.

Gilberte Jacob mentions another completely unforeseeable deportation that occurred at Lévitan, where she had been transferred in the meantime: 'There was one truly awful deportation. One day, the commandant, called Ziemer, on finding some blankets that he thought were in suspiciously good condition, decided that we had taken them from the counters for our beds and he took them away. When one of our comrades recognised his own blanket, he dared to ask for it from this commandant who, after beating him up, sent him to Drancy for immediate deportation.'

Lastly, falling ill and spending more than three days in the infirmary meant going back to Drancy. Both Jacqueline Jacob-Delmas and Marc Garguir's daughter recall the panic which would grip internees who realised they had lice. The incomplete list that we have been able to draw up shows several individuals who were taken back to Drancy alone and then deported.

Punishments could be inflicted for almost any reason. Simon Sarfati wrote thus to his wife on 3 June 1944: 'One of the ladies here, having refused to do these gentlemen's laundry, earned us a collective punishment which consisted in working from 9am to midnight and from midnight to 1am tidying up and cleaning in and on top of the wardrobes ... This morning, these gentlemen will be coming to inspect the work done during the night and, if they aren't happy, they

---

[60] Interviews with Michel Behr, Jean Lévi and Bernard Behr quoted above.

ILLUSTRATION 18. Inmates at Lévitan sorting objects.
Bundesarchiv Koblenz, B 323-311-62.

will suspend all visits for a while.' Similarly, von Behr's visits could give rise to reprimands. 'Sometimes these took a very long time. So, to avoid getting cramps, we would chalk a cross on the floor to mark the position of our feet because if the camp commandant, that lunatic, happened to notice that we had moved, we would be punished. These punishments ranged from a slap in the face to whatever degrading spectacle came into his head and, my God, was he creative in that department', recounts Jacqueline Jacob-Delmas.

CHAPTER 6

EVERYDAY LIFE

WHILE THE INMATES of the Parisian camps remained internees of Drancy, to which they risked being sent back at any moment, the day-to-day running of their lives was almost totally independent of the main camp. The tobacco supply was the only remaining link in this respect. On 5 January 1944, the chief internee at the quai de la Gare thus wrote to the 'internee commandant, Drancy camp' to demand that his monthly cigarette quota, a total of 310 packets, be sent.[1] Apart from these constantly renewed requests, life in the satellite camps was thus independent of that in Drancy, and the contrast in conditions was stark. That inmates ate better, slept better and had a generally easier existence in Austerlitz, Lévitan and Bassano is unquestionably true. However, this statement must be qualified. First of all, the material conditions – in terms of sanitation and food provision – that eventually prevailed in the satellite camps changed over time. Austerlitz, for example, for a long time lacked showers and a goods lift, while access to parcels varied.

In particular, however, and to a greater extent than in other aspects of the internees' lives, their material situation varied enormously between individuals. The wide variety of points of view seen here is the product of widely differing experiences. To differences in position within the camps' organisation must be added socially determined differences in terms of behaviour and the amount of assistance provided (or not) by outside sources. While there were various instances of internees in the quai de la Gare sending money orders (ranging from 450 to 1,595 francs) to their wives outside the camp, others were impoverished to the point of qualifying for assistance given to the 'needy' and for the UGIF's 'free laundry' service. Their circumstances were so dire that the UGIF even organised maintenance payments to their families. In Bassano, this category numbered ten individuals on 30 June 1944, or nearly 20 per cent of the total number of detainees, whereas one month earlier, the list of recipients of UGIF assistance parcels had stood at eight inmates.

---

[1] Centre de documentation juive contemporaine, UGIF 21-653.

Bernard Behr, in a letter to a friend dated 28 May 1944, alluded to this situation of social mixing and the sometimes extreme differences between individuals' conditions of existence: 'The people in here are as different from one another as the people you walk past in the street; four hundred in all, managing directors, industrialists, shopkeepers, actors, craftsman alongside factory workers, shop assistants, travelling salesmen and grocers, of all nationalities, some of whom don't speak French.'[2] This dichotomy between experiences was made all the greater by the presence in the camps of an element drawn from prewar high society.

As Odette Fabius relates in her memoirs regarding Lévitan, 'in this strange camp, Robert [her husband] came across various friends, including the *marquise* de Dampierre, née Colette Cahen d'Anvers, [and] his good friend Georges Lévy, the owner of André shoes.'[3] Among many others, there also were Antoinette Vernes, Countess Jeanine de Casteja and Jean Gradis, scion of a very old Jewish family from Bordeaux whose ancestors had been famous shipbuilders and merchants under Louis XV. There were also well-known lawyers and show business personalities such as Robert Manuel, a young actor expelled from the Comédie-Française in autumn 1940 and Andrée Distel, the sister of Ray Ventura, the French jazz sensation.[4] Lévitan seems to have contained a particularly high proportion of celebrities and members of the upper classes. Freshly transferred from Austerlitz to Lévitan, Gilberte Jacob wrote on 22 February 1944 to her friend Roger Mayer, who remained at quai de la Gare: 'Everything here is different from the quai, especially people's background and mentality.'[5] The UGIF did not deal with any cases of needy internees in the camp until 17 July 1944.[6] However, similar social contrasts seem to have been present in Austerlitz. In letter dated 9 March 1944, for instance, Wolf Epstein made a veiled reference to this 'rather odd mentality'.

Apart from the special category of wives of POWs, the majority of detainees owed their placement in the satellite camps to their family links with non-Jews. They were mostly French Jews, well established within French society. It is thus unsurprising that their socioeconomic status was generally higher than that of most Jews in France, who were often recent immigrants living in poor, exclusively Jewish communities. The presence of a particularly wealthy element within the satellite camps' population risks obscuring the fact that other detainees were deprived of any psychological or material support. The situation of some prisoners' wives was particularly difficult.

---

[2] Private archives of Bernard Behr.

[3] O. Fabius. 1986. *Un lever de soleil sur le Mecklembourg: Mémoires,* Paris: Albin Michel, 215.

[4] R. Manuel. 1975. *Qu'allais-je faire dans cette galère?,* Paris: Émile-Paul. See also M.-A. Joubert. 1998. *La Comédie-Française sous l'Occupation,* Paris: Tallandier, 99 and 147.

[5] Private archives of Roger Mayer.

[6] Centre de documentation juive contemporaine, UGIF 92-1686.

However, while they describe a mosaic of individual experiences, all the internees have referred to the particularly odd experience of day-to-day life in a 'department store'. As Yvonne Klug humorously recounts, 'there was no point in washing the dishes – crash! One crystal glass and plate in pieces on the floor! It was quick and easy; we'd go and find another for the next meal. The amount of waste at Austerlitz was just unbelievable.' While inmates were sometimes searched, this did not happen regularly. Vivette Politi, for example, has found an allusion in an article from *Camp-Camp* to increasing restrictions on the internees' access to the plundered objects. The name of the stock 'Picker's réunis', is a play on the French slang verb *piquer*, 'to steal'.[7]

STOCK MARKET NEWS

PICKER'S RÉUNIS- We have not been surprised by the sudden drop in 'Picker's Réunis'. In well-informed circles, rumours had been circulating for some time that severe restrictions were in the pipeline. And, over the last ten days, only Sunday transports bearing navigation certificates granted following rigorous searches have been allowed. Some freighters have consequently been held in port because of suspicious cargoes. During checks, a degree of agitation was visible among the dockers working for 'Picker's Réunis'. It was not until Monday afternoon that the situation calmed down slightly. Since then, nothing to report.

Our advice is to drop this stock as soon as possible.

Food

'The UGIF supplied us with food. We had just enough not to die of hunger. Some of us suffered greatly from the lack of food. After a while we were allowed to receive parcels, which helped keep those who received them and those with whom they were shared alive. Many internees had no one on the outside.'[8] This account by Mira Lessovoï gives an idea of the food situation for detainees at the bottom of the pile. The UGIF's kitchens, located on the rue Guy-Patin and run by a Monsieur Geismar, had the task of preparing meals, with most ingredients being supplied by the Seine region's *préfecture*. Until July 1943, this establishment had only prepared daily meals for UGIF staff. In April 1944, its team had the job of cooking for 700 people: 700 breakfasts, 700 lunches, 700 dinners and 700 hot drinks.[9] M. Geismar thus had to make enormous organisational efforts. Yet the results often left something to be desired, leading to heated exchanges between Geismar, service 14, the internees and the German commandants of the

[7] It may also have been a pun based on the American lubricant company United Picker.

[8] Bonnet, Jacob-Delmas, Lessovoï in *Le Monde juif* 146, 42.

[9] Centre de documentation juive contemporaine, UGIF-18.

Parisian camps. Meals were delivered in military-style containers, or *bouthéons*, and the camp chief had to arrange their distribution.

Menus were drawn up by the UGIF offices, and examples are preserved in the archives. On 3 September 1943, Lévitan internees were meant to receive:

- for breakfast: coffee;
- for lunch: dressed salad and tomatoes, potatoes, carrots, lettuce and potatoes;
- for dinner: pâté, potatoes, lettuce, tomatoes, leeks, jam, pretzels.[10]

And on Tuesday 5 October:

- for lunch: cabbage salad, potatoes, carrots, apples;
- for dinner: dressed potato salad, potato, cabbage, carrots, grapes.

Internees sometimes had some meat or salted anchovies. The portions, though not tiny, were still modest, and sources of extra food were always necessary.

The cooking and presentation left much to be desired, and the food was often quite inedible. Memories of containers of overcooked pasta congealed into a compacted mass are still strong. Vivette Politi refers discreetly to the chronic wind that resulted.[11] *Camp-Camp* also made humorous references to the food.

> MOTHER'S PRIDE RECIPES
> *-ESKIMO PASTA-*
> Serves 2. Take 8 kg of pasta. Heat some butter separately, stir in flour, then add 20–30 lbs of rhubarb.
> Place on the hob for five minutes before the electricity cuts out.
> At the first whistle, drain the pasta, rinse with the fire extinguisher then serve… out of the window.

Meals were the object of constant negotiations. On 13 November 1943, the chief internee of the quai de la Gare was delighted by a delivery of meat during the week but complained about the 'barely edible' soup in the evenings and the unhygienic conditions in which the food was prepared.[12] While on 15 February he noted a clear improvement in the quality of the soup and pasta, he still requested that onions be delivered separately so that the internees could cook

---

[10] Menus for almost every day have been found in the UGIF archives: Centre de documentation juive contemporaine, UGIF 48.

[11] Centre de documentation juive contemporaine, CMLVI (testimony of Vivette Baharlia-Politi, deported in convoy 76, and camp poems).

[12] Centre de documentation juive contemporaine, UGIF 92-1670.

them themselves. He also suggested that menus should be announced one day in advance.[13] On 23 June, he again set out his 'various requests': '*Guy-Patin.* Containers often taste of medicine. Coffee grounds are often floating around on top of the soup. Bread not cooked properly. Please make suitable remarks to the supplier so that this happens as little as possible ... How is the question of back-up food supplies progressing?'[14]

A constant theme in all these letters is the hard physical work, which increased internees' calorific consumption and hunger. In January 1944, the German offices of the Dienststelle Westen requested a 'snack' from the UGIF, 'seeing as the Jewish internees are engaged in hard physical labour', and prevailed upon them to seek the assistance of the Seine *préfecture* in this matter. The question of this 'snack' cropped up incessantly in the letters from the chief internees to the UGIF. Consisting of biscuits or bread with jam or pâté, it seems to have played an essential role in balancing the internees' diet. On 13 May 1944, Simon Sarfati, at that time assigned to unloading wagons, wrote to his wife: 'I'm so hungry that I'm not even managing to lose any weight. I'm actually convinced I've got fatter and I'm most annoyed about it.'[15] The Germans, who were worried about the progress of the camps' work, gave priority to food supplies. The need for food to be ready early in the morning before a day of labour meant that special dispensation was given by the Dienststelle Westen to the transport business in charge of delivering the food: 'Monsieur BRÉAU Henri' had 'permission to drive from 4am onwards'.[16]

The UGIF seems, as far as it was able, to have taken these comments on board. Von Behr upbraided service 14 on several occasions. On 8 November 1943, after a visit to the quai de la Gare, Kurt Schendel ended his letter to the head of the Guy-Patin kitchens thus: 'The German colonel told me that the food was barely fit for pigs and that this would be our last warning before we all go off to Drancy.'[17] On 2 September 1944, in his report on his activity during the war, Schendel made specific reference to his work 'liaising with the satellite camps':

We had been expressly ordered not to deal with anything except the camps' food (order from Röthke and Brunner). In spite of these orders, the UGIF endeavoured, as far as it was able, to satisfy the desires expressed by the internees of these camps ... Because of this, on several occasions I was the object of remarks from Brunner. *Oberstführer* von Behr frequently summoned me and would repeat again and again, amidst theatrical and threatening scenes, that I alone was responsible for the

---

[13] Centre de documentation juive contemporaine, CDXXV-3.

[14] Centre de documentation juive contemporaine, UGIF 93-48.

[15] Private archives of Jacqueline Ribot.

[16] Centre de documentation juive contemporaine, UGIF 18, 4/04/1944.

[17] Centre de documentation juive contemporaine, UGIF 18.

internees' food and that he did not want to hear about the UGIF. He constantly
threatened that I would be beaten or shot. Despite this, I carried on with this
liaison work, which allowed me to obtain various improvements in the camps'
régime.[18]

Finally, although Kurt Schendel does not mention it, a food shop was eventually set up in Austerlitz. It was a black-market operation run by the Germans.
It sold items that were difficult to find outside, at high prices. Part of its 'stock'
probably consisted of food taken from Jewish apartments. On 16 April 1944, in
a list of requests to his wife, Marc Garguir was careful to tell her, 'No potatoes
because I can buy very good ones here and it's not worth your trouble.' His
daughter even remembers coming home from a visit carrying a big sack of the
vegetables in question.[19] On 7 May 1944, Simon Sarfati described how it was
possible to improve on ordinary rations if one had money. 'This week, we bought
lettuce, radishes, herrings and onions from the canteen, a nice addition to the
usual food ... It's considered a good deal, for a few among us who have money,
to buy butter at 700 francs per kg, meat, ham, eggs, wine, sold at astronomical
prices in the canteen. In spite of this, we've built up a stock of 50 kg of potatoes
at 9 francs per kilo which serves us well.' On 9 July, he observed: 'The people with
money are in luck because you can buy everything and *as much as you like* of it.
Yesterday there was a whole pig sold off at 400 francs per kg, butter at 800 francs,
gruyère cheese at 700 francs, cream cheese at 35 francs for an 8 portion box,
radishes, lettuces, peaches at 60 francs per kg, halva at 400 francs per kg, sugar at
150 francs per kilo.'[20] The details of how this shop was organised are not known.
Was it yet another source of extra revenue for the Germans of the Dienststelle?
However, for those who were lucky enough to receive them, the main source of
supplementary food was the parcels sent by family or friends, meaning that the
role of the canteen would remain marginal.

The meals, eaten in between lines of beds, were often the opportunity to share
rations sent in from outside with one's neighbours in the dormitory. As Marc
Garguir related to his wife on 20 February 1944, he ate and slept in his room
with his 'next-door neighbour Mesguish'. In January, he had told her how he
would cook with his friends using a little stove either improvised or stolen by the
internees. As his 'cook down here' only used butter, he asked for some to be sent.
On Sunday 16 January, a rest day particularly suited to a refined menu, the meal
comprised 'rabbit, herring salad, olives, beetroot and a little jam'. Occasionally,
particularly towards the end, Sunday lunch could be more generous, indeed even

---

[18] Centre de documentation juive contemporaine, CCXXI-26.

[19] Private archives and interview with Denise Bernard, 29/03/2002.

[20] Private archives of Jacqueline Ribot, subsequently placed in the Centre de documentation
juive contemporaine.

festive. On 7 August 1944, Marc Garguir evoked the lunch of the day before with delight:

> Yesterday, Sunday, I was invited out for lunch. (Sorry) eating "out" here means going to share one's dinner or lunch with other comrades in their row, which is to say at the end of their beds, where we lay the table with great taste and cleanliness: tablecloth, porcelain dishes and Baccarat crystal (you either work on the counters or you don't), even flowers on the table, so you can picture the setting. For this particular Sunday lunch it was even nicer as I was invited by my friend from Bordeaux, who is very friendly with a couple of lady chefs who as I told you had left to go to Bassano. This week, we were all delighted here to see that they had come back and so my friend did us a top-notch lunch.

Wolf Epstein told his wife about his 'three comrades who I chat with since we eat together'. These were 'two Marseillais and a chap from Strasbourg'.[21] One of these Marseillais, Simon Sarfati, devoted a large proportion of his forty letters to descriptions of his meals with his friends.

For a select few, parcels were not the only means of improving the quality of the food. Colette de Dampierre, for example, would describe how for Christmas 1943 she had a veritable feast brought in with the complicity of a driver. 'The food we were given was inedible. But most people received magnificent parcels from their families and we would get together in groups for meals that were often better than what most free citizens got', relates Yvonne Klug in a slightly provocative tone. For the poorest internees, however, the UGIF made irregular deliveries of a few 'poverty parcels'.[22] Even if some sharing around seems to have occurred, particularly between neighbours in the dormitories, this inequality in food provision and the periods without parcels explain why some detainees recall having gone hungry while others could complain about putting on weight.

Sleeping and Washing

Like the food, the washing and sleeping arrangements improved somewhat over time. The beds were much better than in the main camp. Yvonne Klug recalls her arrival at Drancy: 'I saw for the first time those rows of bunks with just a straw-filled mattress to lie down on, I nearly fainted.' In Austerlitz, however, 'we had iron beds, like cots, but together we managed to get hold of some very good mattresses. We had very good bedclothes and were very comfortable.' Sleeping in a department store also made it easier for them to equip themselves with furniture, sheets and bedclothes.

---

[21] Private archives of Denise Weill, placed in the Centre de documentation juive contemporaine, letter dated 9/03/1944.

[22] Centre de documentation juive contemporaine, UGIF 18, letter dated 26/10/1943.

Yet it would be wrong to consider the conditions under which the Parisian internees lived purely in relation to those in Drancy. These camps existed in their own right, and the harshness of conditions in Drancy should not blot out the experience of the internees of the satellite camps. Fully aware that conditions there were favourable, and having subsequently survived Auschwitz, Yvonne Klug still remembers the satellite camps as damp, cold places. The cold is mentioned in numerous testimonies. Rats also infested these premises, which were in fact warehouses meant for accommodating goods rather than human beings. Jacqueline Jacob-Delmas describes the 'dozen' rats, 'big, friendly sewer rats' who would get into her bed every night. Vivette Politi, who was also later deported to Auschwitz, also retains a powerful memory of these animals, from which she desperately tried to protect her face using a hat.[23] On 5 January 1944, the chief internee of the quai de la Gare repeated his urgent request to service 14 for '50 BOTTLES of PASTEUR VIRUS. We are literally overrun by rats and I would like to be able, particularly in order to calm the nerves of our female comrades, to act forcefully and without delay.'[24]

Internees' hygiene needs could not be resolved as easily as their furniture requirements. When they first opened, the camps lacked any ablutions apart from a couple of washbasins. It was only in February 1944 that the Germans eventually installed showers in Austerlitz, the work being paid for by the UGIF.[25] They did not function until the following month. In Lévitan, it would take until that same March just to get a simple quotation for installing similar facilities. For the internees, personal hygiene was a constant concern. The Seine region's *préfecture* organised deliveries of '*ZET* mineral soap' and 'toothpaste'. 'I must insist particularly that you urgently send the soap bars that I requested from you. The new arrivals have absolutely nothing' wrote the chief internee of the quai de la Gare on 14 March 1943.

In Austerlitz and Lévitan, there were infirmaries, run respectively by Dr Mathis and Dr Stain. The former was deported to Auschwitz on 30 June 1944 (convoy 76) and never returned. Lévitan also had a dentist, for whom a dentist's chair was provided.[26] Lists of medicines were drawn up and requested from the UGIF. Barely twelve days after the opening of Austerlitz, for instance, the chief internee made the following request: 'Taking into account the exertions that our people have to make, I must look at keeping their strength up by means of the appropriate medicines ... Enclosed is a list of medicines that we need urgently, according to our doctor's recommendations.'[27] Large quantities of medicine also arrived in

[23] Centre de documentation juive contemporaine, CMLVI (testimony of Vivette Baharlia-Politi, deported in convoy 76, and camp poems).

[24] Centre de documentation juive contemporaine, UGIF 18-1318.

[25] Centre de documentation juive contemporaine, UGIF 18-1194, 1195 and 1198.

[26] Centre de documentation juive contemporaine, UGIF 92-1662.

[27] Centre de documentation juive contemporaine, UGIF 92-1671.

the removal crates; Wolf Epstein had the job of sorting these supplies. Detainees who needed medicine would help themselves surreptitiously. Michel and Bernard Behr recall systematically swallowing all the pills they came across while sorting the crates, theorising that they would thus be protected from all ills.

The German command seems to have shown some concern for the health of its workers, whose efficiency depended on their physical condition. Kochan allowed several internees to leave his camp temporarily for medical reasons. On 6 December 1943, he approved a request for 'cough syrup and drops, if possible containing codeine'.[28] People coughing during the night were disturbing the others' sleep. On 3 February, on the Germans' orders, an ophthalmologist from the Rothschild hospital came to the quai de la Gare to examine sixty internees.

In March 1944, washing facilities were finally installed in the quai de la Gare. On 29 March, the editors of *Camp-Camp* sketched a humorous portrait of where they lived.

TO LET

In a fine 'Decadent'-style building pleasantly situated on the banks of the Seine (43, Quai du 2 Décembre) spacious offices and first-, second- and third-floor flats to let, by the week or month. All mod. cons (wash basins, running water, Borniel toilets, electricity at all times, goods lift.) Several entrances, easy to enter and leave the building discreetly. Restaurant service for residents. For any further enquiries, please contact this newspaper.

Entertainment

Working, eating, sleeping: the lives of the internees were highly regulated. Between the end of the working day, 7 or 8 P.M., and lights out at 10 P.M., some time remained for other activities. As a rest day, Sunday assumed particular importance. Detainees could get up one hour later, as coffee arrived at 8 A.M. Sunday was also the day for visits and the brief weekly walk. While interned in Austerlitz, Jacques Stern wrote the following song.

Sunday, holiday...

And once again this week
From Monday to Saturday,
Counting this chain's every link
I await you blessed day

Are you still so far away
O time when for my love
For long weeks on end
Every day will be Sunday?[29]

---

[28] Centre de documentation juive contemporaine, UGIF 18-829.

[29] Centre de documentation juive contemporaine, CMLVI (testimony of Vivette Baharlia-Politi, deported in convoy 76, and camp poems).

Occasionally Saturday afternoon was also free, and these rest hours were given over to leisure activities. One of these was preparing meals in small groups. Games were also played. On 30 April 1944, Simon Sarfati described one of these days: 'After taking a shower, I transformed myself into a civilised man, in blue trousers, Lacoste shirt and sports jacket and, along with some friends from the South of France who had managed to find 4 pairs of *boules,* we played a game of *pétanque* that went on for almost 3 hours in the open air, forgetting for a few hours what we really were. I had the honour of winning an aperitif, water of course.' His letter of 6 February 1944 describes some other activities: 'Our Sunday amusements are reading and music, cards if we can find the time. Otherwise, we take advantage of the day to wash in cold water and sort out our things. As I write, one of our friends is playing the piano.'

The 10 commandments of the perfect internee[30]

At reveille thou shalt wake	At the bell thou shalt go back up
To the castle thou shalt go	With care thou shalt dust thyself off
At the basin thou shalt pause	And thy soup thou shalt get
Shivering	*hungrily*
Then to thy room thou shalt go back	At the office thy parcels thou shalt get
Thy comrades thee shall greet	And treats thou shalt eat
And thy bed thou shalt make up	And with thy comrades thou shalt share
militarily	*fraternally*
To juice duty thou shalt run	In the afternoon thou shalt begin again
The soup containers thou shalt bring	After going down thou shalt go up
And the bread thou shalt give out	After going up thou shalt go down
(if it is *thy turn of course*)	*indefatigably*
On the whistle thou shalt go down	At last the evening air thou shalt breathe
And to thy work thou shalt get	With gusto thou shalt dine
Full of vigour thou shalt be	Soundly thou shalt sleep
every day	*without snoring*
At sorting thou shalt not nick	On Sunday thou shalt rest
At shifting thou shalt not cheat	With thy comrades thou shalt chat
On upper floors thou shalt not hide	About freedom thou shalt think
Surreptitiously	*perpetually*

Reading was not confined to Sundays, and many internees read on a daily basis. The Parisian satellite camps were also, effectively, immense libraries, whose shelves were constantly being restocked from the removal lorries. Gilberte Jacob's letters to Roger Mayer show that in Lévitan, as in Austerlitz, quiet days or periods

---

[30] Text written by internees in the quai de la Gare, Centre de documentation juive contemporaine, UGIF 93-49.

could be an opportunity for intellectual enrichment. On 8 March 1944, after noting that work had been hard recently, Gilberte Jacob goes on: 'First things first, before I forget, something very important! In a 1938 Larousse dictionary I found "letto*nne*" [Latvian], but I'm sorry to say that "letto*ne*" is also acceptable. Visually speaking, this spelling is rather elegant. How hard it is to accept that you were right (I was going to say admit I was wrong, but that's not the same thing).' Her letter of 5 March is entirely concerned with reading and philosophical debates. Others from April mention the creation in Lévitan of an intellectual discussion group.

Many detainees wrote – not only letters, but also articles for *Camp-Camp* and texts of a more literary nature. There were at least two poets, Paul Drori and Jacques Stern. The latter wrote a poem for Vivette Politi on her eighteenth birthday:

> I had so wanted, for your birthday present,
> To give you something suitably pleasant
> To match your love of beautiful things
> But in forty-four nice presents are thin
> On the ground…when you're an internee!
> Of course, I could – you're ahead of me –
> Have rummaged through the bric-à-brac at Austerlitz
> And made a purchase – under the nose of Fritz.
> But no! I preferred my present to come specially
> From outside! From Paris! And for it to be
> A taste of freedom, Spring air, fresh and clean
> That it would bring you as you turn eighteen.[31]

Only one edition of *Camp-Camp* was produced, on 19 March 1944. Permission to print it may subsequently have been withdrawn. Over twelve pages, it described, in a highly sardonic tone, the main aspects of camp life. Its editorial secretary was Georges Simkovitch, who was eventually deported on 31 July 1944 (convoy 77). He did not return.

As Jean Levi, a former internee of Austerlitz and contributor to the newspaper, explains, 'we wanted to produce a sort of *Canard enchaîné* [a well-known French satirical magazine] so that the Germans wouldn't understand it'. There were poems, fake classified ads, editorial columns and even complete short stories. All were packed with puns and double meanings. A degree of self-censorship was imposed by the editors. In the text describing the departure of internees to Bassano (reproduced in chapter 4 of this book), the word 'prison', for example, was crossed out and replaced by 'camp', while 'France will live on' was simply

---

[31] Centre de documentation juive contemporaine, CMLVI (testimony of Vivette Baharlia-Politi, deported in convoy 76, and camp poems).

removed. As the editorial staff had access to at least one typewriter in the camp, the paper could be typed.[32]

It seems likely that the UGIF was involved in its production. We know from a letter of February 1944 that there was no roneo printer or printing press inside the camp. The UGIF had the ability to print a small number of copies of *Camp-Camp*. The organisation's archives have preserved the first drafts of many articles, in particular the uncensored version of page 3 entitled 'Les propos de l'ahuri' ('Dumbfounded observations'). It is clear that the paper's circulation was restricted because only one surviving witness, who was one of the papers' editors, ever laid hands on it.

Leisure activities sometimes went beyond reading and traditional games. Several parties were organised in the Parisian camps, or at least in the quai de la Gare. In 1943, a Christmas Eve party was held during which various artists read poems and sang songs. In the spring of 1944, with the permission of the new commandant, a 'hall' was even constructed. Marc Garguir wrote to his wife: 'I forgot to tell you all about the high-point of this fine Sunday's party. In the evening, after dinner, we had a great show. You should know, girls, that for a week now we've had a concert-hall, theatre and possibly a cinema. I'm telling you, this wonderful hall had some opening last night. Really, you have to have seen it to believe it, there was backlighting, loudspeakers, recorded sound, a stage, curtain, a lighting rig for the stage, etc. We had a great evening. One more thing: there was an interval and, guess what, we were taken to a buffet where there was chilled orangeade and lemonade at 5 francs for a big glass, so you can imagine what a night it was.' On this occasion, the eminently Parisian Robert Manuel is supposed to have said: 'I don't know a theatre with dressing-rooms this good.'

On 9 April, the 'Austerlitz's Folies' took place. The German guards were invited. The show consisted of a series of sketches representing and sending up the internees' everyday lives. One of the latter diligently noted his comments on the programme. Several scripts have been found, among them *The Haunted Floor*:

> *The old internee:* You'll have a lot of work to do, but believe me, you'll get used to it and the time passes much more quickly [i.e., than in Drancy]. Do you know where you've been assigned?
>
> *The newcomer:* Yes. I shall have the pleasure of starting on the second floor. I shall be under a Girl-Guide leader, a delicious young lady, charming and funny...
>
> *The old internee (sounding frightened):* On the second floor... Which department???
>
> *The newcomer:* Porcelain.
>
> *The old internee:* May Kapoo preserve you! ... I'd rather carry 50 full crates up to the third floor than work on that accursed department.

---

[32] Centre de documentation juive contemporaine, CDXXV-2.

Newcomer: But why? Explain yourself!

The old internee: Are we quite alone? Right, listen. The counter is haunted... It's simple, really, the shelves are chock-full of plates, dishes, dinner-services of every sort; and it's like this: each time somebody tells any sort of lie during conversation, the spirit which haunts the place knocks down a piece of crockery to mark its disapproval.

The newcomer (laughing): I can't wait to see this. *(From the wings we hear whistles being blown).*

The old internee: You won't have to wait long... We've got to get back to work.

(Classic crate-maker's equipment. 3 crates. He is banging nails as the curtain goes up. Against the backdrop, a dozen plates of all sizes are hung – on a tea-table a full tea-set. A woman enters)

Her: Are you the new boy?

Himi: Yes, Miss! *(A small plate smashes to the floor)*

Her: Oh, you're too flattering! *(She exits) (Enter another internee carrying a hammer, smartly dressed)*

Internee: Everybody's back?

Him: Oh, but this is alright! It's a pleasure to look at you, the internees up here are so much better dressed than in the sorting rooms, it's true that the work isn't so dirty. In a word, I feel like I've come back to civilisation. What a nice jacket you have! I can tell it's from a proper tailor. I've got almost the same thing in blue. Where's it from?

Internee: From Lanvin's; I had it made a month before I was interned. He used the last of this material for it, I got it for a song – 12000 – *(a plate falls)*

Him: What an odd coincidence!

Internee: Very odd! Were you arrested a while back?

Him: No, a fortnight ago, I was picked up in a swoop, wearing the star. My papers were in perfect order; I was taken away in spite of my protests. And you sir?

Internee: My case, sir, is a tragic one. I am the victim of an abominable plot! As you can see, I am not Jewish *(a plate falls)* in the eyes of the law, my father was ½ Jewish *(half a plate falls)*, that is indisputable, because, listen carefully, as he was being circumcised, the mohel, who came over all faint, had to abandon the operation half-way through, so to speak.[33] What do you think?

Him: That sounds indisputable to me. Yet another miscarriage of justice!

Internee: It's awful, sir, when you think that I've been in France for 30 years *(a plate falls)* that I fought in both wars *(two plates)*, we can safely say that the government's not doing much to protect us *(a plate rises back into place)*.

Him: Well, let's hope all this will be over soon!

Internee: Yes, and, following a conversation with a VIP visitor, I have great hopes for an improvement in our status.

---

[33] The mohel performs the circumcision ritual.

Him: Oh yes? And what did he say?

Internee: That soon we'd all be free workers. (*The entire tea-set crashes to the floor*).[34]

Two months before she was deported, Vivette Politi celebrated her eighteenth birthday in this same 'hall'. A few days later, in a letter to a friend, Bernard Behr enthusiastically described what he did on 28 May: 'Today's schedule is quite different, I think I'll eat lunch with my mother ... then, around six, there's a music-hall show.' Jean Levi recalls a sort of 'troops' revue'.[35] Poetry, songs, short playlets (all written by Gaston Naxara), dances and a raffle were its main components. At the end of the show there was a comedy auction of a painting that had been taken from the stock in Austerlitz.

On 7 July, Simon Sarfati wrote to his wife: 'Some electrician and artist lads are putting on a concert of gramophone records ... To finish on a calm, peaceful note, we'll have a Beethoven symphony.' On 16 July a 'radio roadshow' concert was organised. Preparing and putting on these little events was an important part of the lives of some internees. As an assistant director, Jean Levi recalls with ironic regret: 'When we were liberated, we had begun setting up a theatre for fun, there were some decent singers and a professional pianist. In fact, when we were liberated, that was the end of the theatre. I won't say that I was disappointed [laughs], only ...' Robert Manuel is said to have recited there, as he had done during his months spent in Drancy.

Finally, as in many places of confinement, the satellite camps were the scene of amorous liaisons, some platonic, others not. Jealousies, such as that evoked in the play *The Visit*, were part of camp gossip. Working outside was for some an opportunity for intimate meetings with their wives. The men who moved the pianos from the palais de Tokyo all spoke of these feminine encounters 'between the pianos'.

---

[34] Centre de documentation juive contemporaine, UGIF 93.

[35] Interview with Jean Levi, 17/03/2003.

CHAPTER 7

THE END OF
THE PARISIAN CAMPS

F ROM MARCH 1944, the disciplinary régime in the quai de la Gare became somewhat more relaxed. The internees' everyday living conditions improved as a result. The Allied landings marked a turning point, bringing hopes of liberation. June seems to have seen negotiations regarding the widening of certain prisoner categories. The UGIF archives contain numerous letters and different lists drawn up by category throughout this month. 'Lists of internees aged 60 and over' were established on 8 June for Bassano and Lévitan,[1] on 9 June for Austerlitz.[2] On 10 June, it was the turn of the 'half-Jews' to be counted.[3]

In the end, however, none of these categories were freed. By 24 June, Marc Garguir had stopped believing rumours about the transfer of internees over sixty to the Rothschild old people's home. In fact, the general climate was becoming increasingly tense. Sensing defeat, the Germans were getting nervous, and discipline became stricter. 'One day, the landings happened at last, which had the effect of making this "race of masters" utterly furious. The slightest peccadillo was paid for dearly', relates Jacqueline Jacob-Delmas[4].

The Allied landings had also made hunting down Jews more difficult. In Drancy, Brunner had increasing difficulty in filling the deportation convoys. The detainees who had been transferred to Paris remained under his authority; he could demand their return to the main camp at any time. From June onwards, the internees of the satellite camps were brutally reminded of their true status. Between 30 June and the liberation of Drancy on 18 August, 113 detainees from

---

[1] Centre de documentation juive contemporaine, UGIF 92-1689 and 92-1697-1698-1699-1701.

[2] Centre de documentation juive contemporaine, UGIF 92-1691.

[3] Centre de documentation juive contemporaine, UGIF 92-1694.

[4] *Le Monde Juif.* Special issue 146 (January–March 1993). Testimonies of M. Bonnet, J. Jacob-Delmas, M. Lessovoï, 37.

the satellite camps were sent to Auschwitz or Bergen-Belsen. As for Operation Furniture, it continued until the evacuation of the Parisian camps.

Operation Furniture Goes On

In March 1944, the operation got into difficulty. While the general organisation of the work was adequate, the Dienststelle was, once again, confronted with a crisis of manpower.[5] A total of 115 employees and civil servants were working in the offices on the avenue d'Iéna. They would, however, change regularly as men were sent to the front. Most were not properly trained in their tasks. Von Behr's report expressed fears of work-related accidents, given that, with the intensification of bombing against the Reich, the need for furniture from Jewish apartments was becoming more pressing. Von Behr wanted more workers. Head of the Milice (Vichy's paramilitary police organisation) and Secretary of State for Law and Order Joseph Darnand had previously visited him and agreed terms under which French *miliciens* would help with the work of the Dienststelle.[6] Henceforth, crates were delivered to the Milice in exchange for services rendered, which probably consisted in identifying apartments to empty. The Dienststelle's main concern was to extend its activities into the southern zone. Most of its remaining agents in Paris were wounded veterans.[7] It was suggested that a priority would be the seizure of Jewish furniture assembled in the warehouses at the port of Marseilles and waiting to be sent overseas to its rightful owners.

In March 1944, von Behr summoned several French officials, including the new General Commissioner for Jewish Matters Charles Mercier du Paty de Clam, and announced this extension into the southern zone. Du Paty de Clam opposed this measure vigorously. Enthusiastic collaboration had had its day. Two days later, when he secretly informed Laval of this project, he expressed his hostility to it.[8] He explained that von Behr had claimed that Darnand had agreed to it, which he doubted. The French authorities refused to lend any support to this extension, which therefore rested entirely on the Germans' shoulders. Von Behr sent Bruno Kochan to Marseilles to assess the operation's feasibility, and also to Nice, probably because he expected to find high-quality furnishings in the town's

---

[5] Centre de documentation juive contemporaine, L-188 15 (XIII-47), report signed by von Behr entitled: 'Ergänzungs- und Leistungsbericht des Dienststelle Westen des Reichsministeriums für die besetzten Ostgebiete', 4 pages.

[6] Probably around the beginning of March.

[7] Centre de documentation juive contemporaine, CCLII-8, report on the activity of the Dienststelle, 22/03/1944.

[8] Dépôt central de la justice militaire, Le Blanc, Indre, 'Dossier Utikal et autres', document 28/D/II, statement to the hearing by Charles Mercier du Paty de Clam, 06/05/1947.

villas and holiday homes. In order to resolve the manpower problem, there was even a plan to create an internment camp in Nice, modelled on the three Parisian camps, where spouses of Aryans would be sent.

The idea was refused point-blank by the local head of the SD, Dr Keil, owing to 'political and military difficulties'.[9] In fact, the SD was itself busy plundering these apartments. From a list of 200 premises sent to the local branch of the Dienststelle, most of the apartments had already been cleared out. Competition was fierce, and certain elements of the general staff in Paris had actually given instructions not to let von Behr's department gain a foothold on the Côte d'Azur. However, the *Feldkommandant* of Nice, Major General Eickelmann, was more favourably disposed towards Operation Furniture, especially after being guided around the Nice depot by Kochan on 1 June 1944. There was another depot in Cannes, run by Hauptmann Adamy. The Menton office was run by an agent named Berg, who complained that 70 per cent of the Jewish apartments in his zone had been emptied during the Italian occupation. Cooperation with other German authorities was anything but straightforward. The new head of service IV of the Nice SD, Eckerle, demanded that payment be made to his offices since it was they who indicated which apartments were Jewish-owned. The Alpes-Maritimes section of the collaborationist Parti Populaire Français also took an interest in the Dienststelle's activity, but mainly to complain that they were not receiving any furniture whereas the local Milice were.

For Western Europe, according to the monthly reports of the Dienststelle, the results for Operation Furniture can be seen in Table 1.

TABLE 1. The results of Operation Furniture.

Date	Apartments cleared (total)	Number of wagons (total)
30/09/1943	40,000	18,250
11/12/1943	54,830	19,500
31/12/1943	57,422	23,561
31/01/1944	59,364	24,086
29/02/1944	61,457	24,935
31/03/1944	63,967	25,708
30/04/1944	65,785	26,182
31/05/1944	67,363	26,578
30/06/1944	68,441	26,796
31/07/1944	69,619	26,984

The monthly reports of the Dienststelle are taken from: Centre de documentation juive contemporaine, XIII-47.

[9] Centre de documentation juive contemporaine, CCXXXII-32, inspection report on the southern zone by inspector Schwarze, Gemeinschaftsführer, 16/06/1944. The document is also in: Bundesarchiv, NS 30, 12.

The imminent Allied landings slowed the clearing of apartments somewhat. Just before 6 June, the number of wagons going to the Reich each month had gone down owing to a lack of rolling stock. Nevertheless, Operation Furniture continued up until August. On 12 August, for example, a town house on rue Erlanger was plundered. A Citroën saloon and two lorries converted to run on gas emptied the building entirely.[10] Between 6 June and 1 August, 2,334 apartments were seized; 397 complete sets of furniture were sent to Germany (a total of 16,245 m³) in 408 wagons, making ten entire trains (at an average of 40 wagons per train). Also taken were 80,263 reichsmarks in currency and bonds, as well as 63,400 kg of old metal, old paper and fabric. June 1944 alone saw the equivalent of 5,350 days worked.[11]

The bombing against Germany also targeted rail convoys and stations. Wagons full of furniture from Paris were destroyed, like the four wagons specifically assigned to employees of the ERR in Germany.[12] Facing the Soviet advance westwards, the offices of the ERR located outside the Reich pulled back. Their agents and families needed furniture and, once again, the Parisian depots were called upon, on the orders of Rosenberg himself.[13]

Operation Furniture continued to develop right up to the end. As late as June 1944, the Besançon management created a branch in Chaumont, which functioned until 19 August. Furniture could not be sent to Germany by this branch, which handed it over to the local *Feldkommandatur,* number 769. Medical and cleaning supplies were given to the German military hospital in the town.[14]

Convoy 76

The internees of Austerlitz, Lévitan and Bassano were essential to the smooth running of Operation Furniture. Tension therefore existed between the desire to fill up the deportation convoys and the need to keep the detainees working. In June 1944, the Sipo-SD decided to move the internees back to Drancy in order to deport those who could not prove conclusively that they belonged to a special category.

As Serge Klarsfeld sums up in his *Calendrier,* 'the Allied landings in Normandy led to a comparative reduction in the number of Jews arrested and transferred to

---

[10] Statement by M. Michel Crifo, resident of 1, rue du Général-Balfourier, Paris XVI. Document presented by M. Munnich.

[11] Centre de documentation juive contemporaine, XIII-47, report by the transport department, 08/08/1944.

[12] Ibid., CDXXXVI-5.

[13] Ibid., CDXXXVI-7, letter from Koeppen to Kurt von Behr, 11/07/1944.

[14] Bundesarchiv, NS 30, 12, p. 17, Abschluss-Bericht der Einsatzleitung Nordfrankreich, 05/10/1944.

Drancy in June: about one thousand, split half-and-half between Parisian and provincial Jews'.[15] The letters that Maurice Bensignor, interned in Drancy, managed to send to his family speak of the expectation of the arrival of new internees that characterised that month. The total needed for a convoy was rarely reached. On 18 June, he wrote: 'I would say that the threat of deportation still looms and this is the worst thing for us, especially now that the end is in sight. But as of now we only make up half the number needed to form a convoy.'[16] This lack of prisoners led Brunner to go and bring in Jews from the places where they were assembled, whether they were adults, as in the satellite camps, or children, as on the terrible night of 20–21 July, when he had the 350 residents of the UGIF's boarding houses rounded up.

Maurice Bensignor was finally deported from Drancy in convoy 76, on 30 June. He was accompanied by his young nieces, Reine and Janine Bensignor. The required total had been reached. Several internees of the Parisian camps were among his deported companions. They had been progressively brought back to Drancy from 21 June onwards. Gilberte Jacob recalls: 'On 21 June, during work, while we were carrying crates and wearing long trousers, we were called over the loudspeaker and straight away had to go down without taking anything with us … We were told that we were being taken back to Drancy to have our papers checked.' This day marked the beginning of an operation that would last several days. However, only those internees taken back to Drancy on 22 June seem to have been searched because a complete check through the search register yields only eighteen records, all from this date.

Simon Sarfati left Austerlitz on 24 June. A few hours before his departure, he wrote to his wife: 'I'm going off to have my papers checked with all my buddies and some others as well to the place where I was before. The third convoy is leaving, and when everybody has been checked, we'll make a convoy down there to be taken back … The lads who have come back have told us that, once they see an official document, you're brought back here straight away.' As a postscript, he adds: 'I sent you a letter last night, as last night some convoys had already left, and I thought I wasn't on the lists.'[17]

The complement of the satellite camps' internees found themselves back in Drancy. Gilberte Jacob was thus able to see Roger Mayer again before he left the main camp that same day. Still in Drancy, she wrote to him on the evening of 25 June: 'My dear Roger, it's not been long since you went away. To me it already seems a very long time, and these last few hours this afternoon have been just like a film.'[18] Half the day had indeed been spent inspecting the internees' status.

[15] Klarsfeld, *Le Calendrier de la persécution des Juifs en France*, 1863.

[16] Private archives of Claude Bensignor.

[17] Private archives of Denise Bernard.

[18] Private archives of Roger Mayer.

'This truly bizarre life continued for me until 25 June, on which date we were made to return to Drancy to have our papers checked', relates Yvonne Klug who, like many others, had an interview with Alois Brunner: 'I still did not have my husband's papers and the famous Brunner put me down for the next deportation; it was no use reminding him that my husband had been freed from Drancy itself and … that I had been classified as the spouse of an Aryan and treated as such, he was not having it. So I was assigned to building 2; there was nothing more to be done, it was an irreversible decision.' Michel Behr and his brother Bernard have also left an account of their appearance before Brunner. On seeing their mother's certificate of non-appartenance to the Jewish race, he shouted that it was forged and invalid. The Behr brothers and their father left in utter desperation, convinced that they would be deported. They then encountered Vivette Politi and her father, who had been in the same office a little earlier. They seemed rather confident. Brunner had said nothing to them. The Behr family were taken back to Paris whereas the Politi family went to Auschwitz. The father, Body Politi, did not return.

The details of these interviews with Brunner are not known. Some internees whom we subsequently met were taken back to Paris despite possessing none of the documents, or even forgeries of these, required to prove their 'nondeportable' status. Robert Fabius, whose parents were Jewish and who was married to a Jewish woman, is an example. Might other factors have been at work? This remains unclear. While he possessed documents, admittedly fake but produced by the network in service 6 of the UGIF, who were master forgers,[19] Wolf Epstein would remain convinced that he had benefited from the assistance of Georges Albertini, who had previously got him removed from Drancy and transferred to Austerlitz.[20] It is impossible to say whether this was the case or whether this is just what Wolf Epstein had understood to have happened. With hindsight, it does appear that some prisoners slipped through the net with less in the way of papers than he had, and some with no documents at all. Nor were these necessarily the best-equipped individuals in social terms.

On 25 June, the satellite camps were once again full. Some detainees had been able to meet. Some who had been in Austerlitz were sent back to Lévitan, and vice-versa.[21] Back in Austerlitz, Wolf Epstein spoke of his return journey in a letter written the same day: 'On Wednesday [21 June], we were taken back out to the suburbs [i.e., Drancy]. The POWs' wives are still there', and the same number

---

[19] Service 6 of the UGIF was staffed by former members of the Éclaireurs israélites de France, the French Jewish scouting movement. It was concerned with resistance activities, including the manufacture of fake papers and even running a combat cell in the Tarn.

[20] Centre de documentation juive contemporaine, LXXIV-4, trial of Georges Albertini.

[21] Statement by M. Riese, Dépôt central de la justice militaire, Le Blanc, Indre, 'Dossier Utikal et autres'.

ILLUSTRATION 19. Bassano interior.
Bundesarchiv Koblenz, B 323-311-48.

of 'men – young and old – have been kept there for various reasons.'[22] Bernard
Behr, for his part, recalls that 'the checks were strict ... Out of these 300, more
than 75 were deported and most of them would never return.' Finally back in the
quai de la Gare, Simon Sarfati made great efforts to reassure his wife: 'It's in the
past now.' But, he adds: 'An ugly past'. He had seen some of his comrades remain
in Drancy to be deported.

It is impossible to ascertain how many people were actually kept in Drancy
that day. While Bernard Behr speaks of 75 persons, Yvonne Klug estimates they
numbered 20, plus herself. Either way, many internees of the satellite camps were
deported following these systematic checks. In fact, following this check at least
38 internees of the Parisian camps left for Auschwitz in convoy 76, on 30 June
1944. Georges Wellers, Bernard Pessis, Vivette Politi, Paul and Erna Herzberg,
Sophia Bich, Georges Roueff, Jean Steinberg, Grégoire Afrine, Yvonne Klug and
Marguerite Leger survived; the others perished. There were 1,153 people in this
convoy, including 162 children under eighteen. Georges Wellers would relate
the horror of this journey in *De Drancy à Auschwitz*. One of a small group of
men who had tried to escape, he describes how '[t]his attempt was discovered
by the Germans and all 60 of us were stripped naked and, in this state, placed
in an empty wagon. These 60 naked men, racked with thirst, lying next to each

---

[22] Private archives, access granted by Denise Weill.

ILLUSTRATION 20. Bassano courtyard (2003).
©Gilles Roquelaure.

other on the wagon's filthy floor made a most grotesque, miserable and revolting spectacle.'[23]

Some internees of the Parisian camps were infinitely luckier, and saw their status changed to that of free workers. It was compulsory for them to go to the

---

[23] G. Wellers. 1946. De *Drancy à Auschwitz*, Paris: Éditions du Centre, 222. Quoted in Klarsfeld, *Le Calendrier.*

satellite camp each morning for work and then to leave in the evening. This applied for the most part to those who still had a family member interned. The Behr brothers received this new status whereas their father remained in the quai de la Gare. Replying to a friend's letter on 24 July, Bernard Behr describes his new situation: 'For three or four weeks now I've been free along with Michel, unfortunately Dad can't come out with us. Only twelve of us out of five hundred are in this situation … We pretty much have to work where we were working before, and so we can't go absent … I eat with my father at midday and with my mother in the evening.' Gilberte Jacob hints at Roger Mayer's new 'state' in a letter to her friend (25 June): 'I'm so happy for you and your new state. I don't need to keep telling you to work hard any more.'[24] An *Ausweis* was issued to this handful of atypical workers in order to exempt them from subsequent arrest.

Deportations to Bergen-Belsen

The situation of the wives of POWs changed drastically in June. Having been brought back to Drancy, they returned to Paris only briefly and then were all deported to Bergen-Belsen concentration camp. Following the June checks, not all POWs' wives returned to the satellite camps. The Drancy archives contain a memo, dated 24 June, that probably refers to this decision: 'Until further orders, all female internees from Lévitan, Bassano and Austerlitz to remain in their rooms.'[25] Some of these women were sent back to Paris; seventeen came back to Drancy on 6 July.[26] Transfers of POWs' wives back to the main camp continued throughout July. For Gilberte Jacob and some of her fellow women internees left in Drancy, life started becoming more structured again: 'In July 1944, there was a faint sense of optimism. We ourselves were better informed and engaged in all sorts of speculation.'

On 21 July, the first convoy of wives and children of POWs left for Bergen-Belsen; in it were 48 women and 2 children. It was composed almost entirely of former female inmates of the satellite camps: 45 out of 48. Gilberte Jacob was one of them: 'We left on 21 July in comfortable coaches, passenger coaches. In order to fool any travellers who might have seen us, they put on a charade that quite took us aback. Fifty of us set off, one escaped.'[27] They arrived three days later, on 24 July. On the same day, in Drancy, the second convoy for Bergen-Belsen was getting ready to leave. It consisted of 85 wives and 29 children; of these women, at least 17 had spent time in the Parisian camps. They arrived on

---

[24] Private archives, access granted by Roger Mayer.

[25] Centre de documentation juive contemporaine, DLXIII.

[26] According to the Drancy search register.

[27] Centre de documentation juive contemporaine, XVa-169, statement by Mme Gilberte Jacob to the Department for Research into Enemy War Crimes, 06/06/1945.

26 July. In four days, the Parisian camps had seen the deportation of at least 64 of their former inmates.

Bergen-Belsen was something of an exception within the immense Nazi concentration camp system. Created with the status of a *Krankenlager* (medical camp), it assembled Jews who could be considered hostages whom the authorities had decided not to send to an extermination camp. Although living conditions were far worse, Bergen-Belsen in some ways resembled the Parisian camps. It was a holding place for those Jews that the Nazis either did not want to or could not murder immediately. However, as the German retreat went on, the arrival of detainees from other concentration camps, among them Auschwitz, caused massive overcrowding in Bergen-Belsen and hygiene deteriorated steadily. Starvation and typhus became rife, killing thousands. Conditions were so bad that the detainees continued to die after the liberation of the camp by British troops, who discovered huge piles of corpses.

Evacuation

The deportations to Bergen-Belsen would not be the last for the detainees of the Parisian camps. The final large convoy, no. 77, left Drancy on 31 July 1944. It consisted of 1,300 people, including 330 under eighteen. We have been able to identify eleven detainees from Lévitan and Austerlitz among them; they had been brought back to Drancy between 6 and 24 July. It is not clear whether this was a collective punishment – which seems unlikely, given this dual provenance and the gradual transfer of the group's members – or whether it was due to Brunner's desire to make the most of this last convoy to deport as many people as possible. Some of the prisoners taken from the satellite camps had all the necessary papers to prove that they belonged to special categories – as was the case, for example, for Georges Harden, a former Austerlitz internee, who was the group's only survivor. Raymond Dreyfus, Edmond Masse, André Meyer, Charles Rosenrauch, Isidore Behar, Gitla Seeuws, Marcel Alexandre, André Salomon, Anna Conesco and Georges Simkovitch, the cheeky editorial secretary of *Camp-Camp*, did not return.

Confusion reigned inside the Parisian camps from this point onwards. The various correspondence files indicate that the beginning of August was marked by the suspension of the normal régime as regards both work and discipline. Bassano was evacuated at the beginning of the month, probably on 5 August, Lévitan and Bassano on 12 August.[28] At the quai de la Gare, 'one day, there was great consternation in the camp. We saw lorries arrive, soldiers, yelling as usual.

---

[28] Based on the Drancy search register. We possess no testimony relating to this evacuation. It is likely that, as a satellite camp of the satellite camps, Bassano's workers were split between the two main Parisian camps before final evacuation to Drancy.

Then, beaten by rifle butts, sticks, feet and fists, we were herded into covered lorries and set off for that unknown destination ... known as Pitchipoï ...'[29] But no, we were just going back to Drancy, yet again, to await our departure on another great journey', recounts Jacqueline Jacob-Delmas. 'On 12 August, the SS came to get us and take us back to Drancy and from there deport us ... I had to leave Austerlitz suddenly, leaving behind virtually all my personal effects and, of course, the bags containing your father's papers', Marcel Lob would tell Georges Ascoli's children.

The situation was very similar in Lévitan. In her memoirs, the *comtesse* de Dampierre, the camp's chief internee, describes the sudden announcement at 2 A.M., the lack of preparation and the speed of the evacuation, the atmosphere of panic and how it was impossible for most detainees to gather their few belongings. As there were few buses, the evacuation was done in stages. Out of the 180 people in the camp, each vehicle could carry no more than 40. There was a revolt during one of these transfers, and a group of internees escaped. Michèle Bonnet has described in *Le Monde juif* how she stopped the bus: 'I pressed the bell. By force of habit, the bus stopped. It was every man for himself. I helped as many people off as I could ... As for me, as I was jumping off, the bus started moving again. The *milicien* held onto my arm. In a rage I took a nightshirt with a 1 kg tin in it and smashed him over the head with it, and there I was out in the street, running away.'[30] Robert Fabius and Georges Lévy were in this group. They hid in Paris until the Liberation. However, most of the Jews from the satellite camps had been taken to Drancy.

When they met on 20 September 1944, von Behr reported to Alfred Rosenberg that '[e]ight days before the evacuation from Paris, the 700 Jews of the Dienststelle Westen were cleared out on the order of the SD.' Brunner wanted to deport all the internees now in Drancy. As Drancy included the satellite camps, he had also 'cleared out' the internees assigned to them. Brunner left Drancy on 17 August, along with 51 Jewish deportees whom he thought he could use as hostages. The great convoy that he had longed for was in the end never organised, and the internees of the satellite camps were liberated in Drancy. On 13 August, Wolf Epstein wrote from Drancy to his 'Dear, dear girls': 'You've already heard about the sudden departure to the suburbs [i.e., Drancy] yesterday morning. The idea was that we would all, without exception, continue our journey further this morning. But more pressing practical developments prevented us from leaving. There's a good chance that we'll all stay here until it's over. Personally I think, and many of us are convinced, that time and rolling stock are ranged against the implementation of this plan.'

---

[29] The name given by children in Drancy to the destination of the deportation convoys.

[30] Bonnet, Jacob-Delmas, Lessovoï, *Le Monde juif* 146, 44.

In his last letter to his wife, dated 18 August, Marc Garguir exclaims: 'Phew! At last the day of liberation is here: yesterday evening, at 5 pm the bastards left and the Red Cross took over the camp'.[31] Drancy was indeed liberated that day following an agreement between the Red Cross, the Consul General of Sweden, Raoul Nordling, and the German authorities. Marc Garguir returned home to Enghein-les-Bains (8 miles north of Paris) on foot, carrying his suitcase. As Kurt von Behr would note with regret: 'A few days later, these Jews were walking around … in Paris.'[32] While a number of their inmates ended up in either Auschwitz or Bergen-Belsen, the Parisian satellite camps of Drancy had nevertheless represented for many internees a temporary place of shelter that, upon the liberation of the main camp on 18 August 1944, became permanent. At the end of the war, between 350 and 700 of their former detainees were liberated in Drancy.[33]

Simon Sarfati was liberated on 18 August 1944 after having worked in Austerlitz owing to his status as the spouse of an Aryan. On 17 December 1943, in Drancy, before his transfer to the quai de la Gare, he had had to watch as his sisters, Rosalie Coronel and Victoria Atlas, were sent to Auschwitz in convoy 63, with their young children. They were exterminated. He had been arrested with one of his sisters, a little after the arrest of the other.

The last furniture train of Operation Furniture had been loaded on 1 August at Aubervilliers station. It comprised fifty-two wagons, including five full of the ERR's artworks. Von Behr managed to get approval for the train to leave but it was held on the sidings by French railwaymen and was still there when Paris was liberated.[34] The evacuation of the Dienststelle Westen's German staff took place a few days later, before the liberation of Drancy. In her statement, Miss Nehring acknowledged that she left Paris on 16 or 17 August, heading east. Once back in Germany, Bruno Kochan rejoined his unit at Guben in September and was given medical duties. He then worked as a courier and lorry driver. Wounded in the hand by a grenade on 30 March 1945, he was hospitalised in Berlin. When this establishment was evacuated, he was among the walking wounded who took to the road. In April 1945, the Red Army took him prisoner and interned him at Zillau, from where he escaped. He was then picked up by American soldiers (or so he claimed) and freed because he was wounded. In 1948, he was living in

---

[31] Private archives of Denise Bernard.

[32] Bundesarchiv Berlin, Reichsministerium für die besetzten Ostgebiete, R6, 236, Report of September 1944.

[33] In his *Calendrier,* Serge Klarsfeld gives the figure of 350 while von Behr speaks of 700 Jews. Maurice Rajsfus appears to have used the former figure in his book, *Drancy, un camp de concentration très ordinaire.* A calculation using the Drancy register and the list of entries and departures in Klarsfeld's *Calendrier* increases this number to 500 people.

[34] L.H. Nicholas. 1994. *The Rape of Europa: The Fate of Europe's Treasures in the Third Reich and the Second World War,* New York: Alfred A. Knopf, 292.

Hanover.[35] Von Behr and his wife left Paris with enormous quantities of baggage, full of souvenirs of these most unusual camps, which would so rapidly be forgotten.[36] Their little convoy comprised 11 private cars (including a Cadillac) and four lorries.[37] Most of the archives had been burnt.

On 24 August, the Nancy branch of the Dienststelle was dissolved and its agents evacuated to Germany. The Belfort branch still managed to send off seventeen wagons of furniture, which arrived near Offenbach, next to Frankfurt am Main.[38] On 26 August, no. 43, quai de la Gare was blown up. Warehouses 5 and 6, which had housed the camp and the furniture depot, were completely destroyed in the ensuing fire.

---

[35] Dépôt central de la justice militaire, Le Blanc, Indre, 'Dossier Utikal et autres', dossier II, information G, cote 40/G, statement by Bruno Kochan, 09/07/1948.

[36] Ibid., sous-dossiers, A 'Ordre d'informer'.

[37] Bundesarchiv, NS 8 230, Bericht über die Übernahme des Dienstgutes der Dienststelle Westen des Reichsministerium für die besetzten Ostgebeite, 213–218, 213.

[38] Bundesarchiv, NS 30, 12, Abschluss-Bericht, 5.

CHAPTER 8

The Silence of History

B Y THE TIME of the exodus of the German occupation authorities, who headed east in August 1944, the Dienststelle Westen had seen its staff steadily diminish as its employees were mobilised following the Allied landings. After a journey lasting three weeks, von Behr, his wife and nine agents finally reached Staffelstein, in Franconia, and made themselves comfortable in Banz castle. An inspector from the Ministry of the Eastern Territories paid them a visit at the beginning of December. By now, France and Belgium had been liberated, although a portion of the Netherlands remained occupied and Operation Furniture, along with the other activities of the ERR, continued there. On 5 December 1944, Rosenberg decided that responsibility for Operation Furniture would be officially transferred from the Dienststelle Westen to the ERR.[1] The Dienststelle was mothballed, and its assets – including the cars – brought back from Paris were distributed among various German agencies. Von Behr held on to those few documents that had been saved. Among them were the books recording the apartments that had been emptied (the *Wohnungsbefundbücher*). He also held on to the equipment used to place seals on these apartments. The liquidator assigned to the Dienststelle, Wesemann, took the jewellery and the register of correspondence.

At the beginning of 1945, the last employees of the ERR who were still active went and joined the von Behrs in Banz castle.[2] On 23 January, Alfred Rosenberg sent the head of the Dienststelle Westen a letter thanking him for the work he had done. When the Americans reached Franconia, Herr and Frau von Behr committed suicide in their apartments in Banz castle. Theirs was a theatrical end: Kurt von Behr wore his uniform and drank a last glass of champagne, vintage 1918. On 4 May, the few archives that remained were taken by U.S. troops to the castle of Neuschwanstein, in Bavaria.

If most of the detainees of the Parisian camps survived the war, many, many more than anyone had thought were deported. The surviving archives give no details of detainee numbers or of movements between or transfers within the

---

[1] Bundesarchiv Berlin, R6/272, pp. 15–17, 19.
[2] De Vries, *Sonderstab Musik,* 99.

three camps. There is no entry register giving internees' names. It is not even clear whether the Germans bothered to create one, in contrast to the perfectly kept accounts of every piece of furniture, every crate, every object. However, by combining various sources it is possible to obtain accurate figures regarding the detainees of the Parisian camps.

Total Number of Deportations

The question of the camps' populations can be approached using two methods. The first builds up a cumulative total, taking into account individual trajectories to give the total number of people who went through the three camps, and establishing what happened to them. The second shows 'snapshots' at given moments. Here, the number of internees can remain unchanged even though, on an individual level, substitutions had occurred. It is thus startling to realise, for example, that in July 1943 when it was created, Lévitan camp held 180 internees, and that one year later in July 1944, it still held 180. However, not all of them were the same people.

So, how many people did the satellite camps hold? The number fluctuated greatly. The Drancy register only mentions the Dienststelle Westen's internees from August 1943 onwards. Here and there, however, we have managed to locate a few short lists that, though only scribbled down on scraps of paper, nevertheless had decisive consequences for those whose names were on them.

The changing picture of the camps' populations can be observed using two main sources. The first are the records of the estimated amounts of food needed by each of the three satellite camps.[3] The second comes from the Drancy register, which recorded movements into and out of the camp, including transfers to the Parisian camps. The former can lead to an overestimation of the camps' populations as the figure, produced for logistical purposes, did not take into account any small reduction in the number of detainees, and in fact assumed an increase in numbers with time. These figures thus possess a certain inertia of their own. They may also have been a means of obtaining extra food from the Seine *préfecture*.

The second source often appears to contradict other documents produced by the Drancy administration, such as the search register and various transfer orders.[4] Lastly, unlike the food figures, the Drancy register does not give details of the respective share of the three satellite camps in the overall number of detainees detached to the Dienststelle Westen in Paris. The resulting statistics can be assembled in table form (see Appendix).

There was a high degree of mobility between Drancy and the satellite camps, with constant comings and goings. The dates of the creation of the different satellite camps are also marked: 1 November for Austerlitz and sometime around 14

---

[3] Centre de documentation juive contemporaine, UGIF 48-840 to 48-1120.

[4] From 19 January onwards. See Klarsfeld, *Le Calendrier*.

March 1944 for Bassano. The UGIF's records between 15 and 17 March again show how Bassano was established, a satellite of the satellites, created not through an increase in the Dienststelle's workforce but through the transfer of detainees out of Lévitan and Austerlitz. From 15 to 17 March, the overall total still stood at 657 internees, whereas on 15 March it was made up of 250 detainees in Lévitan, 393 in Austerlitz and 14 in Bassano; two days later the balance had shifted to 227, 383 and 47 internees respectively in the three Parisian camps.

Finally, the sometimes large discrepancies between the two methods of calculation, along with the great instability of the total number of prisoners, make accurate estimates difficult. However, the resulting picture allows us to follow the evolution of events. From July 1943 to August 1944, the Parisian camps contained, at different times, between 180 and 686 internees. Whereas Bassano never held more than 63 internees, the camps at Lévitan and Austerlitz saw large variations in their populations. Up until February 1944, Lévitan seems to have held the greater number. This relationship was then reversed.

All of this provides various 'snapshots' of the camps. What happens, though, if we move the focus onto the detainees themselves? How many people lived at some time in the satellite camps of Drancy? Transfers to these camps could be of short duration. Jacob Robert's son, for example, knows that his father spent time in Austerlitz but has not been able to establish the dates.[5] Unlike other movements, transfers from Drancy to the satellite camps did not usually result in any specific note being placed on internees' individual file cards. Only the mysterious note '0$^{18/13}$ German list' written on the back of the card seems occasionally to refer to such a transfer. Explicit reference to Lévitan, Bassano or Austerlitz is extremely rare.[6]

The satellite camps saw at least 795 internees identified by name pass through them. At least 64 of these were wives of POWs.[7] The distribution of these 795 people among the various German categories of classification has not been pos-

---

[5] Email received from Claude Léon, 19/09/2002.

[6] For this reason we have not undertaken a systematic examination of the entire Drancy records. Movements into and out of Drancy, when they are recorded, do not allow us to determine whether or not the individuals who came back were the same as those who subsequently went out again. Following certain individual trajectories has shown us that both cases were possible.

[7] Three other sources for these lists have been located. The first is on roll 92 of the UGIF archives (Centre de documentation juive contemporaine, UGIF 92-1679 and following). It is undated, but can be placed, through cross-referencing, at the end of January 1944. It has a heading for each camp, under which work teams are placed side by side. The second list was drawn up in Drancy between 28 October and 1 November 1943 (Centre de documentation juive contemporaine, CCCLXXVI-4). It was part of the preparations for the opening of Austerlitz. Finally, the laundry lists, which were produced throughout the period from July 1943 to August 1944, are one last major source. Pieces of information found here and there, in particular from an examination of the entire Drancy search register, can also be added.

sible, owing to a lack of detail in the sources. However, the occupiers always allowed themselves some (limited) room for manoeuvre in the choice of detainees
to be sent to the satellite camps. The same was true of the convoys to the East.
The only category for which the link between membership and deportation was
systematically checked was that of the wives of POWs. These women were all
deported to Bergen-Belsen in July 1944.

Of all the internees in the Parisian camps, at least 166 were deported, 21 per
cent of the total – one-fifth of all detainees. This contradicts to some extent the
image of the Parisian camps as places of protection. The figure is also certainly
an underestimate, as any internees who were deported would by definition have
spent less time in the camp and would have had fewer opportunities to find their
way onto one of the partial lists we have discussed.

On almost every convoy leaving Drancy between July 1943 and August 1944
there was at least one internee of the Parisian camps, a further demonstration of
their administrative dependence on the main camp. The Table 2, below, clearly
indicates how the Parisian camps constituted one of the many links in the chain
of the organisation and implementation of these deportations.

TABLE 2. Deportations from the Parisian camps towards Auschwitz and
Bergen-Belsen.

Convoy no.	Date	Towards Auschwitz No. of deportees identified as internees of the Parisian camps	No. of survivors from the group
59	02/09/1943	1	0
61	28/10/1943	1	0
62	20/11/1943	12	1
64	07/12/1943	2	0
63	17/12/1943	3	0
66	20/01/1944	6	1
67	03/02/1944	11	2
68	10/02/1944	6	1
70	27/03/1944	2	0
71	13/04/1944	3	0
72	29/04/1944	1	0
74	20/05/1944	3	0
75	30/05/1944	4	0
76	30/06/1944	38	11
77	31/07/1944	11	1
		Towards Bergen-Belsen	
80	21/07/1944	47	No figure available
80	24/07/1944	17	No figure available

Some detainees waited in Drancy for a long time following their return from the Parisian camps, before being deported. The chaotic process of filling the convoys gave rise to widely differing, often arbitrary outcomes. This flow of detainees between the Parisian camps and Drancy on the one hand, and the death camps and Bergen-Belsen on the other, was echoed in the trains carrying furniture, objects and crates, most of which went to Germany, although these of course did not leave from the same station.

Operation Furniture: The Final Tally

During its two years of operation, the Dienststelle Westen sent out monthly reports that were widely circulated. These allow us to follow, month by month, the results of the plunder of apartments in France, Belgium and the Netherlands. However, the figures they contain do not give a detailed picture of the works of art, books and other cultural goods delivered to the Einsatzstab Reichsleiter Rosenberg in accordance with the decree that created the Dienststelle. The items thus transferred to the ERR were marked 'MA' (Möbel Aktion). In all they numbered 3,148, including 1,364 paintings and drawings, 462 Asian antiquities, 51 sculptures and 100 antique weapons. Six of these pieces were destroyed by the ERR as examples of degenerate art. Thirty-four were put aside to be traded in the future but nevertheless remained part of the ERR's collection.

The Dienststelle's financial documents were destroyed in Paris in August 1944. A final account drawn up a few months later was based on the reports sent back to Berlin. It calculated that the Dienststelle had disbursed a total of 9,260,560 reichsmarks, at that time worth almost 200 million francs (around 1.8 million pounds).[8] The Besançon branch calculated that it alone had filled 207 wagons with furniture and other objects between September 1943 and August 1944, a total volume of 9,374.1 m³ worth 964,500 reichsmarks.

The last of the Dienststelle's reports, dated 8 August 1944, provided figures for the whole of occupied Western Europe. As of 31 July 1944, the Dienststelle Westen had emptied 69,619 Jewish homes and sent 69,512 complete sets of furniture for apartments to the Reich. A total of 1,079,373 m³ had been moved using 26,984 wagons, making up 674 trains. However, only half of the total volume of looted furniture was ever distributed to German refugees. The rest went to various agencies and administrative bodies of the régime. The looting of apartments had also yielded currency and bonds to a value of 11,695,516 reichsmarks, along with 2,191,352 kg of metal, paper and fabric that had been recovered and sent to Germany. The report also specified that furnishings and other objects had been distributed among German employees in France, to a value of

---

[8] Bundesarchiv, NS 8 230, Bericht über die Übernahme des Dienstgutes der Dienststelle Westen des Reichsministerium für die besetzten Ostgebiete, 213–218, 217. This figure breaks down as follows: for 1942, RM 2,600,000; for 1943, RM 4,337,560; for 1944, RM 2,323,000.

1,516,816 reichsmarks. However, the official total was an underestimate, as we know that 29,000 apartments in the Netherlands and 38,000 in Paris (giving a total of 67,000) were emptied.[9] Yet at least 100,000 m³ of furniture was looted in Belgium.[10] Even allowing for large-scale distribution within these countries and a high rate of 'fiddling', a great deal seems unaccounted for.

It is impossible to check the veracity of these figures. Was it in the Dienststelle Westen's interest to inflate them, in order to demonstrate its efficiency and the financial value of the enterprise, or to understate them, in order to build up its own stocks? In any case, great efforts were made to show that the volume of goods plundered was equal to that sent to Germany, in order to conceal the unofficial distribution of goods and the straightforward theft that occurred at every stage of the sorting process in Operation Furniture. Similarly, it is impossible, given that we do not have access to the complete archives of the Dienststelle, to know how the looting was statistically divided between France, Belgium and the Netherlands.

As far as France is concerned, other figures do exist. These were produced by the removal companies at the request of the Commission du coût de l'occupation (Commision for the Cost of the Occupation), which was created on 21 October 1944 and renamed the following year as the Commission consultative des dommages et des réparations. This was an official body that undertook to calculate the damages suffered by France, with a view to later negotiations over reparations. Three general reports were published in 1945 and 1946 on the damages sought respectively from Germany, Italy and Japan. These were followed by specialised reports on individual sectors of economic activity. One of these concerned removal companies and storage businesses.[11] Its authors devoted a chapter to 'the valuation of furniture taken by the Germans.'[12] The amount of furniture looted from Jews was estimated at 15,000 m³ for Paris and 5,000 m³ for the provinces. It was also stated that 60,000 m³ had been seized from storage companies. According to the report, then, the total was 80,000 m³. Since we know that around 38,000 homes belonging to Jews were emptied in the northern zone of France, this gives about 2 m³ per apartment, which is obviously too low.

The authors of the report added 43,000 m³ taken from antique dealers and non-Jews. Even taking this new total of 123,000 m³, we are well below a realistic estimate of the size of Operation Furniture. The removal companies no doubt systematically understated the level of plunder in which they had participated.

---

[9] Aalders, *Geraubt!* 364.

[10] Letter from the *Einsatzleiter Belgien* to the Ministry of the Ocupied Eastern Territories, dated 18/08/1944, quoted in Pezechkian, 'La Möbelaktion en Belgique', 157.

[11] Commission consultative des dommages et des réparations. 1948. *Ingérences allemandes dans l'activité industrielle, Monographie A.I.41. Entreprises de déménagement et garde-meubles,* Paris: Imprimerie nationale.

[12] Ibid., 10.

This is all the more likely given that any compensation payments in such cases would not have gone to them.

The report also gives details of the volume of furniture shipped away by rail. It gives a total of 111,708 m³ sent from France, which once again seems too low. The total paid to the SNCF for these removals is also indicated: 4,652,188 francs at 1938 prices. The study's authors mention an interesting fact: a proportion of the material sent to Germany was taken there by requisitioned lorries, mainly from Bordeaux and Paris, giving a figure of 300 vehicles covering a total of 3,200,000 km. The cost of this transport was put at 81 million francs, 69 million of which had come out of the occupation expenses paid by France. Twelve million francs were never paid.

While the removal companies calculated how much the war had cost them (they had also had equipment stolen, in particular lorries), the Jewish survivors, who had come back to apartments that were empty, or often occupied, sold or relet, were left looking in the papers for news of measures regarding the recovery of, or compensation for, their property. There was, at the time of the Liberation, a real willingness to try to recover any looted property that could be returned to its owners. This project encountered various difficulties due to the complexity of the processes of Aryanisation and looting.[13] The most important law in this regard was not passed until 21 April 1945. It was primarily concerned with businesses and buildings. As rent agreements had already been dealt with, it remained to be determined how stolen money (in particular the *amende du milliard*, the collective 'billion-franc fine' imposed on France's Jewish population, for the payment of which money was siphoned from Jewish bank accounts and share portfolios were sold) was to be restituted or compensated, along with furniture plundered through schemes such as Möbel Aktion. As the government and the Restitution Service set up within the Ministry of Finance considered that these were cases of German looting, and that the French state had not decided on or implemented them (which was untrue in the case of the billion-franc fine), these two types of confiscation were provisionally left out of this legislation.

The Question of Furniture Found in France

The only measure concerning furniture was the placing of recovered items under state control. From 5 October 1944, enemy goods (including German properties) were placed in sequestration.[14] The French Territorial Administration sold them

---

[13] On the restitution of looted property, see Dreyfus, *Pillages sur ordonnance*, 275–322; A. Prost et al. 2000. *Aryanisation économique et restitutions*, Paris: Mission d'étude pour la spoliation des Juifs de France, La Documentation française, 71–93.

[14] *Journal officiel de la République française*, 7/10/1944. Law of 5 October 1944 relating to the declaration and sequestration of goods in the possession of the enemy.

through the Central State Auction Service. In the period up to 1946, 138,000 lots were sold, among which were, without doubt, objects that had come from Operation Furniture.[15] No attempt was made to return this furniture to its owners. However, in April 1945, following pressure from Émile Terroine, the head of the Restitution Service for the Property of Victims of the Dispossession Laws and Related Measures, the legal status of furniture found in warehouses and accommodation under the control of the occupying authorities was modified.[16] An interministerial commission was charged with classifying the furniture into two categories: those items that were in use and whose owners could not be identified, and those whose owners could potentially be located. Items in the second category were placed in the hands of the French Territorial Administration, and those in the first were handed over to the Secours national, which had been renamed Entr'aide française (French Mutual Help) following the Liberation.[17] Entr'aide française would then distribute this furniture not only among needy families who had been dispossessed by the Nazis but also among the general population who had lost essential items due to the war. Terroine's judgement acknowledged that the vast majority of furniture seized as enemy property had originally come from Jewish apartments. It is not known what happened to the furniture that remained in the six depots of the Dienststelle Westen, which included the three Parisian camps. We do know that Austerlitz was visited by agents of the Restitution Service.[18] All that remained of the buildings of the Magasins généraux on the quai de la Gare was a pile of rubble.

Each administrative region classified the furniture found on its territory. In Paris, recovered items were displayed on stand 60 at the Paris Trade Fair, at the porte de Versailles. On request, dispossessed owners could come and visit. These visits, almost a mirror image of those of von Behr and German dignitaries to the Parisian camps, are still remembered by many, as are those to the palm house of the Botanical Gardens in Paris, or to stand 63 at the porte de Versailles, where the 2,000 pianos found in Paris, including several hundred from the basement

---

[15] A. Wieviorka and F. Azoulay. 2000. *Le Pillage des appartements et son indémnisation: Mission d'étude sur la spoliation des Juifs en France,* Paris: La Documentation française, 28. For general remarks on the restitution of furniture and compensation, see 27–72.

[16] *Journal Officiel de la république française,* 12/04/1945, 'Ordonnance du 11 avril 1945 relative à la devolution de certains biens meubles, récupérés par l'État à la suite d'actes de pillage commis par l'occupant'.

[17] The Secours national (National Assistance), a vast quasi-governmental assistance agency, had been a branch of the Vichy régime and so had strong ideological associations. It could not be disbanded with the Liberation, however, as it provided essential services to the displaced population.

[18] Archives nationales, AJ38 5931, 'Liste des immeubles réquisitionnés par les Allemands et par les Alliés.'

of the palais de Tokyo alone, where detainees from the satellite camps of Drancy had been sent, were displayed. Only half of these instruments were ever returned to their owners.

It was in this context that the removal firms took steps to protect themselves from possible legal action. It is possible that their attention was drawn to this problem when their managerial union was questioned during the drawing-up of the national report on war damages. The Organisational Committee was dissolved in 1945 and a provisional administrator, a Monsieur Catherine, appointed. The managerial union again became the sole legal representative for these removal and furniture storage firms. On 6 July 1945, an 'assembly of companies requisitioned by the German offices on avenue d'Iéna' was organised by the managerial union, which had taken over the premises and furniture (which it kept) of the Organisational Committee at 20, rue Chauchat.[19] These companies set up a commission comprising six members to investigate the contents of accounts relating to the removal of Jewish furniture. An expert would then be appointed in order to 'sort out legalities', and finally decide what to do with the money (and furniture) they had acquired through Operation Furniture. Adrien Bedel took charge of these matters. The minutes of this first meeting show that the money paid by the Dienststelle Westen was considered as having been legitimately earned by these requisitioned firms because it had been received for actual services rendered, because the firms had not wanted to carry out the work in question and because it had not been profitable.[20] No one from these removal firms was prosecuted, unlike in Belgium, where the directors of the Arthur Pierre removal company were put on trial. Some Jews tried to take these companies to court, but it appears that no case was ever brought. Some firms issued certificates to dispossessed claimants that attested to their participation in the looting.[21]

The profession carried on working, with considerable modernisation and internationalisation in the 1960s. The fact that a large proportion of these family businesses had participated in the clearing of Jewish apartments (in Paris, at any rate) and perhaps only survived because of this, was never subsequently mentioned. There were rumours, though, that certain heads of these firms had such well-furnished apartments because they had taken the opportunity to pick

---

[19] Archives de la chambre syndicale du déménagement, letter from the commission representing the assembly of companies requisitioned by the German offices on avenue d'Iéna to M. Catherine, provisional administrator of the CODGM, 18/07/1945.

[20] Ibid., minutes of the meeting of the assembly of companies requisitioned by the German offices on avenue d'Iéna, 06/06/1945.

[21] An example of one of these certificates is reproduced in Wieviorka and Azoulay, *Le Pillage des appartements*, 94.

up some nice pieces…[22] There was a deafening silence on this subject for many years.[23]

Möbel Aktion and the Parisian internment camps should have been mentioned, if only briefly, in at least two trials, one in Germany and the other in France. The first of these was the trial at Nuremberg of Alfred Rosenberg.

The Trial of Rosenberg

During his questioning by the delegation from the French legal office, assistant prosecutor Monneray questioned Rosenberg on Operation Furniture and presented three pieces of evidence: a note dated 3 October 1942 from the *Reichsleiter* to Hitler explaining the organisation of the operation and two reports from the Dienststelle.[24] Rosenberg denied that the looting of apartments had any relation to deportations and declared that he had not known the destination of the trainloads of Jewish deportees.

It should be noted here that one document showing the existence of the Parisian camps, presented amongst a mass of other material, was published at Nuremberg. However, it was not referred to by the prosecution, who were mainly concerned with proving that Rosenberg had been one of the organisers of the deportation of the Jews. The defence attempted to separate the looting from the deportations. Monneray asked the accused directly about the deportations:[25]

> *M. Henry Monneray:* I have only a few questions to ask the accused. Accused Rosenberg, is it correct that the deportation and execution of the Jews in France allowed your service to seize furniture and valuables belonging to these Jews?
>
> *Accused Rosenberg:* It is correct that I had received an order from the government to confiscate archives, works of art and later on furnishings from Jewish citizens in France.
>
> *M. Monneray:* The large-scale deportation of the Jews could only increase the productivity of your seizure and confiscation operations. Is this not the case?

---

[22] Interview with Jean-Noël Cannioni, general secretary of the removal firms' managerial union. In an illustrated history published to mark the centenary of the managerial union in 1990, the clearing of Jewish apartments was described at some length. See R. de Foucauld. 1990. *Il était une fois…le déménagement,* Paris: Éditions Saurat.

[23] Interview with Raymond Cornuau, former General Secretary of the removal firms' managerial union, appointed in 1946.

[24] In all, five documents relating to Möbel Aktion were presented by the prosecution.

[25] International Military Tribunal. *Trials of War Criminals before the Nuremberg Military Tribunals under Control Council,* 16 volumes, vol. 14 November 1945–1 October 1946 (Washington, 1949), 594–598.

Accused Rosenberg: No, the deportation of the Jews has nothing to do with that. This measure was put into force when I was informed that the Jews in question were no longer residing in their institutions, their castles or their apartments, that they had left Paris and other residences, and had not returned.

M. Monneray: Once the Jews were deported, they were nonetheless absent, were they not?

Accused Rosenberg: When German troops arrived, Paris was almost completely depopulated. Most Parisians and inhabitants of towns in the North of France gradually returned; but, as I have been told, the Jewish population did not come back, in particular not to Paris. It had therefore not been deported, but had fled; I believe that the number who fled was estimated at 5,000,000, 6,000,000 or 7,000,000 or even more.

A dialogue of the deaf ensued, during which Monneray attempted to prove that Rosenberg knew the destination of the Jewish deportation convoys (which was likely) and that the looting operations were part of the Final Solution. The accused flatly denied having been aware of the latter's existence. It should be noted that throughout his false testimony he continued with his anti-Semitic rants on the number of Jews, their wealth (such as his remarks regarding 'castles') and their power.[26] Absorbed in its argument, the prosecution at no point mentioned the Parisian camps, whose existence it was nonetheless aware of and many of whose internees had eventually been deported. Alfred Rosenberg was condemned to death on 1 October 1946. The sentence was carried out.

The Trial of the ERR

The subject of the Parisian satellite camps of Drancy could have been brought up in another trial, but they were not even mentioned. On 1 and 2 August 1950, the permanent military tribunal in Paris tried the heads of the ERR. In the dock, Gerhard Utikal, who had succeeded von Behr, was seated next to some of the other men responsible for the looting of works of art. The trial received a fair amount of publicity, with particular attention being given to stolen artworks.[27] Operation Furniture was not mentioned once during the cross-examinations,

---

[26] Möbel Aktion was mentioned a second time on 16 April 1946 (the 109th day of the trial), when Rosenberg justified the looting by declaring that he had written down 'in a big ledger the addresses, the names of owners and an outline description of their furniture as a basis for possible future negotiations': ibid., vol. 11, 480. We have seen that this was untrue.

[27] 'Quatre dirigeants du service Rosenberg répondent du pillage des collections d'art israélites', *Le Monde*, 02/08/1950, 12; 'Hitler considérait comme une faible indemnité le vol des collections d'art israélites', *Le Monde*, 03/08/1950, 5.

even though the prosecution had carried out extensive investigations into the looting of apartments. *Commandant* (Major) Roux, the chief examining magistrate of the 2nd military tribunal at Reuilly barracks, Paris, led the inquest and indicted twenty-seven people. Most had been involved in running the ERR, although they also included a number of officials from the Dienststelle Westen, including one woman, the famous Sigrid Nehring, owing to a degree of confusion between the activities of the Einsatzstab and those of the Dienststelle.

Investigations into the looting of furniture had been pursued in the provinces, with mixed results, during which numerous witness accounts of the Parisian camps and 'Operation Furniture' were carefully assembled, although their outcome was inconclusive. One file in particular on 'the general organisation of the "Rosenberg bureaux"' contained a witness statement and a cross-examination of Arthur Garbas, the head of personnel and accounts at the avenue d'Iéna (he was eventually found guilty). Documents from Germany were included as evidence, and London-based investigations were completed. Von Behr, his wife and the camp commandants Fritz Ziemer, Bruno Kochan and Redhardt were among those indicted for 'looting in wartime'.[28] Gilberte Jacob, a former internee of Austerlitz, gave her testimony, as did Georges Kohn, Jean Reich, Félix Lichtenauer and chief Rabbi Cohen of Bordeaux. Charles Mercier du Paty de Clam, Sigrid Nehring, Arthur Garbas and many others provided invaluable details on Operation Furniture and the Parisian camps over a long period of investigation that began in 1946.

Commandant Roux had everything he needed to bring the trial of the Dienststelle Westen to a speedy conclusion, even though most of the indicted individuals had not been found. In fact, only Arthur Garbas and Sigrid Nehring had been located in Germany, where the former was already in prison. Miss Nehring, who had not lost her liking for soldiers, was still single in 1948 and working as a secretary in the officers' mess at Ploen, in Holstein, in the British occupied zone. The search for Bruno Kochan, which was particularly actively pursued owing to the testimony of former detainees, was abandoned in June 1949, when the British authorities decided that the evidence against him was insufficient (Kochan was living in their occupation zone at this time). Since September 1948, the Allied authorities had been refusing extradition requests for individuals accused of anything other than serious violent offences. The deportations from the Parisian camps had already been forgotten. Since von Behr was dead and his wife presumed also to have committed suicide, only minor accomplices, and relatively few of them at that, could be sent to the dock. Furthermore, the prosecution's main thrust concerned the theft of artworks, and the military tribunal did not want to begin a second trial in relation to the apartments. In 1949, the hour of

---

[28] These evidence files were of particular value to us in retracing the history of the Parisian camps.

the post-Liberation purges and high-profile trials had passed, and the first amnesties had already been declared.

The trial of Operation Furniture and the Parisian camps therefore never took place. Arthur Garbas was considered separately and the case against him dropped on 31 August 1948. Only the heads of the ERR ever stood trial. One case was dropped on the grounds of mistaken identity, one defendant was acquitted and three, Walter Hofer, Gerhard Utikal and Robert Scholz, received ten years' imprisonment and were banned from entering France for ten years. They were released less than one year later.[29]

Compensation for Victims

Compensation took a long time to arrive. While attempts were made to retrieve items located in Germany, the results were very disappointing, except in the case of works of art that had been safely stored away and, particularly for the most important pieces, catalogued.[30] French legislation on restitution, compensation, and the general restoration of Republican legal norms dealt with a vast array of issues. The question of compensation for sums extracted from bank accounts, a practice whose victims had mainly been Jews, was only resolved in June 1948. The question of stolen furniture was left hanging. It was true that one decree governing postwar reconstruction and compensation allowed for payments to victims to cover property taken away by or put under the control of the enemy. However, we do not know how many Jewish victims of looting attempted to use this law to obtain compensation. Only a small sample of the six million war damages files has been archived.

It would not be until 1957 that Jews who had lost their furniture could glimpse the possibility of receiving compensation with the passing in the Bundestag of the so-called *Brüg* law on restitution.[31] France's Jews could now file claims, either through the Fonds social juif unifié (the Unified Jewish Social Fund) or individu-

---

[29] Curiously, Austerlitz camp was mentioned in another postwar trial, that of Georges Albertini. Wolf Epstein, an internee of Austerlitz, gave evidence in defence of the accused, who was on trial for collaboration with the enemy. Epstein stated that Albertini had saved his life by intervening on three occasions, and concluded by certifying that Albertini was not an anti-Semite. Albertini was only sentenced to five years' forced labour, the confiscation of his property and 'national indignity'. Attenuating circumstances were recognized. For this testimony, see Centre de documentation juive contemporaine, LXXIV-4. This testimony is also mentioned in N. Weill. 2003. *Une histoire personnelle de l'antisémitisme*, Paris: Robert Laffont, 23 and 185–186.

[30] On the recovery of property from Germany, see C. Lorentz. *La France et les restitutions allemandes au lendemain de la Seconde Guerre mondiale, 1943–1954*, Paris: ministère des Affaires étrangères, direction des archives et de la documentation.

[31] The *Bundesrückerstattungsgesetz*, 'federal law on restitution'.

ally by writing to Berlin, where the local tax office centralised all requests from abroad. It took ten years to deal with the French claims (their total number is not known). What with forms to fill in, documents to produce, endless waiting and appeals to file, Operation Furniture was a continuing bureaucratic presence in the lives of Jewish households right up to the end of the 1960s.

AROUND A MEMORY HOLE

ILLUSTRATION 21. Austerlitz camp before its destruction in 1999.
©Le Parisien/Guy Gios.

W.G. SEBALD WAS PERHAPS the last great German writer of the twentieth century. In one of his last books, he recounts the search for memory undertaken by a certain Jacques Austerlitz. At the end of a lengthy peregrination around the railway stations of Europe, Austerlitz finds himself in Paris, in the new National Library. There he meets a character by the name of Henri Lemoine, who takes him up to the eighteenth floor of the southeastern tower. From this vantage point, he has a vision of Paris in the gathering dusk. 'Thus, on the waste land between the marshalling yard of the Gare d'Austerlitz and the Pont Tolbiac where this Babylonian library now rises, there stood until the end of the war an extensive warehousing complex to which the Germans brought all the loot they had taken from the homes of the Jews of Paris', Lemoine explains to him.[1] He then talks about Operation Furniture, about the French removal men, the complicity of the government. 'In the years from 1942 onwards everything our civilisation has produced, whether for the embellishment of life or merely for everyday use, from Louis XVI chests of drawers, Meissen porcelain, Persian rugs and whole libraries, down to the last salt-cellar and pepper-mill, was stacked there in the Austerlitz-Tolbiac storage depot.'[2]

It thus fell to a novelist to evoke one of the Parisian camps, Austerlitz, and even to give its name to a great, deeply layered novel that seeks to describe the impossibility of remembering and the inexorable burying of all traces of the past. Sebald describes Austerlitz camp as being entombed beneath the vast and grandiose French National Library, which is incorrect. The library is nearer Austerlitz railway station, several hundred metres from where the camp was situated. The detail of the camp's description is entirely at odds with the reality to which it seeks to bear witness. Its site was not where the author imagines it to be, and there was no 'contingent of soldiers from Indochina' guarding the detainees.

Following his liberation from Drancy, Marcel Lob returned to the quai de la Gare to retrieve Professor Ascoli's papers: 'I went back there, but all I found, where our building had stood, was a smoking pile of rubble: the Germans had come in the night following their withdrawal from Paris and bombarded the place.'[3] Yet the porcelain cup and silver fork spirited out of Austerlitz by Marc Garguir are material evidence of this vanished past.

All traces of the existence of the Parisian camps disappeared with the departure of their detainees. From that point on, silence surrounded this particular piece of the still very recent past. The evacuation of the internees marked the beginning of a long hiatus that, up until the publication of this book, covered the history of these places of confinement and hoarding. The memory of the satellite camps of Drancy is in every respect situated 'outside the frame of memory'. Simultaneously an instance of forgetting and of borrowed memory, it still struggles to find its identity.

The places once inhabited by the internees of the Parisian camps have crystallised a true memory hole, 'a form at once hollow and solid, hollow because it cannot be filled with images drawn from the collective memory, yet solid because it is not really absence, emptiness, or nothingness, but rather a feeling of lack, a feeling which works on us to produce a mnemonic effort.'[4] It is out of the

---

[1] Sebald, *Austerlitz*, 401.

[2] Ibid., 402.

[3] Singer, *Un universitaire face au destin*, 6.

[4] R. Bastide. 1970. 'Mémoire collective et sociologie du bricolage', *L'Année sociologique* 21, 95.

memory hole formed by the quai de la Gare that the present historical work was born, itself the end result of a work of memory. As this book draws to its close, it seems fitting to revisit these sites in search of lingering memories of the Parisian camps.

The buildings that housed the three camps have changed in terms of both form and function. Some of those who know them well have nevertheless retained the vague recollection that something had happened in them. What this past really consisted of, however, has been completely forgotten. It has gradually been concealed by the superimposed collective memorial representations of the Occupation.

The building on rue de Bassano was put up for sale by its owners and bought in 1947 by the General Union of the French Foundry Association, who made no modifications to the interior save the addition of some partition work and modern bathrooms. In 1951, an outbuilding was constructed (or possibly reconstructed) to the left of the porch covering the main entrance and the entrance to the courtyard. In it was installed a conference room and auditorium seating 230 beneath a glass roof, hidden from the street by the façade built in 1900. The decorations chosen by Louis Cahen d'Anvers and his wife remained in place. In 1987 the building was bought by the French bank Crédit Mutuel, which then put it up for sale. It stood unoccupied for over ten years. Eighteen works of 'grande décoration' – statues, panels and tapestries – were sold off at auction.[5] The building was acquired by a property investment company, which also has a small luxury tailoring department. Today, sewing machines once again occupy the ground floor and basement of 2, rue de Bassano: luxury men's suits are being made in the very place where von Behr and his cronies came to have their uniforms and suits tailored. To the eyes of informed visitors, such as the authors of this book, this realisation gives the scene an almost surreal aura, as if the 'phantom work' characteristic of the unconscious had this time come to haunt the premises.[6]

As of 2 September 1944, the Lévitan building was again requisitioned, this time by the French army, who used it to house its quartermasters' offices. The building was not returned to its owners until December 1945, in poor condition. As it was difficult to tell whether the damage had been done by the Germans or the French, the buildings requisitioning department decided to cover only 50 per cent of the repair costs.[7] The furniture store reopened in 1946, the sale

---

[5] See the announcement in the *Gazette de l'hôtel Drouot* advertising the sale by the auction house Calmels, Chambre and Cohen on 27 March 1997.

[6] 'Travail de fantôme'. N. Abraham and M. Torok. 1987. *L'Écorce et le noyau*, Paris: Flammarion.

[7] Archives de Paris, 4W 115, dossier 5724, réquisition du 85–87, Faubourg-Saint-Martin. The building at 54, avenue d'Iéna was also requisitioned, this time by the Americans, until 31 March 1947. The owners then rented the building to the Société nouvelle de vente des surplus. See Archives de Paris, 4W 103, dossier 5431.

to the Liebig corporation having been annulled. At the time of the Liberation, Wolff Lévitan was still the legal owner of the building, but he chose in any case to go to court to have his rights confirmed.[8] The Lévitan stores were sold in the 1970s and the brand disappeared. The shop in the Faubourg-Saint-Martin closed, and the building turned into a garage. It was bought up in the 1990s by an advertising and public relations company, a subsidiary of a large French conglomerate. Major building works were undertaken, and the interior of the building comprehensively redesigned. Walls were knocked down and replaced by glass panels. The roof terrace was rebuilt. Today, 250 people work there in elegant surroundings, for which top designers and architects have produced furniture and ornamental pieces.

For the most part, neither the occupants of the building nor neighbouring residents know, or at least claim to know, anything – except the local chemist, whose shop window is like a porthole compared to the façade of no. 85–87. He says that he knows that during the war there had been Jews there, men and women waiting to be deported from the nearby Gare de l'Est to the concentration camps and liquidation. He says that he knows that these Jews were put to work packing up works of art taken from the Louvre and Jewish collections that were also being sent from the Gare de l'Est to Germany.[9] He was given some of this information by some ladies living nearby. Two ladies in the neighbourhood, whom we subsequently met, still recall the image of Jews walking around on the roof, guarded by Germans. They believe that these people were waiting to be put into wagons to be deported from the Gare de l'Est.[10]

Neither memory nor forgetting, a memory hole is a trace of a past whose contents are no longer known, leaving only the frame, which is given physical form by the buildings left standing. Now empty, this frame comes to be filled by the two canons of socially shared memory: the deportations on the one hand, the looting of works of art on the other. Widely portrayed in the media and endlessly evoked, these two motifs of the past force their way into the reading of everything that happened, and hence all that we know happened without actually knowing the real details. This 'borrowed memory' has long filled the memory hole that characterised recollections of Lévitan.[11] The same was true of Austerlitz.

Damaged and destroyed, the buildings of 43 quai de la Gare were either repaired or entirely rebuilt to their original specification. In 1952, the Grands Moulins expanded further, annexing the premises of the stationery firm Bergès;

---

[8] He obtained a ruling from the Seine region's civil tribunal on 6 June 1945, which pronounced the sale void according to the decree of 21 April 1945.

[9] Interview with the chemist opposite 85–87, rue du Faubourg-Saint-Martin, 13/03/2003.

[10] Interviews of 15/05/2003 and 16/05/2003 quoted previously.

[11] 'Mémoire empruntée'. M. Halbwachs. 1992. On Collective Memory, edited, translated and with an introduction by Lewis A. Coser, Chicago, London: University of Chicago Press.

the Vichy-État warehouses were swallowed up in 1956.[12] Flour milling continued on the site until 1996. It was not until the 1980s that redevelopment plans were drawn up. However, the buildings were not particularly suited for conversion into residential developments; it was decided to level the whole area. The ZAC Rive gauche (Left-bank mixed development zone) undertook the total remodelling of the last remaining large undeveloped area of Paris. In 1988 a decision by François Mitterrand initiated the building of a new national library on the banks of the Seine.

The Grands Moulins left in 1997, and the rebuilt Austerlitz camp building was razed to the ground in June of that year. The main building of the complex, which overlooks the old quai de la Gare, renamed quai Panhard-et-Levassor, is being totally transformed. It will house Paris-7 University, formerly based at Jussieu. A new building will occupy the site of the camp, which will also be part of the university. In the midst of these new constructions, only the buildings of the Grands Moulins and the Frigos artists' collective bear witness to the industrial past of a zone that today houses major banks, consulting companies and new housing.

Despite all these changes, a trace of the past had for a long time remained: a plaque that had been placed at the site of the camp after the war. It bore witness to the fact that something had happened here. As with Lévitan, this plaque, while it referred to the past, did so through the motifs of a collective memory that completely submerged the reality of events. Internees indeed lived in this place between 1943 and 1944. However, while some were indeed deported, it was not from here. Nor were there 'thousands' of them, and the overall tone of the inscription leaves a rather misleading impression:

1943–1944
On these premises taken and occupied by the enemy were interned thousands of victims of Nazi persecution. Many of them were deported and perished in the extermination camps.

For a long time this plaque encapsulated the memory hole that surrounded the camp's history. Neither memory nor forgetting, the text it bears nonetheless formed the starting point of the work of memory and then of history, which finally resulted in the present book. Again, the path it took began outside France, in Germany, a trace as it were of the exchanges between Paris and Berlin that were at the heart of the life of the Parisian camps. The Jews of Austerlitz, Bassano and Lévitan had been put in a special category following a demonstration in support of the spouses of Aryans that had taken place in Berlin. German apartments were furnished with the contents of Jewish apartments sent from Paris. The Parisian

---

[12] Langlois, *De la Salpêtrière à la Bibliothèque nationale*, 91.

camps came back to the surface of memory following an article published in a German magazine.

The abandoned refrigerated warehouses that stand next to the Grands Moulins were occupied in 1971 by a group of artists who turned them into a workspace.[13] The painter Jean-Michel Frouin and two puppeteers, Marie Guastalla and Claude Bensignor, became interested in the history of the area, as they saw the old buildings being gradually demolished one by one. Having noticed the plaque in front of no. 43, quai de la Gare, near their studios, they met with survivors, including Maurice Wolf. When the construction of the Bibliothèque nationale de France had finished, a German journalist with the magazine *Die Zeit* went looking for evidence of what had happened there during the war. He met with the three artists from les Frigos, who told him what they knew, and wrote a long article entitled 'The Towers of Silence', in which he talked of Austerlitz camp and suggested that the '*très grande bibliothèque*' was built on the site of the camp.[14] In the wake of this article, a piece written by the journalist Nicolas Weill, the great-grandson of Wolf Epstein, was published on the front page of *Le Monde*.[15] Not long before this, Jean-Michel Frouin, Claude Bensignor and Marie Guastalla had placed a groundbreaking advertisement in the same newspaper's evening edition calling for former internees to come forward.

The replies they received led to the creation of an association for former detainees, perhaps the last such association to have been formed in France. Roger Mayer, a former internee of Austerlitz, became its president; Denise Weill, the granddaughter of Wolf Epstein, took on the role of secretary and Mira Lessovoï, who had already attempted to launch a similar initiative several years earlier, was very active in locating more detainees. Various former prisoners and relatives of deceased internees answered the call, and it was decided to commission a historical study of the camps. After several false starts, the two authors of the present book were brought on board in October 2001.

The memory hole surrounding the satellite camps of Drancy may no longer exist, yet no real collective memory has been formed. The preparatory work undertaken for this book revealed the difficulties involved in this. It was hard to find witnesses, and many letters went unanswered. 'Half-Jews', 'spouses of Aryans': the complex identities of certain internees of the Parisian camps may explain the impossibility of constructing a collective memory of this period, given that existing shared representations tend to separate Jews into one group and non-Jews into another. On the margins of both groups, many witnesses and their descen-

---

[13] G.-A. Langlois. 1996. *Le Guide du promeneur, 13e arrondissement*, Paris: Parigramme, 107.

[14] A. Smoltczyk and M. Weiss. 1997. 'Die Türme des Schweigens', *Die Zeit*, 23 January 1997, 11–17.

[15] 'La bibliothèque François-Mitterrand à l'ombre d'un camp nazi', *Le Monde*, 23 October 1997.

dants have trouble finding social frames in which to express their past. It is thus telling that one former detainee of the quai de la Gare, who had been interned as the spouse of an Aryan, consented to meet us only following the death of his wife and let us know from the outset that he was a 'militant atheist'. Indeed, before agreeing to meet us, he telephoned to make sure that the association had 'no religious agenda'.

Another witness, the daughter from the first marriage of a man interned at Austerlitz (as the spouse of an Aryan), has described the difficulty of reconstituting past events along with others when one is, in fact, isolated: 'We can't say that we knew anyone who was deported, apart from some very old acquaintances. We were a bit like survivors shipwrecked on an island compared to what was going on around us. Well, I should make one thing clear: we were complete atheists. We had never been religious. And so my sister's children had married Catholics. So the only Jews left were me and my sister. So, what were we going to do with these letters [written by her father from Austerlitz]? I'm eighty-three. Well, I met Denise Weill, who told me to go to the Centre de documentation juive contemporaine.'

The wives of POWs seem, for their part, to possess an identity that was superficially more unified in terms of collective representations of the Second World War. They could have given their testimony – and did, although their accounts related to another experience that also brought them together: their deportation to Bergen-Belsen. The only testimony from the wife of a POW relating to the Parisian camps was part of a witness statement made immediately after the war.[16] Another interned wife of a POW, when we contacted her during the research for this book, declined to meet us, although she wished us well, explaining that: 'In that camp [Lévitan], many unfortunate things must have happened but, as far as I'm concerned, it was always just a brief transitional passage between Drancy and Bergen-Belsen.'[17] We have been unable to meet any of these women.

Most of the spontaneously written accounts from former detainees of the satellite camps were in fact produced by people who were eventually deported to Auschwitz. Recounting the journey leading up to their deportation, they speak of how the Parisian camps constituted something of a breathing space.[18] Having escaped death, they have no complexes or feelings of embarrassment in this respect, less still of shame at having spent time in places that at the end of the day represented, for some of them, a refuge from deportation.

Indeed, an unwillingness to speak out linked to the relatively 'privileged' situation of the Parisian internees can be added to the mechanisms of memory in explaining the sparseness of recollections of Austerlitz, Lévitan and Bassano. Roger

---

[16] Statement by Gilberte Jacob.

[17] Letter from Paule Lévy dated 04/11/2002.

[18] See for example the memoirs of Maurice Wolf, Yvonne Klug and Vivette Baharlia-Politi.

Mayer, the president of the internees' association, when asked by us whether he had talked about his experiences after the war, replied: 'Well, with the deportees it's quite simple, really, I think I can say that they didn't want to talk about it. They thought nobody would believe them. So I felt ashamed to talk about what happened to me ... Obviously, when you consider what happened to the deportees, I was privileged.' This feeling is very powerful, even though, as Roger Mayer himself added, 'in fact, it's very complicated, as not a week went by without people being deported from Austerlitz and Lévitan.'[19]

The Parisian camps have their own history, which can now be fully appreciated. Yet writing this book has shown us that, in more than just historical terms, recollections of the Parisian camps in turn occupy a subsidiary position in relation to the memory of Drancy. An interview with a former inmate of Austerlitz was revealing in this respect. We were going to talk about the history of the satellite camps, a subject he had worked tirelessly to promote, yet more than two-thirds of the conversation was devoted to Drancy. For several minutes we had been unambiguously talking about Austerlitz, when we asked him: 'Could you draw the camp?' Our host replied, most obligingly: 'Yes, I can try.' Picking up a pen, he started to sketch an outline: 'Buildings here, here and here. So, there were three wings, like a U, do you see...' Drancy concentration camp gradually appeared on the sheet of paper. Taken aback, we asked him: 'Really, so it had the same layout as Drancy?' 'Yes, that's Drancy, that's it [silence]. Oh, you meant the quai de la Gare?'

We did not get a drawing of Austerlitz camp that day.

---

[19] Interview with Roger Mayer, former internee at the quai de la Gare, Paris, 8/4/2002.

APPENDIX

TABLE 3. Numbers of Internees According to Sources

Date	According to UGIF menus	Lévitan	Austerlitz	Bassano	According to Drancy register
18/07/1943	180	180			
20/07/1943	200	200			
17/08/1943	215	215			
21/08/1943	209	209			210
23/08/1943					208
30/08/1943					206
03/09/1943					204
04/09/1943	220	220			
06/09/1943					223
08/09/1943					222
09/09/1943					221
10/09/1943					219
12/09/1943					218
03/10/1943	240	240			
04/10/1943					237
05/10/1943	247	247			
06/10/1943					243
08/10/1943	337	337			
21/10/1943	344	344			248
23/10/1943					252
25/10/1943	348	348			
30/10/1943					302
31/10/1943	402	402			
01/11/1943	538	344	194		438
06/11/1943					437
10/11/1943	537	344	194		

Date	According to UGIF menus	Lévitan	Austerlitz	Bassano	According to Drancy register
12/11/1943					433
24/11/1943					435
27/11/1943					433
28/11/1943	541	344	197		441
29/11/1943	537	344	193		
01/12/1943					444
11/12/1943	587	344	243		
12/12/1943					437
14/12/1943					485
17/12/1943	615	369	246		510
18/12/1943					512
22/12/1943	511	255	256		
30/12/1943					507
07/01/1944	520	264	256		
08/01/1944					509
09/01/1944					507
18/01/1944					506
24/01/1944	505	264	241		
25/01/1944	520	264	256		
29/01/1944					520
04/02/1944					518
08/02/1944					497
11/02/1944	537	264	273		
28/02/1944					501
13/03/1944	637	264	373		591
14/03/1944	657	254	393	10	588
15/03/1944	657	250	393	14	608
16/03/1944	657	233	393	31	
17/03/1944	657	227	383	47	
21/03/1944					607
28/03/1944	674	227	398	49	
29/03/1944					
06/04/1944	661	227	385	49	
12/04/1944					576

Date	According to UGIF menus	Lévitan	Austerlitz	Bassano	According to Drancy register
13/04/1944					575
22/04/1944					574
01/05/1944					564
02/05/1944					563
05/05/1944					562
06/05/1944	691	227	415	49	592
09/05/1944	675	227	398	50	
15/05/1944	677	225	398	54	
17/05/1944					591
14/06/1944					590
15/06/1944	682	225	398	59	
25/06/1944	654	180	411	59	
26/06/1944					584
27/06/1944					579
28/06/1944					569
29/06/1944					554
01/07/1944	686	225	398	63	
06/07/1944					545
07/07/1944					543
10/07/1944					543
12/07/1944					540
15/07/1944					537
16/07/1944	652	180	411	61	
17/07/1944					535
18/07/1944					533
21/07/1944					532
22/07/1944					531
24/07/1944					530
31/07/1944					542
02/08/1944					541
05/08/1944					536
09/08/1944					533

REFERENCES

ARCHIVES

An appendix to the Dienststelle Westen's liquidation report lists the archives burnt in Paris in August 1944. These included all the records of emptied apartments, documents concerning the furniture trains (*Abtransport*), accounts, records of 'special tasks' (furniture and other objects sent to individuals) and general correspondence.[1]

Archives de Paris (Archives of the Seine)
    Entr'aide française: 24 W1, 24 W2, 24 W3, 24 W13, 24 W15.
    Permis de construire, VO11/1329, VO12/257, VO13/112.
    Entrepôts et magasins généraux de Paris, D.8J 74 Dommages de guerre, D.8J 236, plans de sites, D.8J 237, plans de site.
    Réquisitions immobilières, série 4W: 101, 103, 111, 115, 142, 153, 415, 416.

Archives nationales (National Archives, Paris)
    Commissariat général aux questions juives: AJ38 146, 404, 405, 796, 797, 799, 2423 dossier 8839 'rue de Bassano', 2585, dossier 23272 'Deutsch de la Meurthe 4 place des Etats-Unis', 2626 '85–87 Faubourg Saint-Martin', 5929, 5930, 5931, 5934.
    Etat-major militaire allemand: AJ40 411, 412, 456, 459, 591, 627, 1366, 1359, 1683.
    Fichier de Drancy et cahier de transfert: F9/5675 to 5749, F9/5781 to 5788.

Service historique de la gendarmerie, Maison-Alfort (Archives of the gendarmerie)
    Compagnies de Paris Minimes et Exelmans, cartons n°s 11 83, 11 832, 11 835, 11 837, 11 838, 11 839, 11 858, 11 859, 11 861, 11 864, 11 865, 11 866, 11 870, 11 871.

Centre de documentation juive contemporaine (Shoah Memorial, Paris)
    V-119, VI–24, XI–1, XIII–47, XVa–169, XV-183, XIXa–38, 42, XX–48, 50, XXV–31, XXVIIIa-293, 307, XXVIIIb-13, LXII-17, LXXI-120, LXXIV-4, LXXV-94, CIVb-210, CVI-17, 96 , CVII-7, 13, 14, 23, 27/30, 41/43, 55, 63, 75, 78, 81, 86, 88a, 92, 99, 104, 108, 116, 117, CXII-46, CXL-74, 88, 95, 105, 127, CXLI-160, 168, 178, 184, 185, 186, 187, 193, 195, CXLII-8, CXLIII-357, 380, CXLV-645, 568, 569, CXLIV, 396, 443, 454, 454a, 457, CCXI-71, 96, 126, CCXVI-55, CCXXI-26, CCXXXII-23, 30, 30b, 31, 32, 33, CCXLIV3-1, CCL-14, CCLII-8, Abl.1, CCLXI-18, CCI-1, CCCLXXVI-12, CCCLXXVI-1, 4, CCCLXXVII-1, 3,

---

[1] Bundesarchiv, NS 8 230, Bericht über die Übernahme des Dienstgutes der Dienststelle Westen des Reichsminiterium für die besetzten Ostgebiete, 213–218, 218.

6, 10, 13, 16, CCCLXXVIII-5, CCCLXXIX-21, CDXI-195, CDXXIV-1, 2, 25, 31, 38, 44, 45, 46, 47, CDXXV-2, 3, 6, 8, 9, 17, CDXXVI-5, CDXXVII-1, 9, DLXIII, DCXXVIII-3, 7, 9, 21, CDXXXVI-3, 4, 5, 7, 9 à 20, CDXXXVIII-21, CDXCV-10, CMVII-13, CMXVII-13, CMLVI.

Microfilms from the UGIF Archives (the original documents are kept at the YIVO in New York): Nrs 17, 18, 21, 23, 28, 48, 49, 92, 93.

The 8616 came back or Doors that open only from the outside, memoirs of Yvonne Klug.

La Mémoire blessée, memoirs of Maurice Wolf, unpublished

Dépôt central de la justice militaire, Le Blanc (Central Archives of French Military Justice)

Dossier 'Utikal et autres'.

Bundesarchiv Berlin (German Federal Archives)

Reichsministerium für die besetzten Ostgebiete, R6 : 1, 2, 3, 17, 19, 30, 201, 204, 225, 226, 236, 272.

Dienststelle Rosenberg – Kanzlei Rosenberg NS 8: 230.

Dienststelle Rosenberg – Beauftragter des Führer dür die Überwachung der gesamten geistigen und weltanschaulichen Schulung und Erziehung der NSDAP, NS 15, 101a, 103.

ERR, NS 30 : 12, 13, 27, 28, 30.

SS-HO : 1478, 1479.

O.915 : 136/326, 136/341.

O.916.

O. 211/111.

Archives of Beit Lohamei HaGhetaot : Dutch Archives Section BLH, Dossier Josef Weiss Nr 317.

The archives of the SNCF do not provide the needed information on the furniture trains to Germany.

Archives de la Chambre syndicale du déménagement (Union of Movers' Companies), Paris: Dossiers du Comité d'organisation des entreprises de déménagement et garde-meubles (loose documents. In December 1957, some files from the Organisational Committee were handed over to *Joint,* which was dealing with preparations for the application of the Brüg law).

Private Archives

of the daughter of Roger Altmann, former internee at the quai de la Gare

of Jacqueline Ribot, daughter of Simon Sarfati, former internee at the quai de la Gare, subsequently placed in the Centre de Documentation Juive Contemporaine

of Roger Mayer, former internee at the quai de la Gare

of Bernard Behr, former internee at the quai de la Gare

of Michel Behr, former internee at the quai de la Gare

of Jean Levi, former internee at the quai de la Gare

of Odette Dassonville, former internee at Lévitan

of Denise Bernard, daughter of Marc Garguir, former internee at the quai de la Gare, also placed in the Centre de Documentation Juive Contemporaine

of Denise Weill, granddaughter of Wolf Esptein, former internee at the quai de la Gare, also placed in the Centre de Documentation Juive Contemporaine. Bulletins of the association « Austerlitz-Lévitan-Bassano ».

of Erna Herzberg, former internee at Lévitan and Bassano

of Claude Bensignor

Memoirs of Colette Dampierre, née Cahen d'Anvers, written in English, held by her nephew, Christian de Montbrison.

INTERVIEWS

Odette Dassonville, former internee at Lévitan, Orly, 4/11/2002

Jacqueline Ribot, daughter of Simon Sarfati, former internee at the quai de la Gare, Paris, 24/2/2003

Michel Behr, former internee at the quai de la Gare, Angers, 5/2/2003

Roger Mayer, former internee at the quai de la Gare, Paris, 8/4/2002

Bernard Behr, former internee at the quai de la Gare, Paris, 31/3/2002

Samuel Pintel, son of Thérèse Pintel, former internee at Lévitan, deported to Bergen-Belsen, Paris, 14/3/2003

Jean Levi, former internee at the quai de la Gare, Paris, 17/3/2003

Félix Lichtenauer, former internee at Lévitan, Paris, 12/4/2002

Denise Weill, granddaughter of Wolf Epstein, former internee at the quai de la Gare, Paris, 15/4/2002

Denise Bernard, daughter of Marc Garguir, former internee at the quai de la Gare, Paris, 29/3/2002

Francine Christophe, survivor of Bergen-Belsen, Versailles, 20/5/2002

Christian de Montbrison, nephew of Colette Dampierre, former internee at Lévitan, Paris, 10/5/2002

Mme Haymans, daughter of Robert Fabius, London, 14/12/2002

Gilles-Antoine Langlois (by telephone), historian of the 13th *arrondissement*, 23/12/2002

Jean-Michel Frouin, painter

Marie Guastalla and Claude Bensignor

M. Roquelaure, architect, 5/6/2003

M. Raymond Cornuau (by telephone), former general secretary of the Chambre syndicale des entreprises de déménagement (from 1946), 24/4/2003

M. Jean-Noël Cannioni, general secretary of the Chambre syndicale des enterprises de déménagement, 23/4/2003

Claude Léon, son of Jacob Robert Léon, former internee at the quai de la Gare, email of 19/9/2002

Paule Levy, former internee at Lévitan, deported to Bergen-Belsen, letter of 4 November 2002.

Georges Delorme, son of Michel Kaplan, former internee at the quai de la Gare, 3/6/2002

Boris Delorme, son of Michel Kaplan, former internee at the quai de la Gare, 9/6/2002

Hélène Grunwald, daughter of Adèle Warchawski, former internee of Lévitan, deported to Bergen-Belsen, 15/6/2002

Erna Herzberg, former internee at Lévitan and Bassano, deported to Auschwitz, 20/6/2002

Interview with two neighbours of 85–87 rue du Faubourg Saint-Martin, 15/5/2003 and 16/5/2003

Interview with the chemist opposite 85–87 rue du Faubourg Saint-Martin, 13/3/2003.

BIBLIOGRAPHY

Aalders, Gerard. 2000. *Geraubt! Die Enteignung jüdischen Besitzes im Zweiten Weltkrieg*, Cologne: Dittrich Verlag.

Abraham, Nicolas, and Maria Torok. 1987. *L'Ecorce et le noyau*, Paris: Flammarion.

Adler, H.G. 1974. *Der Verwaltete Mensch: Studien zur Deportation der Juden aus Deutschland*, Tübingen: Mohr.

Arendt, Hannah. 1994. *Eichmann in Jerusalem: A Report on the Banality of Evil*, Harmondsworth: Penguin.

Assouline, Pierre. 1997. *Le dernier des Camondo*, Paris: Gallimard.

Bajhor, Frank. 2001. *Parvenüs und Profiteure: Korruption in der NS-Zeit*, Frankfurt am Main: S. Fischer.

Bastide, Roger. 1970. « Mémoire collective et sociologie du bricolage », *L'Année Sociologique* 21, 65–108.

Berg, Roger. 1947. *Documents pour servir à l'histoire de la persécution raciale*, Paris: Service d'information des crimes de guerre, Office français d'édition.

Bergeron, Louis. 1991. *Les Rothschild et les autres: la gloire des banquiers*, Paris : Perrin, «Histoires et fortunes».

Les Biens des victimes des persécutions anti-juives en Belgique. Spoliation. Rétablissement des droits. 2001. Résultats de la Commission d'étude. Rapport final de la Commission d'étude sur le sort des biens des membres de la Communauté juive de Belgique spoliés ou délaissés pendant la guerre 1940–1945, 2 vols. Brussels.

Billig, Joseph. 1963. *Alfred Rosenberg dans l'action idéologique et administrative du Reich hitlérien, inventaire commenté de la collection de documents conservés au Centre de documentation juive contemporaine, provenant des archives du Reichsleiter et ministre A. Rosenberg*, Paris: Editions du Centre.

Bleustein-Blanchet, Marcel. 1960. *La rage de convaincre*, Paris: Robert Laffont ; reissued by Livre de Poche, 1974.

Bloch, Marc. 1925. « Mémoire collective, tradition et coutume: A propos d'un livre récent », *Revue de synthèse historique* vol. 40, issue 118–120, 73–83.

Briggs, Asa. 1995. *The Channel Islands: Occupation and Liberation 40–45*, London: BT Batsford Ltd, Imperial War Museum.

Bunting, Madeleine. 1995. *The Model Occupation: The Channel Islands under German Rule. 1940–1945*, London: HarperCollins.

Commission consultative des dommages et des réparations. 1948. Ingérences allemandes dans l'activité industrielle, Monographie A.I.41. Entreprises de déménagement et garde-meubles, Paris: Imprimerie nationale.

Cruikshank, Charles. 1975. *The German Occupation of the Channel Islands*, London, New York: The Trustee of the Imperial War Museum, Oxford University Press.

Delarue, Jacques. 1968. *Trafics et crimes sous l'Occupation*, Paris: Fayard.

Dreyfus, Jean-Marc. 2000. *L'aryanisation économique des banques pendant l'Occupation et leur restitution à la Libération, 1940–1952*, PhD dissertation under the supervision of Pr Antoine Prost. University of Paris 1-Panthéon-Sorbonne.

Dreyfus, Jean-Marc. 2003. *Pillages sur ordonnances: Aryanisation et restitution des banques en France 1940–1953*, « Pour une histoire du XXe siècle », Paris: Fayard.

Drori, Paul. 1948. *Matricule 5586 : Poèmes*, Paris: Polyglottes.

Fabius, Odette. 1980. *Un lever de soleil sur le Mecklembourg: Mémoires*, Paris: Albin Michel.

Foucauld, Régis de. 1990. *Il était une fois... le déménagement*, Paris: Editions Saurat.

Geissmann, Georges. 1944. Article in *L'Homme libre*, 15 September.

Gensburger, Sarah. 2002, « Les figures du Juste et du Résistant et l'évolution de la mémoire française de l'Occupation », *Revue française de science politique* 52(2–3), 291–322.

Gensburger, Sarah. 2010. *Images d'un pillage: Album de la spoliation des Juifs à Paris. 1940–1944*, Paris: Textuel.

Gerlach, Christian. 1998. *Die Wannsee-Konferenz, das Schicksal der deutschen Juden und Hitlers politische Grundsatzentscheidung, alle Juden Europas zu ermorden*, Hamburg: Hamburger Edition HIS Verlag. Translation into French: 1999. *Sur la conférence de Wannsee*, preface by Annette Wieviorka, «Opinion », Paris, Liana Levi.

Ginzburg, Carlo. 2001. *A distance: neuf essais sur le point de vue en histoire*, Paris: Gallimard. In English, 2002, Wooden Eyes. Nine Reflections on Distance, London : Verso.

Gros, Dominique (ed.). 1996. *Le droit antisémite de Vichy*, Le Genre humain (30/31), Le Seuil.

Gruner, Wolf. 1997. *Der geschlossene Arbeitseinsatz deutscher Juden: zur Zwangsarbeit als Element der Verfolgung, 1938–1943*, Berlin: Metropol.

Gruner, Wolf. 2005. *Wiederstand in der Rosenstrasse: Die Fabrik-Aktion und die Verfolgung der "Mischehen" 1943*, Frankfurt am Main: Fischer.

Gutman, Israel (ed.). 1990. *Encyclopedia of the Holocaust*, New York: Macmillan.

Halbwachs, Maurice. 1992. *On Collective Memory*, edited, translated and with an introduction by Lewis A. Coser, Chicago, London: University of Chicago Press.

Halbwachs, Maurice. 1994. *Les Cadres sociaux de la mémoire*, Paris: Albin Michel.

Herbert, Ulrich. 1998. « Die deutsche Militärverwaltung in Paris und die Deportation der französischen Juden », in Ulrich Herbert (ed.), *Nationalsozialistische Vernichtungspolitik 1939–1945: Neue Forschungen und Kontroversen*, Frankfurt am Main: Fischer.

Heuss, Anja. 2000. *Kunst-und Kulturgutraub: Eine vergleichende Studie zur Besatzungspolitik der Nationalsozialisten in Frankreich und der Sowjetunion*, Heidelberg: Universitätsverlag C. Winter.

Hilberg, Raul. 1985. *The Destruction of the European Jews*, 2 volumes, New York, London: Holmes & Meier.

Hilberg, Raul. 1992. *Perpetrators, Victims, Bystanders: The Jewish Catastrophe 1933–1945*, New York: Aaron Asher Books.

Hillairet, Jacques. 1997. *Dictionnaire historique des rues de Paris*, 2 vols, 10th ed., Paris: Les Editions de Minuit.

International Military Tribunal. *Trials of War Criminals before the Nuremberg Military Tribunals under Control Council,* 16 volumes, vol. 14 November 1945–1 October 1946 (Washington, 1949),Joubert, Marie-Agnès. 1998. *La Comédie française sous l'Occupation,* Paris: Tallandier.

Kaspi, André. 1991. *Les Juifs pendant l'Occupation,* Paris: Le Seuil.

Klarsfeld, Serge. 1983. *Vichy-Auschwitz: Le rôle de Vichy dans la solution finale de la question juive en France,* 2 vols, Paris : Fayard. Reprinted in 2001, Fayard.

Klarsfeld, Serge. 1993. *Le calendrier de la persécution des juifs en France 1940–1944,* Paris : « Les fils et filles des déportés juifs de France » and the Beate Klarsfeld Foundation. Reprinted in 2001, Paris: Fayard.

Klarsfeld, Serge, and Beate Klarsfeld. 1978. *Le Mémorial de la déportation des Juifs de France,* Paris: Serge and Beate Klarsfeld.

Kohn, Georges. 1999. *Journal de Compiègne et de Drancy,* presented and with commentary by Serge Klarsfeld, Paris: Editions de l'association « Les fils et filles de déportés juifs de France ».

Lambauer, Barbara. 2001. *Otto Abetz et les Français ou l'envers de la Collaboration,* « Pour une histoire du Xxe siècle », Paris: Fayard.

Langlois, Gille-Antoine. 1996. *Le guide du promeneur 13ᵉ arrondissement,* Paris: Parigramme.

Langlois, Gilles-Antoine. 2000. *De la Salpêtrière à la Bibliothèque nationale de France: Histoire d'un quartier de Paris,* Paris: Somogny.

Le Masne de Chermont, Isabelle, and Didier Schulmann. 2000. *Le pillage de l'art en France pendant l'Occupation et la situation des 2000 œuvres confiées aux musées nationaux,* Paris: Mission d'étude sur la spoliation des Juifs de France, La Documentation française.

Manuel, Robert. 1975. *Qu'allais-je faire dans cette galère?* Paris: Emile-Paul.

Marrus, Michael M., and Robert O. Paxton. 1981. *Vichy France and the Jews,* New York: Basic Books.

Molau, Andreas. 1993. *Alfred Rosenberg: der Ideologe des Nationalsozialismus: eine politische Biografie,* Koblenz: S Bublies.

Lorentz, Claude, 1998. *La France et les restitutions allemandes au lendemain de la Seconde Guerre mondiale, 1943–1954,* Paris: ministère des Affaires étrangères, direction des archives et de la documentation.

Le Monde Juif. Special issue 146 (January–March 1993). Testimonies of M. Bonnet, J. Jacob-Delmas, M. Lessovoï, 37.

Nicholas, Lynn H. 1994. *The Rape of Europa: The Fate of Europe's Treasures in the Third Reich and the Second World War,* New York: Alfred A. Knopf.

Peschanski, Denis. 2002. *La France des camps: L'internement 1938–1946,* Paris: Gallimard.

Pezechkian, Johanna. 2002. « La Möbelaktion en Belgique », *Cahiers d'Histoire du Temps Présent* 10 (Brussels), 153–180.

Philipp, Elisabeth. 2000. *Histoire d'une entreprise de son temps: Compagnie des Entreprises et Magasins Généraux de Paris,* Paris: EMGP Textuel.

Pollak, Michael. 1990. *L'Expérience concentrationnaire,* Paris: Métailié.

Prost, Antoine, et al. 2000. *Aryanisation économique et restitutions,* Paris: Mission d'étude pour la spoliation des Juifs de France, La Documentation française, 71–93.

Rajsfus, Maurice. 1989. *Des Juifs dans la collaboration 2. Une Terre promise?* Paris: L'Harmattan.

Rajsfus, Maurice. 1996. *Drancy, un camp de concentration très ordinaire, 1941–1944,* Paris: le cherche midi éditeur.

Redgis, Yvonne. 2010. *Survivre: Souvenirs d'une rescapée d'Auschwitz (1945),* with commentary by Jean-Marc Dreyfus, Paris: Larousse.

Revel, Jacques (ed.). 1996. *Jeux d'échelles: la micro-analyse à l'expérience,* Paris: Seuil.

Rigg, Bryan. 2002. *Hitler's Jewish Soldiers: The Untold Story of Nazi Racial Laws and Men of Jewish Descent in the German Military,* Lawrence: University Press of Kansas.

Roseman, Mark. 2002. *The Villa, the Lake, the Meeting,* London: Penguin Press.

Safrian, Hans. 1993. *Die Eichmann-Männer,* Vienna: Europaverlag.

Schatzmann, Muriel, 1944. «Au Galeries Austerlitz », *Fraternité* (September).

Sebald, W.G. 2001. *Austerlitz,* London: Penguin.

Shirman, Israël. 1973. « Un aspect de la solution finale: la spoliation économique des Juifs de Belgique », *Cahiers d'Histoire de la Seconde Guerre mondiale* 3 (Brussels), 65–83.

Singer, Claude. 2000. *Un universitaire face au destin Georges Ascoli (1882–1944),* Paris: Association des anciens élèves de l'Ecole normale supérieure.

Smoltczyk, Alexander and Weiss, Maurice. 1997. 'Die Türme des Schweigens', *Die Zeit,* 23 January 1997, 11–17.

Stoltzfus, Nathan. 1996. *Resistance of the Heart: Intermarriage and the Rosenstrasse Protest in Nazi Germany,* New York: Norton.

Szajkowski, Zosa. 1966. *Analytical Franco-Jewish Gazetteer,* New York: American Academy for Jewish Research, The Lucius N. Littauer Foundation, The Gustav Wurzweiler Foundation.

United Restitution Organization. 1958. M. Aktion Frankreich, Belgien, Holland und Luxemburg, 1940–1944.

Verheyde, Philippe. 1999. *Les mauvais comptes de Vichy: L'aryanisation des entreprises juives,* Paris: Perrin.

Vries, Willemn de. 1996. *Sonderstab Musik : Music Confiscations by the Einsatzstab Reichsleiter Rosenberg under the Nazi Occupation of Western Europe,* Amsterdam: Amsterdam University Press.

Weill, Nicolas. 2003. *Une histoire personnelle de l'antisémitisme,* Paris: Robert Laffont.

Weill, Nicolas. 'La bibliothèque François-Mitterrand à l'ombre d'un camp nazi', *Le Monde,* 23 October 1997.

Wellers, Georges. 1946. *De Drancy à Auschwitz,* Paris: Editions du Centre.

Wellers, Georges. 1991. *Un juif sous Vichy,* Paris: Editions Tirésias.

Wieviorka, Annette. 1992. *Déportation et génocide: Entre la mémoire et l'oubli,* Paris: Plon.

Wieviorka, Annette, and Floriane Azoulay. 2000. *Le pillage des appartements et son indemnisation,* Paris: Mission d'étude pour la spoliation des Juifs de France, La Documentation française.

INDEX